The New Public Personnel Administration

Fourth Edition

The New Public Personnel Administration

Lloyd G. Nigro
Georgia State University

Felix A. Nigro
Emeritus, University of Georgia

F. E. Peacock Publishers, Inc.   •   Itasca, Illinois

Cover photo by The Image Bank: Marc Romanelli

Copyright © 1994
F. E. Peacock Publishers, Inc.
All rights reserved
Library of Congress Catalog Card No. 92-061962
ISBN 0-87581-374-7
Printed in the United States of America
10 9 8 7 6 5 4 3 2 1
1998   1997   1996   1995   1994

This book is dedicated to the memory of Marilyn and Vinnie

Contents

Preface

The study of public personnel administration has come a long way since the days when it essentially was about how to run traditional merit systems. It is today a challenging and important area of public policy and administration. During the coming decade, fundamental choices about the future of the public service on all levels of government will be made, and the resulting personnel policies will certainly do much to determine government's role in shaping American society as it enters the next century.

The 1980s were marked by a growing realization that the public service was in crisis. It was a decade of severe political challenges, rapidly fading public confidence, and weakening capabilities. The possibilities to be realized from the personnel policies and institutions that emerged from the civil service reforms of the early 20th century seemed to have run their course, and the political leadership seemed more intent on dismantling than on revitalizing the public service.

The language of reform stressed private or market-driven alternatives to public administration, and privatization was advanced as the solution to many of government's supposed inadequacies. Private-sector management techniques, including pay-for-performance systems used in major corporations, were said to be far superior engines of efficiency compared to anything the public sector had come up with. Above all, the reformers said, the regulatory concept of personnel administration embodied in the merit systems produced by turn-of-the-century civil service reform was to be replaced with a management-centered approach stressing efficiency and effectiveness through human resources management.

Specific areas of policy debate and political controversy included public employee pay, unions and collective bargaining, and affirmative action plans. Questions concerning what public employers needed to do in order to recruit, select, and retain a quality work force assumed center stage. Performance appraisal methods and job evaluation and classification systems were critically examined; reforms were urged. Pay for performance became a centerpiece of proposals on all levels of government to reform the civil service by making it more efficient and effective.

While the fundamental values and traditional practices of public personnel administration were being challenged and public pressures for sweeping reforms were building in the 1980s, public employers were facing new problems and responsibilities that demanded immediate attention. The demography of the nation's labor force was changing at a pace that threatened to overwhelm public employers' capacity to respond with appropriate policies and practices. AIDS became an epidemic that had to be taken seriously in the workplace, and drug and alcohol abuse could no longer be ignored or handled through traditional means. Sexual harassment surfaced as a major concern for women, the single most rapidly growing segment of the work force. Gender discrimination in pay became a divisive issue, raising demands for comparable worth as a standard for setting wages in the public sector. Laws requiring equal employment opportunities for women and minorities were expanded to include people with mental and physical disabilities.

All in all, the 1980s were turbulent years for public personnel administration, years in which the need for change became painfully apparent and the search for a "new public personnel administration" took on great urgency. The early 1990s have revealed no lessening of the pressures for change and reform; if anything, they have increased. The policy choices made in response to these challenges during this decade are likely to transform the practice of public personnel, and the stakes are high for all concerned.

In this fourth edition, we focus on a number of major trends, controversies, and human resources problems that public employers and their personnel specialists will have to grapple with during the 1990s. Several of these, such as those related to position classification, pay, and equal employment opportunity, have roots that reach deep into the history of the public service in the United States. Others, including AIDS, sexual harassment, and pay for performance, are more recent developments.

Accordingly, we have divided this edition into three major sections. The first provides an overview of the American public service today, puts into historical perspective the new public personnel administration in the United States, and offers a description of how personnel contributes to organizational effectiveness. The second concentrates on six long-term problem areas that continue to represent important challenges to those who design and manage modern public personnel systems. The third section covers several new or emergent problems now requiring serious attention from policymakers as well as those responsible for the day-to-day operation of personnel systems on all levels of government. In an effort to allow for instructors' preferences with regard to topic sequences and conceptual framework, individual chapters in Sections II and III are designed to be largely freestanding.

In order to discuss all of these important topics, we have deleted several of the chapters that appeared in the third edition. These choices were painful, since subjects such as training, career systems, and grievances and appeals are themselves highly significant areas of public personnel policy and administration. To the degree possible, we have incorporated some of this material into new or revised chapters, but a comprehensive treatment of all of the field's important facets was simply beyond the scope of this text. We hope instructors using it will be able to fill in some of the gaps. However, we believe that the material presented in this edition offers a useful (and very usable) introduction and background for more advanced and specialized studies.

□

We greatly appreciate the support and encouragement we received from friends and colleagues at Georgia State University and the University of Georgia. We owe special thanks to the many public agencies and public administrators who very generously provided us with a great deal of the information we needed for this edition. Particular thanks go to Professor Bill Waugh, who shared his extensive collection of government documents and reports.

Our families have now endured four editions of *The New Public Personnel*, and they surely have reason to wonder how anything can be new for that long. Edna, Carol, Kimberly, and Michael deserve to be recognized because this edition, as well as the previous three, would not have been possible without their patience and active support.

Ted Peacock told us he would put his best editor on this project, and he did. We are greatly indebted to Gloria Reardon for her careful and highly effective editing of this text.

Finally, thanks to all those wise students who suggested new topics, recommended needed revisions, and let us try out new ideas on them.

Lloyd G. Nigro
Felix A. Nigro

Public Personnel Administration in the United States

I

The American Public Service Today: Issues and Challenges

Personnel administration plays an important role in the efforts of public agencies of all kinds to achieve their goals, because American society relies on government workers at various levels to provide a wide range of necessary services. The American people expect that, among many other things, their children will be educated, their roads will be maintained, their food will be safe to eat, and their mail will reach its intended destination. Quite literally, the quality of American life depends on the performance of those who work for government—the quality of the public service.

An Internal Revenue Service unable to recruit and retain competent accountants is unlikely to make sure that everybody pays a "fair share." A badly trained police officer is a threat to the public safety, and overworked air traffic controllers may make disastrous mistakes. Incompetent or self-serving procurement and contract administration practices may waste huge sums and threaten the public's health, safety, and welfare. Partisan and discriminatory personnel practices fuel social conflict and limit the capacities of public agencies to be responsive to the legitimate interests of many groups in society.

This first chapter is divided into two major parts. The first presents a demographic sketch of the public service in the United States, with facts and figures to provide a sense of the scale and scope of the public service and its importance to the society. The second part describes what some have called the quiet crisis of the American public service. Its quality can no longer be taken for granted, and questions of personnel policy have emerged as prominent items on the public agenda of issues and problems to be resolved. This brief discussion of the quiet crisis introduces the many serious challenges faced in public personnel administration today that will be addressed in later chapters.

A DEMOGRAPHIC PORTRAIT OF THE AMERICAN PUBLIC SERVICE

The public service upon which Americans depend is large. Out of a U.S. civilian labor force of 124.8 million in 1990, 18.4 million were public employees. Of these, about 4.5 million worked for the states and about 10.8 million were on the payrolls of local governments (some 5 million in school districts alone). The federal government employed a little over 3 million civilians, or about 17 percent of the total number of public employees.[1]

The public service is distributed across many jurisdictions. In addition to the national government, the public sector includes the 50 states, over 3,000 counties, more than 19,000 municipalities, and almost 30,000 special-purpose districts. Add in townships and school districts, and the total exceeds 83,000 governmental units. Attention tends to be focused on the larger units, but many have populations under 5,000, and most are under 50,000.[2]

The public service is expensive. During 1986 the combined payrolls of the federal, state, and local governments approached $400 billion. For the same year, their total expenditures were $1.7 trillion. In other words, of every $4 spent by government in the United States, $1 went into the paycheck of a public employee.[3]

The public service is different at each level of government. Under the federal system, each level has certain responsibilities, some that are exclusive to a single level and others that overlap. What the various governmental units do and how much of it they do vary considerably. Education and law enforcement are primarily local responsibilities. States administer welfare programs, construct and run prison systems, and build and maintain freeways. The federal government has exclusive control over national defense, currency, and first-class mail services. These differences can be seen in the relative sizes of federal, state, and local governments and the occupational profiles of their work forces (see Table 1.1).

Table 1.1   Governmental Employment by Level of Government and Function, 1990

Function	Employees (1,000)		
	Federal Civilian	State	Local
National defense	1,038	—	—
Postal service	816	—	—
Space research/technology	25	—	—
Education	13	1,984	5,974
Highways	4	261	308
Health/hospitals	291	730	772
Public welfare	10	217	272
Police protection	79	89	664
Fire protection	—	—	327
Sanitation/sewerage	—	2	236
Parks/recreation	24	45	266
Natural resources	225	164	38
Financial administration	140	147	202
Other government administration	28	53	308
Judicial/legal	43	110	195
All other	369	701	1,198

Source: U.S. Bureau of the Census, *Statistical Abstract of the United States: 1992* (Washington, DC, 1992), Table 482.

Functional differences contribute to wide variations in the size and composition of city work forces. New York City, which operates a university system as well as elementary and secondary schools and delivers other services typically handled by counties, had more than 350,000 employees on its payroll in 1990. This is more than the entire population of many U.S. cities; only 63 had populations of over 250,000 in 1990. The same year, the city of Los Angeles (population 3.5 million) had 51,000 employees and Chicago (population 2.8 million) had 42,000.[4]

The public service is where the people are; public employees are concentrated in the large metropolitan areas and heavily populated states. Collectively, for example, in 1990 the nation's cities employed some 46,000 people in the area of housing and urban renewal and another 43,000 in public libraries. The majority of public service workers are in cities of 50,000 or more. Of the 5 million inhabitants of Cook County, Illinois, some 205,000 were local government workers in 1988. On the other end of the spectrum, in Jones County, South Dakota, 1,500 residents supported 50 or so government employees. There were over 1 million full-time positions in the 50 state systems of higher education in 1990, over 113,500 of them in California. Texas had 81,000, and there were fewer than 4,000 in either Wyoming or Alaska.[5]

Since under 10 percent of the federal work force is located in Washington, D.C., the distribution of the remaining 90 percent has a major impact on the states and localities. Over 1.3 million federal civilian employees were concentrated in eight states in 1989: New York, Pennsylvania, Illinois, Maryland, Virginia, Florida, Texas, and California. More than 315,000 worked in California. Maryland, Virginia, Alaska, and Hawaii had over 250 federal employees per 10,000 population. Wisconsin, in contrast, had only 60 per 10,000.[6]

The public service reflects the policy priorities that flow from public attitudes and political trends. Much of the recent growth in state bureaucracies was the result of federal policies designed to shift administrative responsibility for public welfare and regulatory services to the state governments. They, in turn, have sought to pass on certain program mandates and costs to local governments. The federal executive branch is a good example of how political change affects the public work force. President Ronald Reagan did not preside over a shrinking executive force; the executive departments grew by 6.2 percent between 1980 and 1989. The independent agencies, having lost the Veterans Administration to the cabinet-level Department of Veterans Affairs, collectively declined by 9.5 percent.[7] Table 1.2 tracks the shifting fortunes of executive-branch departments and independent agencies during the Reagan and early Bush years. A few, such as the Justice and Treasury Departments, the Federal Deposit Insurance Corporation, and the Postal Service, experienced substantial growth, but most lost positions; note, for example, what happened to the Office of Personnel Management and the General Services Administration.

The Changing Public-Service Work Force

The demography of the public service is changing at an accelerating pace. In certain respects, it is becoming more representative of the diverse and pluralistic society for which it works. Equal employment opportunity laws and affirmative action programs have contributed to rather dramatic increases in the overall employment of minorities and women over the past 30 years. By 1990, for example, half of all federal white collar jobs were held by women, and over a quarter of these positions were occupied by minorities. In 1990, 27.3 percent of *all* federal jobs were held by racial and ethnic minorities.[8]

Changes in the labor pool available to government are likely to more than compensate for any retreat from aggressive affirmative action policies by the executive, legislative, or judicial branches. Pub-

Table 1.2   Federal Civilian Employment in Executive Branch, by Department and Agency, 1980 and 1989

Department	1980	1989	Percent change
State	23,497	25,327	7.8%
Treasury	124,663	152,548	22.4
Defense	960,116	1,075,437	12.0
Justice	56,327	79,667	41.4
Interior	77,357	76,545	0.2
Agriculture	129,139	122,062	−5.5
Commerce	48,563	45,091	−7.1
Labor	23,400	18,125	−22.5
Health and Human Services	155,662	122,259	−21.5
Housing and Urban Development	16,964	13,554	−20.2
Transportation	72,361	65,615	−9.3
Energy	21,557	17,130	−20.5
Education	7,364	4,696	−36.2
Veterans Affairs	228,285	245,992	7.8
Independent Agencies			
Environmental Protection Agency	14,715	15,590	5.9%
Equal Employment Opportunity Commission	3,515	2,743	−22.0
Federal Deposit Insurance Corp.	3,520	9,031	156.6
Federal Emergency Management Agency	3,427	3,048	−11.1
General Services Administration	37, 654	20,063	−46.7
National Aeronautics and Space Administration	23,714	24,165	1.9
Nuclear Regulatory Commission	3,283	3,288	0.2
Office of Personnel Administration	8,280	6,859	−17.2
Small Business Administration	5,804	4,653	−19.8
Tennessee Valley Authority	51,714	26,676	−48.4
U.S. Postal Service	660,014	826,310	25.2

Source: U.S. Bureau of the Census, *Statistical Abstract of the United States: 1991* (Washington, DC, 1991), Table 529.

lic-sector recruitment, hiring, training, and career development programs will by necessity have to respond to a labor force that is increasingly made up of women, racial and ethnic minorities, and immigrants. Public administrators will have to be able to manage a diverse work force effectively.

The public service has steadily become more professional, well educated, and highly trained. The term *professional state,* applied to a system of government in which experts who work in a wide variety of specialized fields are key actors in making as well as implementing public policies, represents the central role government plays in American society. On all levels of government, functions such as social welfare and insurance, regulation, economic policy, research and development, and public works require people with highly developed technical skills and training. The federal government employs over 100,000 engineers and about 80,000 scientists. The U.S. Department of Agriculture houses close to 25,000 biologists and physical scientists, and another 40,000 work for other agencies.[9] The list of occupational specialties and professions needed by the public sector is very long, and it is growing.

Variability in Personnel Systems

The demographic heterogeneity of the public service is compounded by the extraordinary variability of its personnel systems. Federal and state laws and policies, professional standards of good practice, political traditions, and social norms do impose certain commonalities (e.g., no public employer may legally discriminate against racial minorities). Nevertheless, many small and large differences may be found across the 83,000 governmental units. It can fairly be said that while a general familiarity with public personnel administration will tell you what to look for, it frequently will not tell you what you will find in specific cases.

There are numerous examples of this variability. Many jurisdictions operate highly formalized, impersonal, and legalistic merit systems; many others are quite informal and personal in their approaches. In some places, independent civil service commissions function as central personnel agencies, but in others personnel departments reporting to city or county administrators make and administer policy. One state may bargain collectively with its employees, while its neighbors steadfastly refuse to do so. In one city, the police chief is a political appointee; in another, the chief occupies a career or merit position.

Within large governments there may be several personnel systems. Employees of the U.S. Departments of Justice, Agriculture, and State are in separate systems, and the federal Senior Executive Service operates under rules and procedures that are very different from those covering General Schedule and Wage Grade workers (see Chapters 2 and 7). In some jurisdictions a substantial proportion of the work force serves at the discretion of agency heads, chief executives, boards, and commissions; in others, only a few at the top do not enjoy the job security and procedural protection afforded by a classified civil service. Diversity is a hallmark of public personnel systems in the United States.

THE QUIET CRISIS OF THE AMERICAN PUBLIC SERVICE

The Framers of the U.S. Constitution were very much aware that the administrative *competence* of the new government would be a crucial factor in the citizens' willingness to support it in both material and political terms. They also understood that a successful democracy requires a deep-seated confidence in the essential *fairness, honesty*, and *responsiveness* of the public service. Today, there is reason for concern that the public service is gradually losing its capacity to function effectively on these terms.

In its 1989 report, the National Commission on the Public Service (also known as the Volcker Commission) observed that the need for a highly competent and trustworthy public service in the United States was steadily growing, not diminishing. However, the commission found serious problems with both competence and trust.[10] Its recommendations for changes in federal personnel policies and practices were intended to address what some have called the "quiet crisis" of the civil service. The commission's central message is clearly stated: We need to build a national consensus on the importance of a truly excellent public service. It called for:

> ... a renewed sense of commitment by all Americans to the highest traditions of the public service—to a public service responsive to the political will of the people and also protective of our constitutional values; to a public service able to cope with complexity; to a public service attractive to the young and talented from all parts of our society and also capable of earning the respect of all our citizens.[11]

The Volcker Commission's elevated vision of the values that should be embodied in the American public service is as old as the Republic. Translating that vision (or elements of it) into specific policies and administrative practices that enjoy broad public support has always been difficult, however. In part, this may be attributed to deeply entrenched public suspicions about "big government" and "bureaucrats." Over the past 20 years, the fragile base of public support enjoyed by the public service on all levels of government has been visibly eroded by a continuous barrage of partisan attacks, unsatisfied expectations, scandals such as Watergate, fiscal stress, and outright neglect by those in positions of political leadership. In 1990, Larry Lane and James Wolf described the condition of the federal personnel system in discouraging terms:

> Today's federal personnel system is the product of years of ne-
> glect—the offspring of a condition where political and ideological agen-
> das predominated over professional concerns. As a result, the
> personnel mechanisms in place are in disarray and ill-prepared to deal
> with the problems facing the nation....Piecemeal attempts by the exec-
> utive branch and the Congress to address specific problems in the sys-
> tem have not arrested its decline.[12]

While the federal government has by far been studied the most
in these terms, many states, localities, and school districts appear to
have similar problems. By the end of the 1980s, evidence of declining competence, existing or impending shortages of needed human
resources, and slumping morale in many areas of the nation's public
service was accumulating at a rate that could no longer be ignored.
In many instances, the public sector is fighting a losing battle to recruit and retain people with the skills and abilities needed to meet
the complex technical and social challenges confronting governments on all levels. Civil service reforms calculated to improve productivity, agency effectiveness, and responsiveness to political
leadership have produced at best mixed results. Public indifference,
partisan attacks, and increasingly noncompetitive rates of pay and
fringe benefits have lowered morale and dampened enthusiasm for
careers in the public service.[13]

Recommendations of the Volcker Commission

The Volcker Commission was concerned with the policies and practices of the federal public service, but its recommendations also
apply to other levels of government employment. To revitalize the
service and restore confidence in it, the commission urged the pursuit of 15 goals related to personnel policies and human resources
management. Each of these goals addresses a specific issue, but the
commission's general purpose was to focus attention on three basic
problem areas: reforming policies and practices at the top level of
the civil service, recruiting and retaining qualified personnel, and
improving performance and productivity.

The Higher Civil Service

In the first problem area, the Volcker Commission recognized
the need to reform personnel policies and practices affecting the
quality of the top levels of the civil service, including senior career
administrators and presidential appointees. A competent personnel
system is essential at this level because these administrators are re-

sponsible for the effective and efficient operation of the federal government.

It is the higher civil service that provides much of the day-to-day expertise and leadership necessary for successful governance. Public confidence and trust in government depends heavily on the extent to which those at the top of the civil service are seen to be competent, responsive, and consistently honest and fair.[14] The commission's evaluation of the condition of the higher civil service, along with those of other knowledgeable observers, must be considered alarming:

> Unfortunately, there is growing evidence that the supply of talented managers, political and career, in government is dwindling. Among presidential appointees...turnover rates have become a serious problem.... Among career senior executives...over half say that if a suitable job outside government became available, they would take it....Today, sadly, fewer than half the government's most senior and most successful executives are willing to recommend a career in public life to their children.[15]

Attracting and Keeping Talented People

In the second problem area, the Volcker Commission added its voice to those warning of serious weaknesses in government's ability to attract "the best and the brightest" to the career public service (see Chapter 4). Recruiting talented people with the needed technical and professional skills is difficult in an increasingly competitive labor market. Some agencies, such as the National Aeronautics and Space Administration, the National Institutes of Health, and the Department of Defense, have not been successful in efforts to hire scientists, nurses, or engineers from the nation's best universities. Turnover and early retirements also threaten to weaken the foundation of experience and skill government needs to function smoothly.

The tarnished image of the federal service and its cumbersome recruitment and hiring procedures discourage college students who might otherwise choose careers in the public service. Generally, public employment is not held in high esteem by today's college students, and the commission's own survey of honor society students revealed their overwhelmingly negative impressions of the rewards and career opportunities offered by the federal government. It is not hard to understand why federal agencies might have trouble recruiting from this group; 86 percent of the students expressed the belief that a "federal job would not allow them to use their abilities to the fullest," and about 50 percent said "most federal jobs are routine and monotonous."[16]

Government's ability to offer competitive pay and benefits has steadily deteriorated over the past decade. Studies have found that pay and benefits in the federal service are below those in the private sector by an estimated 7 to 24 percent for comparable jobs, and the gap has been growing larger every year.[17] On the executive level, the differences are even more striking. For responsibilities comparable to those of Level II executives, private executives make about eight times the pay of their federal-service counterparts.[18] In specific "shortage" occupations such as accountants and computer specialists, federal pay may be as much as 45 percent behind the private sector. Examples cited in a 1990 report to the Congress by the U.S. General Accounting Office (GAO) include the following:

> An official at the Naval Facilities Engineering Command in Philadelphia said that journeymen environmental engineers at the GS–12 level earn about $36,645 in the federal government; in the private sector in Philadelphia, he said, they could earn over $20,000 more. The official said "[t]his office has been reduced to a training ground. We hire good but inexperienced personnel, train them, only to lose them in 1 or 2 years to higher paying outside jobs."...The chief of pharmacy at the Boston Veterans Affairs Medical Center (VAMC) told us that salaries for newly graduated phamarcists were $7,000 to $15,000 a year higher at chain drug stores and other hospitals in Boston than at VA, where the entry-level salary was $32,121.[19]

Performance and Productivity

The third area of concern addressed by the Volcker Commission was the ability of the federal personnel management system to stimulate and sustain what it called a "culture of performance." The American public has every right to expect that civil servants will work hard to deliver services in an efficient, timely, and responsive manner. However, simply demanding high levels of performance is not enough. The personnel system must provide a supportive infrastructure of policies and programs. According to the commission, commitment to performance cannot survive if the government fails to provide adequate pay, recognition for jobs done well, training programs, and decent working conditions: "Quality service must be recognized, rewarded, and constantly reinforced. It is not enough to exhort the work force to do better—government must provide tangible signals that performance matters."[20]

Pay for performance has been a popular idea on all levels of government in the United States for some time, but efforts to implement it have been proven to be a challenge. Funding of merit pay and bonus plans has frequently been so inadequate that the intended connections between performance and compensation often have not been achieved, especially in the minds of public employees.[21]

The development of performance appraisal systems that discriminate among levels of performance and enjoy broad-based support in the work force has not been easy. In 1989, for example, the GAO reported that its preliminary examination of the federal government's Performance Management and Recognition System (PMRS) had revealed widespread unhappiness with the system. The PMRS was designed to overcome the weaknesses of the agency merit pay plans initially established under the 1978 Civil Service Reform Act, and the GAO concluded that after four years in operation it was far from a complete success. Nevertheless, the GAO considered PMRS an important program because it is a principal means for providing incentives to motivate and reward federal managers, and the lack of an effective program to do this could impede the creation of a culture of performance in government.[22]

Other Problems and Issues

In addition to the problem areas in public service highlighted in the Volcker Commission report, public personnel systems also are facing other performance-related issues such as those considered in Section III. One of these has to do with the changing nature of the American work force, which has already been noted: The labor pool from which public service personnel can be drawn is increasingly being composed of women, ethnic and racial minorities, and immigrants. These groups now make up about half of the public work force, and over the next ten years it is estimated that they will contribute well over 50 percent of the net additions.[23] The public service also, along with the rest of the population, is gradually aging. As the skills demanded by jobs in the public sector continue to increase, heavy investments in pre-entry, entry-level, and midcareer training and education will be required to keep pace. Successfully managing and developing the competencies of a diverse work force and creatively adapting personnel policies and practices to its needs are high priorities.

Public as well as private employers are also facing a series of social, legal, and organizational issues flowing from problems such as drug addiction and alcoholism (substance abuse), AIDS, the needs of handicapped workers, arguments for comparable worth and pay for performance, and sexual harassment. Such problems, once largely ignored or dealt with in the workplace by excluding or getting rid of employees who could be troubling to the organization, must now be confronted by public employers on legal grounds or as a matter of public policy. Balancing the needs and rights of individuals against those of the organization or the society has become a major challenge for public personnel administrators.

The controversies surrounding mandatory drug testing and the treatment of workers suffering from alcoholism provide a good example. In the federal service, a policy on such matters was set as a provision of the Civil Service Act of 1883 (the Pendleton Act), which stipulated that "no person habitually using intoxicating beverages to excess shall be appointed to, or retained in, any office, appointment, or employment to which the provisions of this act are applicable."[24] Over 100 years later, this mandate no longer applies; education, prevention, and rehabilitation are the goals of public personnel policies and programs addressing addiction. Similarly, employers are now asked to take positive steps to remove barriers to the employment of the disabled and to provide facilities that allow them to be productive, fully functional members of the work force. Workers suffering from AIDS are also protected from discrimination in employment under the Americans with Disability Act of 1990 (see Chapter 10).

The Challenge for Public Personnel Administration in the 1990s

If it is to contribute to the capacity of government to serve the public interest, public personnel administration must engage the many dimensions of the quiet crisis. The Hudson Institute, in a report prepared for the U.S. Office of Personnel Management, describes the challenge confronting federal agencies in the 1990s in terms we believe are equally applicable to state and local governments:

> Without reforms, some agencies may find the quality of services they can deliver will slowly erode, undermining public faith and support. For others, business as usual carries a genuine risk of failure to fulfill the basic public responsibilities they are charged with...the time to address these issues is now, before a slow decline or crisis has irrevocably damaged the reputation for competence, honesty, and fairness that the Federal civil service still enjoys.[25]

Modern democratic governments can be successful only to the degree that their agencies are staffed by motivated people who are technically able, politically responsible, and ethically committed to serving the public interest. The responsibilities of today's public personnel administration, therefore, are anything but mundane. The results of its efforts to meet the human resources challenges now confronting governments on all levels will deeply influence social, economic, and political developments in the United States.

■

NOTES

1. U.S. Bureau of the Census, *Statistical Abstract of the United States: 1992*, 112th edition (Washington, DC, 1992), Tables 481, 612.
2. U.S. Bureau of the Census, *Statistical Abstract of the United States: 1989*, 109th edition (Washington, DC, 1989), Table 445.
3. Ibid., Table 479.
4. U.S. Bureau of the Census, *Statistical Abstract: 1992*, Tables 490, 37, 38.
5. City employment, U.S. Bureau of the Census, *Statistical Abstract: 1992*, Table 489; county employment, U.S. Bureau of the Census, *City-County Data Book: 1988* (Washington, DC, 1988); state employment, *Statistical Abstract: 1992*, Table 486.
6. 1989 data from the U.S. Bureau of the Census, *Statistical Abstract: 1992*, Table 519.
7. U.S. Bureau of the Census, *Statistical Abstract: 1992*, Table 529.
8. U.S. Office of Personnel Management, *Federal Staffing Digest*, August 1991, p. 1; U.S. Bureau of the Census, *Statistical Abstract: 1992*, Table 522.
9. U.S. Office of Personnel Management, *Federal Staffing Digest*, Spring 1990, p. 8.
10. National Commission on the Public Service, *Leadership for America: Rebuilding the Public Service* (Washington, DC, 1989), pp. 1–9.
11. Ibid., p. 1.
12. Larry M. Lane and James F. Wolf, *The Human Resource Crisis in the Public Sector: Rebuilding the Capacity to Govern* (New York: Quorum Books, 1990), p. 17.
13. Charles H. Levine and Rosslyn S. Kleeman, *The Quiet Crisis of the Civil Service: The Federal Personnel System at the Crossroads* (Washington, DC: National Academy of Public Administration, December 1986).
14. U.S. Merit Systems Protection Board, *The Senior Executive Service: View of Former Federal Executives: Report to the President and Congress of the United States* (Washington, DC, October 1989).
15. National Commission on the Public Service, *Leadership for America*, p. 12.
16. Ibid., p. 26.
17. Levine and Kleeman, *Quiet Crisis*, p. 6.
18. *Report of the Commission on Executive, Legislative, and Judicial Salaries, 1985*, cited in Levine and Kleeman, *Quiet Crisis*, p. 22.
19. U.S. General Accounting Office, *Recruitment and Retention: Inadequate Federal Pay Cited as Primary Problem by Agency Officials* (Washington, DC, September 1990), pp. 32–33.

20. National Commission on the Public Service, *Leadership for America*, p. 34.
21. U.S. General Accounting Office, *Pay for Performance: State and International Public Sector Pay-For-Performance Systems* (Washington, DC, October 1990).
22. U.S. General Accounting Office, *Pay for Performance: Interim Report on the Performance Management and Recognition System* (Washington, DC, May 1989).
23. The Hudson Institute, *Workforce 2000* (Washington, DC, August 1990), p. xx.
24. "The Pendleton Act," in Frank J. Thompson (ed.) *Classics of Public Personnel Policy* (Oak Park, IL: Moore Publishing, 1979), p. 19.
25. The Hudson Institute, *Civil Service 2000*, report prepared for the U.S. Office of Personnel Management Career Entry Group (Washington, DC, June 1988), p. 44.

Public Personnel Administration: A Historical Overview

2

Public personnel administration did not emerge as a specialized field of study or established practice in the United States until the early 1900s, but governments have been recruiting, hiring, paying, managing, and firing public employees since the founding of the Republic. In these terms, public personnel administration has been around as long as governments have existed. This chapter traces the development of public personnel concepts and practices in the United States. It is intended to provide a background or context for the more detailed discussions of long-standing issues and current problems found in Sections II and III.

RESPONSIVENESS: THE ERA OF PATRONAGE AND SPOILS

For roughly the first 100 years of its existence, civil service in the United States was highly partisan in nature. Government workers were expected to actively support a political party's candidates for elective office. This was the norm. Government jobs traditionally were awarded to those who had faithfully served the winning party, its candidates, and the policy agenda they advanced. Hence the saying, "To the victor go the spoils."

Arguments for patronage or spoils approaches to public employment rely heavily on the idea that democratic governance requires public employees who are responsive to public priorities and electoral mandates. In addition to providing a strong incentive to work for the party, spoils systems virtually guaranteed responsiveness to legislators and elected executives, because those hired were at once loyal and fully aware that they could be dismissed for partisan reasons. In theory, by hiring and firing on the basis of political loyalty and active support for the party or candidate, the personnel system helps to assure bureaucratic responsiveness to elected officials and, through them, to public opinion.

Presidents, as well as governors and mayors throughout the country, have used patronage to build powerful political coalitions. Some students of American history maintain, in fact, that the presidents' control of federal patronage in the 18th and 19th centuries greatly strengthened the executive branch's position in the constitutional system of separated powers.[1] Abraham Lincoln freely dispensed federal jobs in an effort to build loyalty to and support for the Union cause. The White House was often overrun by job seekers during his tenure, and he is said to have remarked that "the spoils system might in the course of time become far more dangerous to the Republic than the rebellion itself."[2]

Policies of the First Presidents

The spoils system that Lincoln adeptly used and privately feared bore little resemblance to that used by presidents in earlier days. In general, the policy of the first six presidents (1789 to 1829) was to make appointments to federal offices on the basis of "fitness." In those days, fitness meant that the person was of good character, was able to do the work involved, *and* was in conformity with the views of the chief executive and his political associates. Normally, all three standards had to be satisfied. These early presidents did remove some people on purely partisan grounds, but they habitually replaced them with persons they believed to be both loyal *and* capable of effectively doing the administrative work of government.

Even after the Federalists lost control of the presidency to Thomas Jefferson in 1800, the national government's work force was drawn almost exclusively from the upper class. American society was highly stratified, and the government was led by the well-educated, the well-born, and the prosperous.[3] The early presidents were looking for men who had backgrounds like theirs, who shared their commitment to the Constitution, and who believed in governance as a responsibility of their social class. During this rather brief period, the federal service was very exclusive.

Taking into account the demand for political loyalty, it can hardly be said that the first six presidents implemented a merit system in the modern sense of that term. Nevertheless, the national government did have a "good reputation for integrity and capacity."[4] The situation was very different at the state and local levels, however. By 1829, the practice of handing out jobs simply on the basis of partisan support had entrenched itself in large states like New York and Pennsylvania.

Development of the Spoils System

When President Andrew Jackson was inaugurated in 1829, the United States was in the midst of a profound social, political, and economic transformation. The old social and political order established during colonial times was being replaced by a modern capitalist system based on the belief that wealth, power, and position should be and could be *achieved* rather than *inherited*. All that was needed were equality of opportunity, imagination, and hard work. Democracy and an expanding franchise were giving rise to organized parties and majoritarian politics. The country was expanding westward, urbanizing, and industrializing.[5] Swelled by large numbers of immigrants, the population, especially in the cities, was growing rapidly.

Jackson's stated views on public personnel policy reflected this changing scene. He rejected the elitist views of his predecessors in favor of a much more democratized approach to public service. Jackson is often called the father of the spoils system because he argued that the public service should be open to all segments of society, and there was no need for permanence because the duties of most federal jobs were simple and did not require experience. Accordingly, Jackson considered rotation in office the best policy. In the new era of democratic politics, Jackson's position was popular, responding as it did to "widespread resentment at the monopolizing of public office by representatives of the upper classes." Indeed, some families were said to have "maintained themselves from father to son in the civil service."[6]

In light of what was to happen to the civil service during the second half of the 19th century, Jackson could hardly be called a practitioner of unmitigated spoils. His appointments to top-level federal positions mirrored earlier attention to ability and competence. The available pool of qualified persons was still relatively small, and most of them came from upper-class backgrounds.[7] Nonetheless, his egalitarian rhetoric did much to open the gates for spoils on the national level. Those who followed were far more inclined to sweep out incumbents and to replace them with party loyalists. Their objective was a practical one: to win elections by strengthening the party machinery from the grass roots up.

During the second half of the 19th century, the spoils system developed to the point that it had "an adhesive grip upon the political machinery of the United States."[8] This was particularly true in the states and cities, especially the large cities where the "machines" prospered and the "bosses" ruled. For example, the goals of New York City's Tammany machine during the 1880s were: "To nominate candidates for public office, to get out the vote, and win elections. Once in power, the organization enjoyed a patronage feast."[9]

George Washington Plunkitt was a Tammany district leader or ward boss who happily explained his political "philosophy" to William Riordon of the *New York Evening Post* in a series of interviews conducted around the turn of the century. Plunkitt colorfully described the logic underpinning the spoils system:

> What is representative government anyhow? Is it all a fake that this is a government of the people, by the people and for the people? If it isn't a fake, then why isn't the people's voice obeyed and Tammany men put in all the offices?...We stood as we have always stood, for rewardin' the men that won the victory....Say, the people's voice is smothered by the cursed civil service law; it is the root of all evil in our government....First, this great and glorious country was built up by political parties; second, parties can't hold together if their workers don't get the offices when they win; third, if the parties go to pieces, the government they built up must go to pieces.[10]

CIVIL SERVICE REFORM I: UNDERMINING THE MACHINES

The civil service reform against which Plunkitt railed was an element of the Progressive movement of the late 19th and early 20th centuries in the United States. This movement had many political objectives, one of which was the destruction of the party machines and bosses who ran the nation's major cities. In the reformers' eyes, these machines institutionalized administrative inefficiency and waste, fostered rampant corruption, and ignored the legitimate interests of electoral minorities while taxing them heavily. Advocates of the reform agenda included members of the banking and commercial sectors, middle- and upper-income groups, and the growing numbers of university-trained professionals.

By advancing "neutral competence" as the standard that should be applied in the selection and retention of civil servants, the reformers sought to undermine a critical element of the machine's base of electoral power and administrative control—patronage. Plunkitt had reason to be alarmed.[11] He understood that the reformers were trying to fundamentally alter the political landscape. His fears would be realized as more and more governments enacted legislation designed to limit the scope of patronage in public employment.

Plunkitt certainly would have agreed with Justice Lewis F. Powell's dissenting opinion in *Elrod* v. *Burns* (1976).[12] In this decision, a majority of the Supreme Court ruled that dismissing "nonpolicy-making" employees solely for reasons of their affiliation with a political party violated their First Amendment rights. Powell disagreed, saying that it was naive to think that political activities were motivated by "some academic interest in 'democracy' or other public service impulse." He stated, "For the most part, as every politician knows, the hope of some reward generates a major portion of the local political activity supporting parties." Powell concluded, "History and long prevailing practice across the country support the view that patronage hiring practices make a sufficiently substantial contribution to the practical functioning of our democratic system to support their relatively modest intrusion on First Amendment rights." Plunkitt would have applauded, but Powell was in the minority, and *Elrod* v. *Burns* was the first of several Court decisions[13] that limited constitutionally acceptable patronage to situations where the hiring authority could "demonstrate that party affiliation is an appropriate requirement for the effective performance of the public office involved." Through these decisions, the Court provided a strong (if belated) constitutional underpinning for the merit principle.

Implementing Neutral Competence with Merit Systems

American democracy and egalitarianism have historically supported the ideal that people should get and keep jobs on the basis of their relative ability and performance. The belief that rewards such as job status and income should be *achieved* by the individual also enjoys widespread popular support, and disinterested, nonpartisan administration of the law is highly valued. With regard to the public personnel function, these norms are the foundation of the *merit* concept or principle. Basing the administration of public personnel systems on the merit principle was high on the agenda of the civil service reformers, who sought to legitimize their point of view by appealing to such deeply rooted American values.

In application, the merit principle dictates that appointments, promotions, and other personnel actions should be taken exclusively on the basis of the employees' relative ability and job performance. Since the turn of the century, this has usually meant the administration of competitive examinations for appointments and promotions. Test scores have been relied upon to distinguish accurately among candidates according to their capacity to perform satisfactorily on the job. For other personnel actions such as pay raises, reductions in force, and dismissals, it has also been assumed that employees' "merit" could be determined through performance appraisals, and they should be treated accordingly.

Government personnel systems based on these values and assumptions are called *merit systems*. In O. Glenn Stahl's words: "In its broadest sense a merit system in modern government means *a personnel system in which comparative merit or achievement governs each individual's selection and progress in the service and in which the conditions and rewards of performance contribute to competency and continuity of the service.*"[14]

On the federal level, after several unsuccessful initiatives, legislation establishing the foundation for a rudimentary merit system was passed by Congress in 1883. This was the Pendleton Act, which was enacted following President James A. Garfield's assassination by a disappointed office seeker in 1881. The more immediate and less sentimental reason for its passage, however, was the incumbent Republicans' fear that the next president would be a Democrat who would remove all Republican officeholders. The victory for reformers was not overwhelming at the time, because the law's coverage extended only to about 10 percent of the positions in the executive branch. But it would be successful in the long run; by 1952, well over 90 percent of the positions were covered, and presidents were beginning to complain about their inability to establish policy control over an "unresponsive" bureaucracy.

The administrative machinery set up to carry out the Pendleton Act was the bipartisan Civil Service Commission (CSC), rather than an executive agency. This meant that the CSC would enjoy considerable independence from the president in its policy-making and day-to-day administrative activities. However, the CSC was far from autonomous. The president appointed the three commissioners, subject to Senate confirmation, and could remove them. The president also had to approve civil service rules and regulations recommended by the CSC before they could be implemented. Another key provision was presidential authority to place additional positions under the classified civil service (the positions covered by the merit system), as well as to remove positions from it.

As state and local governments adopted merit systems, they tended to follow the federal example by creating commissions or boards to administer them. The first merit systems were poorly funded and struggled to survive (many did not). Besides being limited in coverage, they were narrow-gauged; basically, they gave routine tests to applicants, kept employee records, and did little else. Commissions were staffed largely by clerks, and it was the clerks who took care of the departments' personnel chores.

The first state to adopt civil service legislation applying the merit principle was New York in 1883, followed by Massachusetts in 1884. The limited success of the reform movement on the state level is revealed by the fact that no new state laws were approved during the next 20 years. Albany, New York (now a stronghold of old-style machine politics) was the first municipality to establish a merit system, in 1884. During the 1890s, Milwaukee, Philadelphia, New Orleans, and Seattle were among the cities approving charter amendments which established civil service regulations. The first county to do so, in 1895, was Cook County, Illinois. As the machines and reform parties struggled for control of the nation's cities and counties, it was not unusual for merit systems to come and go, depending on election outcomes. Often, commissions established under reform administrations became fronts for spoils when the machines gained the upper hand.[15]

The number of civil service systems at least nominally based on the merit principle continued to expand between 1900 and 1930, but the scope of their activities remained quite limited. At best, the merit principle was making sure that public employees were appointed through competitive entrance examinations, prohibited from engaging in partisan politics, and compensated on the basis of equal pay for equal work. In practice, little if any attention was paid to potential connections between personnel practices and organizational productivity and effectiveness. For the most part, merit systems concentrated on "keeping the rascals out." In many localities and states, of course, the spoils system was still deeply entrenched.

EFFICIENCY AND PRODUCTIVITY: MODERN PERSONNEL ADMINISTRATION

The explosive growth of the federal government during the Great Depression of the 1930s quickly outpaced the Civil Service Commission's capacity to handle day-to-day personnel operations. As President Franklin D. Roosevelt dramatically expanded the size of the classified civil service to encompass the New Deal agencies, it became clear that much of the commission's work would have to be decentralized to the agency level. It had become a serious bottleneck. This practical reality, in combination with the recognition that skilled personnel administration might help agencies function more efficiently, led to Roosevelt's 1938 executive order requiring professionally staffed personnel offices in federal agencies.

Historically, Roosevelt's order signaled the arrival of "modern" personnel administration. In this case, *modern* meant expansion of personnel services to line management, and improvement of such functions as position classification, selection, and training. It also meant that the definition of the CSC's responsibilities would shift from established routines to policy formulation, research and development, and program evaluation. Since these mandates required the CSC and departmental personnel offices to develop expertise across a wide variety of topics, college graduates began to replace clerks. Personnel administration gradually became more professionalized and specialized.

The concept of personnel administration as a tool or arm of management began to take hold, not only in the federal government but also in some states and localities. World War II greatly increased the pressure for personnel offices to be responsive and supportive, and by the end of the war, the old perception of personnel administration as a routine activity with limited technical content and little relation to managerial needs had been largely abandoned. Thus, in 1950, Herbert Simon, Donald Smithburg, and Victor Thompson stated in a widely read public administration text that personnel specialists dealt with matters "that are of the greatest long range importance to the organization."[16]

Developing and Managing Human Resources

The definition of the role of personnel administration continued to evolve. Between 1945 and 1960, public personnel administration became more people-oriented and less fixated on rules and regulations designed to protect the merit principle. Two general criticisms of the earlier approach to personnel administration were often heard. First, while increasingly professionalized and formalized personnel opera- tions were efficient in their own terms, they frequently worked to frustrate line officials. Personnel offices typically acquired reputa- tions as being centers of bureaucratization in which rules and proce- dures were all-important. A familiar complaint was that personnel workers carried a rule book (a personnel manual) that they followed rigidly, in a deliberate effort to severely limit line officers' discretion in personnel matters.

This kind of criticism was probably inevitable, given the increas- ingly technical nature of the personnel function and the establish- ment of personnel offices staffed by specialists. Those in staff roles normally will exert considerable control because they have a monop- oly on the expertise needed to administer complex policies and pro- cedures. In the public sector, they commonly have the legal as well as organizational authority to enforce and adjudicate the rules that managers must follow. Nevertheless, as part of a trend that would culminate on the federal level in the 1978 Civil Service Reform Act, appeals for flexibility and a management orientation were often heard during the late 1950s.

The second criticism was that personnel specialists tended to as- sume a highly legalistic definition of their responsibilities, while ne- glecting the social or human dimensions of organizational productivity. Personnel specialists did not seem to be at all "people minded." They concentrated on day-to-day tasks, applying technical skills but showing little interest in developing a broad-gauged ap- proach to the development and management of the organization's human resources. The human relations approach was having some limited influence in the private sector prior to World War II, but this was not the case in the public sector.

This situation began to change after the war as a people orienta- tion gained followers. Advocates believed that the insights of human relations could be applied to the personnel function in the following specific ways:

1. Attending to social and psychological factors in productivity, such as supervisory leadership, incentives, and the design of jobs and work settings.
2. Focusing attention on the behavioral as well as technical skills and conditions people need to develop their potential and to function effectively in the workplace. This includes enhancing job satisfaction and commitment to organizational goals through psychologically rewarding work settings, supportive

management styles, and opportunities for career development and training.
3. Recognizing the importance of effective supervision on the social and psychological levels. Since supervisors are the point
at which employees relate most directly to the organization,
they must be prepared to deal with a broad range of interpersonal and group processes which may affect morale and productivity. Personnel specialists should be able to provide
training and other programs to help supervisors be effective
in human as well as technical terms.
4. Increasing the knowledge base of personnel administration.
At least some personnel specialists should conduct applied
research into the social and psychological effects of personnel
policies and practices. This is vital if personnel administration
is to be firmly grounded in an understanding of the human
side of organizations.
5. Requiring personnel workers to have sufficiently broad backgrounds of training and experience to understand human behavior. The value of personnel specialists should not be
judged only in terms of command of techniques such as position classification and testing; they should also be schooled in
human relations theory and its practical applications.

By 1960, some progress could be reported on the federal level
and in a growing number of state and local jurisdictions in making
personnel systems more professional, better related to management
needs, and more attuned to a human resources management point of
view. The concept of public personnel, as set forth in textbooks, jour-
nals, and the recommendations of professional societies and commissions, firmly supported all of these values, in addition to the merit
principle. However, just how much progress toward realizing them
in practice had been made was a matter of opinion.

For many governments, patronage was still the dominant and accepted way of doing business. Congress had amended the 1935 Social
Security Act in 1940 to require merit-based personnel systems in state
agencies administering social security funds, and this method of
"forcing" merit was extended to the broad array of federal grants-in-
aid to states and localities that developed during the 1960s and 1970s.
In most states, prohibitions against partisan activity covered only
agencies administering federal funds (as required by the 1940 Hatch
Act). Moreover, even nonpartisan merit systems tended to be inward-
looking and unresponsive to many of management's concerns.

The "state of the art" as set forth in the personnel texts of the

1950s would be rendered obsolete (or at best incomplete) by the changes that took place beginning with the 1960s. Stimulated by social and political forces such as the civil rights movement, laws were enacted and court decisions were handed down on a variety of issues that had profound effects on modern public personnel administration. Among these issues were the legality of collective bargaining in the public sector, equal employment opportunity for minorities and women, and the constitutional rights of public employees.

COLLECTIVE BARGAINING IN GOVERNMENT EMPLOYMENT

Public-sector collective bargaining (negotiations between management and unions collectively representing workers) is now commonplace in many regions of the country (see Chapter 8). Prior to 1960, however, most merit system administrators thought of collective bargaining as peculiar to the private sector, a process that had no place in government. They had little or no familiarity with collective bargaining or appreciation of its institutional significance as a system of internal governance in private business. Therefore they saw it as a real menace to the merit principle, believing that the unstated goal of most union leaders was to wipe out civil service laws and regulations and replace them with agreements negotiated under the threat of strikes and other disruptions of public services.

For many personnel administrators, public employee unionization and collective bargaining were in the same category as spoils: practices to be vigorously resisted on legal, legislative, and organizational levels. By 1968, the federal courts had firmly established the right of public employees to form and join unions under the First Amendment of the Constitution. The courts had ruled that public workers have no constitutional right to collective bargaining or to strike against employers, but, more important, they also had identified no constitutional reason why public employers could *not* bargain collectively. Thus the decision was essentially political, and state legislatures could enact laws that required localities to engage in collective bargaining, proscribed collective bargaining, or took any position in between. The state also might say nothing, thus making collective bargaining a local option. And state legislatures could decide whether or not the state was to bargain collectively with all or some of its workers.

Once the question of their constitutionality had been resolved, laws enabling collective bargaining were warmly received by public employees in many states where pay and benefits had fallen behind those of the private sector. The spread of collective bargaining during the 1960s was to dramatically change the nature of public personnel administration. In 1959, Wisconsin was the only state to have passed legislation requiring municipal employers to bargain collectively with unionized workers. At that time, none of the states bargained with its own employees, and in the federal service there was no law or executive order providing for collective bargaining. By contrast, in the private sector most nonagricultural workers had been guaranteed the right to bargain collectively by the 1935 National Labor Relations Act. While Franklin Roosevelt had supported this act, he had also expressed strong opposition to any form of collective bargaining in the federal government.

The present situation is very different. By 1985, 40 states and the District of Columbia had statutes or executive orders setting up frameworks for collective bargaining with some or all government employees. In the federal government, collective bargaining was authorized initially by executive order in 1962, and since 1978 it has been a statutory requirement of the Civil Service Reform Act. Postal workers have been bargaining collectively since 1970. Currently, while the proportion of private-sector workers represented by unions and covered by negotiated contracts has declined to under 20 percent, in the public sector this proportion has grown to over 40 percent.[17]

Slightly less than half of all state and local government full-time workers are now members of employee organizations of one kind or another, and the percentage of organized employees is higher in such functions as education, highways, public welfare, hospitals, police, fire fighting, and sanitation. Close to 70 percent of all federal employees also are represented by unions serving as bargaining agents. No longer a novelty in the public sector, collective bargaining has become an accepted aspect of public personnel administration in many jurisdictions.

In collective bargaining, the relationship between management and the worker is transformed. Management deals directly with the union in the formulation and implementation of the rules of the workplace, and employees' views usually are expressed through the union and its leaders. In addition to requiring new areas of expertise of personnel administrators, collective bargaining has forced them to recognize and adapt to conditions under which power must be shared with one or more employee organizations. One highly visible result has been the emergence of a new specialty within the field:

labor relations and collective bargaining. Offices of labor relations, either within personnel departments or as free-standing units, also have become common.

EQUAL EMPLOYMENT OPPORTUNITY IN THE PUBLIC SECTOR

Today, the term *equal employment opportunity* (EEO) means that an employer may not discriminate in any aspect of employment for reasons of race, sex, age, religion, national or ethnic origin, or disability (see Chapter 9). In Stahl's definition of merit systems cited earlier, there is certainly no room for hiring or other personnel actions based on anything other than the individual's qualifications and job performance. However, there is no doubt that numerous public employers on all levels of government were systematically discriminating against minorities and women in 1962, when Stahl's book appeared. Patronage systems did much to exclude them, and in practice the merit principle often applied only to white males.

Discrimination of this kind has deep roots in the American public service. President Woodrow Wilson, a strong advocate of civil service reform, nevertheless ordered African Americans removed from all but menial jobs in the federal service, in an effort to build the southern base of the Democratic Party. Like ethnic and racial minorities, women have historically been confined to lower-grade jobs in government, as they have been in the private sector. Traditionally, their job opportunities have been restricted largely to clerical, secretarial, and service positions ("women's work," according to the stereotype).

Before the civil rights movement of the 1960s, the failure of public personnel systems to assure equality of opportunity had gone virtually unchallenged. Clearly, social norms, unequal educational opportunities, barriers to political participation, and intentional discrimination by personnel administrators all had played roles in keeping minorities and women out of all but the lowest levels of the public service.

A passive approach to the administration of merit systems had reinforced the pattern. Typically, those in charge of merit systems argued that the very low representation of minorities and women and their concentration in the lowest-ranking jobs did not violate the merit principle. They reasoned that as long as no *overt* discrimination was to be found, the absence of minorities and women was unfortunate but no fault of the merit system. But the U.S. Commission on

Civil Rights concluded in a 1969 report that many cases of overt discrimination could be found, and "static" and arbitrary civil service procedures were doing much to exclude minority groups. It cited as examples the use of unvalidated tests, rigid educational requirements, and automatic disqualification for an arrest record. The commission also stressed that most merit system agencies were making no positive effort to recruit minorities and seldom visited black colleges and universities.[18]

At the time this report was issued, the civil rights movement was having an impact on public policy. Several lower court decisions, based on the Fourteenth Amendment and the Civil Rights Acts of 1866 and 1871, had made it clear that the federal judiciary was inclined to void discriminatory practices and to impose affirmative action programs to redress their effects if public employers did not do so voluntarily. Then the Civil Rights Act of 1964, under which the Equal Employment Opportunity Commission (EEOC) was established, was amended in 1972 to cover the public sector as well as the private sector. Under Presidents Lyndon Johnson, Richard Nixon, and Jimmy Carter, federal affirmative action programs were implemented. Federal rules and regulations requiring that affirmative action plans be put into place by private contractors and governments receiving federal funds also were set forth during this period.

The federal courts have interpreted the prohibitions in the Civil Rights Act of 1964 on sex discrimination in employment. They have clearly established that sex-based job classifications must have a rational basis; there must be an occupationally valid reason for excluding men or women from a particular category of jobs. Because affirmative action programs now typically include women in recruitment, hiring, and career development initiatives, women are being hired to fill many kinds of positions previously assumed to be too strenuous or otherwise unsuitable for them (e.g., police and fire services). Intentional as well as traditional forms of discrimination against women such as sexual harassment are illegal, and the EEOC is empowered to investigate complaints by women against employers.

Nevertheless, women are still very poorly represented in higher-grade professional and executive positions, and many employers still appear to be placing a "glass ceiling" on their upward mobility. Veterans' preference is also a meaningful barrier for women. In *Personnel Administrator of Massachusetts* v. *Feeney* (1979),[19] the Supreme Court ruled that a Massachusetts statute granting veterans absolute preference in civil service appointments did not constitute sex discrimination and was not a violation of the equal protection clause of the Fourteenth Amendment. While the number of female veterans will increase, the vast majority are male, and absolute preference will continue to have an adverse impact on the hiring and promotion of women in the public sector.

Equal employment opportunity protections have been extended to cover discrimination based on age or disability. The Age Discrimination in Employment Act of 1967, as amended in 1978, prohibits public as well as private employers from discriminating against persons on the basis of age. Employers must be able to show that age is a legitimate employment qualification, and the courts now require reasonable evidence that a certain entrance or retirement age is disqualifying for a particular position. Thus employers may not favor younger workers if age is unrelated to ability to do the job in question. The Rehabilitation Act of 1973, which applies to public and private agencies that receive federal funds, requires them to have written affirmative action programs for the handicapped. Employers must make reasonable accommodations in facilities and tasks to facilitate the employment of persons with disabilities, a category that now includes victims of AIDS. The Americans with Disabilities Act of 1990 expanded coverage to most public and private employers.

Establishing the Rules for Equal Employment Opportunity

The U.S. Supreme Court issued a landmark decision in *Griggs* v. *Duke Power Company* (1971)[20] in which it established the following standard: An employer using a selection requirement that has disparate effects on the basis of race, sex, religion, or national origin must prove the requirement is job-related. If the employer cannot do this, the requirement constitutes illegal discrimination. The Court found that Duke Power was using job standards that were not demonstrably related to successful job performance, and this had served to disqualify black workers at a substantially higher rate than white workers. As to the company's claim that its intentions had been good, the Court said that "good intent or absence of discriminatory intent does not redeem employment procedures or testing mechanisms that operate as 'built-in headwinds' for minority groups and are unrelated to measuring job capability."

For public as well as private employers, *Griggs* was a bombshell. For the first time, the employer would have to prove that its personnel practices were valid and job-related if "the numbers" showed that the success of minorities was not proportional to that of nonminorities; that is, the practices were having a disparate impact. Before *Griggs*, plaintiffs had been required to show an intent by the employer to discriminate or to prove that a personnel policy or practice was invalid or not job-related. Under *Griggs*, once disparate impact was shown to exist, the burden of proof shifted to the employer. Individuals were not required to show that they had been harmed by a discriminatory practice in order to be covered by a court-ordered remedy. Remedies were to be applied to affected *classes* such as racial minorities and ethnic groups.

Numerous lower court decisions have since enjoined the use of selection methods that have not been proven to be related to satisfactory job performance. Judges have ordered personnel agencies to prepare new tests, issued guidelines for validating tests, required outreach recruitment, and mandated other changes in personnel programs intended to increase the hiring of minorities. In some cases, remedies took the form of consent decrees under which, for example, public employers agreed to use remedial hiring ratios and to alter seniority rules to protect minorities under reduction-in-force conditions.

Relevant actions taken by the Supreme Court have included ordering back pay for victims of discrimination and, in *Regents of the University of California* v. *Bakke* (1978),[21] ruling that college admission programs that take race into account are constitutional. In a widely publicized private-sector case, *United Steelworkers of America* v. *Weber* (1979),[22] the Court decided that voluntary affirmative action plans calling for preferential treatment of African Americans are not in violation of the Civil Rights Act of 1964. Justice William Brennan stated that the legislative history of the act indicated clearly that it was not the intention of Congress to "prohibit all race conscious affirmative action plans."

Progress under Affirmative Action

Despite some complaints that affirmative action is a form of "reverse discrimination"—against white males in particular—beginning in the 1970s significant progress was made in breaking down barriers to the hiring and career progress of minorities and women in the public sector. On the state and local levels, by 1990 minorities made up 27 percent of the public-sector work force, compared to 18 percent in 1973. The proportion of women among state and local government workers grew from 35 percent in 1973 to 43 percent in 1990. But the continued concentration of minorities and women in the lower levels of the public service is reflected in the fact that minorities in state and local jobs earned on average 85 percent of what white employees did in 1973 and 92 percent in 1990. The income gains for women were proportionately about the same but improved only from 73 percent of what men earned in 1973 to 80 percent in 1990.[23]

In the federal service, also, minorities and women have improved their positions, as indicated by an analysis of the data for 1976 and 1986 by Gregory Lewis. By 1986, their combined share of General Schedule (GS) positions was over 58 percent; for women only it was about 49 percent. In 1976, white males had occupied over 50 percent of all GS positions. Minorities and women also made gains in terms of their movement into management-level jobs. Fully 89 percent of GS–13 and above jobs were held by white males in 1976, but this number was down to 79 percent by 1986. The proportion of women in these grade levels grew from under 6 percent to 13 percent, and the gains for minority males were from about 5.5 percent to over 8 percent. White women made the largest gains in this category, from under 5 percent in 1976 to over 10 percent in 1986.[24] Minorities and women have made commensurate progress in closing average-pay gaps that cannot be explained by differences in age, education, or experience.

These discrepancies are still large, however, and not likely to disappear until well into the next century if current policies are maintained. Lewis concluded in 1988 that:

> Women and minorities made progress toward greater representation and more equal job rewards throughout the 1976–86 period. The pace was not rapid. It will take another 30 years before women and minorities fill half the positions at GS–13 and above and unexplained salary differences will still remain, but progress does appear to be steady.[25]

In state governments, women do appear to be making steady progress toward achieving pay equity and rates of promotion comparable to those of men in managerial positions. They may actually be doing somewhat better in this respect than their federal counterparts.[26]

The Battle over Quotas

In the 1980s, executive-branch support for affirmative action, especially programs calling for quotas, or remedial hiring ratios, and other forms of protection for groups or classes as opposed to individuals, evaporated. Presidents Ronald Reagan and George Bush declared remedial hiring ratios to be a form of reverse discrimination that violates the Fourteenth Amendment and the Civil Rights Act, though both also stated their commitment to EEO and "color-blind" personnel policies and practices. Under Reagan's appointment of Clarence Thomas as chairman of the EEOC, the agency became far less aggressive in its efforts to investigate complaints.

The U.S. Justice Department urged the Supreme Court in 1983 to rule unconstitutional an affirmative action plan entered into voluntarily by the Detroit Police Department providing for the hiring and promotion of whites and blacks in equal numbers. In this instance, the Court declined to hear the case, but over the next few years, it issued a series of decisions that had the practical effect of making it harder to bring discrimination suits and to obtain consent decrees designed to compensate for past discrimination. Among the more important of these decisions were *Patterson* v. *McLean Credit Union* (1989), *Wards Cove Packing Co.* v. *Atonio* (1989), *Price Waterhouse* v. *Hopkins* (1989), and *Martin* v. *Wilks* (1989).[27] Other decisions made it more difficult to recover compensatory damages and attorney's fees.

In *McLean*, the Court ruled that an 1866 statute guaranteeing all persons the same right to make and enforce contracts did not prohibit racial harassment on the job and other kinds of racial discrimination after the formation of a contract. *Wards Cove* was particularly significant because it reversed the *Griggs* rule that employers are responsible for showing that practices having disparate impact are job-related and required by "business necessity." Under *Wards Cove*, employers were simply required to show that the practice in question is significantly related to a legitimate business objective. This was, of course, a far less stringent standard than that imposed by *Griggs*. In *Price Waterhouse*, the Court ruled that a discriminatory employment action motivated by prejudice did not violate the Civil Rights Act if the employer could demonstrate that the same decision would have been made for reasons unrelated to prejudice.

Wilks was important because it allowed a person to challenge a consent decree settling a job discrimination suit by filing a separate lawsuit. Under this decision, for example, it was possible for a white male to sit on the sidelines until a decree protecting minority or female employees from reductions in force based strictly on seniority was implemented, and then initiate a lawsuit against the employer, seeking to overturn the court order. This would in effect prevent anything resembling finality or closure. After *Wilks*, in fact, suits challenging long-standing, widely accepted decrees were filed in over a dozen cities, including Birmingham, Boston, and Cincinnati.

Congress responded to these rulings of the Court by passing an amendment to the 1964 Civil Rights Act known as the Civil Rights Act of 1990. This legislation was designed to overturn key aspects of the rulings and to strengthen existing protections and remedies. President Bush vetoed the bill on grounds that it would force employers to impose racial and gender quotas in order to avoid expensive lawsuits. He pointed in particular to language that required employers to demonstrate *business necessity*, a term defined in the act as "essential to effective job performance." The veto was upheld by a narrow margin, but the following year a compromise bill was passed which established that practices having disparate impact on women or minorities must be "job-related for the position in question and consistent with business necessity" in order to be legal. The president signed the Civil Rights Act of 1991, arguing that it was no longer "a quota bill." According to its sponsors, though, the changes required to pass the 1991 act were minor, and it accomplished their objectives with regard to strengthening EEO and protecting affirmative action remedies.

CONSTITUTIONAL RIGHTS OF PUBLIC EMPLOYEES

Since the 1950s, the federal courts have significantly strengthened the individual's constitutional position in the employment relationship. As late as the mid-1950s, however, this relationship was dominated by the employer. The public employer was free to impose many conditions on workers that they had to accept in order to keep their jobs, and the only responsibilities of the government were those set forth in laws which could be revoked by the legislature. Historically, the courts had ruled that employees do not have any rights in the job, based on the Constitution. Thus, in fixing terms of employment, the public employer could and often did deny workers civil and political rights that were universally enjoyed by those in the private sector.

The due process clause of the Fifth and Fourteenth Amendments was held not to apply to public employees because, as the Court stated in *Bailey* v. *Richardson* (1951), "Due process of law is not applicable unless one is being deprived of something to which he has a right."[28] Government employment could not be considered property, it could be "perceived" to be liberty, and it "certainly" was not life. Accordingly, public employees were not entitled to substantive or procedural due process; they could, for example, be barred from political activity and denied the right to a hearing in loyalty cases. In

1892, Justice Oliver Wendell Holmes had stated for the majority that "The petitioner may have a constitutional right to talk politics, but he has no constitutional right to be a policeman."[29] This point of view held for the next 60 years, and the scope of judicial review of personnel actions taken by managers was very limited. As Arch Dotson observed in 1955, "from the assertion that there exists no constitutional right *to* public employment, it is also inferred that there can be no constitutional right *in* public employment. The progression is that, since there are no fundamental claims in employment, employment is maintained by the state as a privilege."[30]

Beginning in the 1950s, under the leadership of the Warren Court, the federal judiciary issued a series of decisions that effectively demolished what was called the "doctrine of privilege." In its place, the courts applied the following standard: "whenever there is a substantial interest, other than employment by the state, involved in the discharge of a public employee, he can be removed neither on arbitrary grounds nor without a procedure calculated to determine whether legitimate grounds exist."[31] Using this standard, the courts have narrowed management's discretion by extending certain constitutional protections and guarantees to public employees on all levels of government.

For public employees, one of the most important changes was a series of Supreme Court decisions in the 1970s establishing that they may have property and liberty interests in their jobs that warrant protection of the due process clause of the Fifth and Fourteenth Amendments. As defined by the Court, property interests include whatever affects the livelihood of an individual (e.g., welfare benefits, eligibility for occupational licenses). Liberty interests may come into play in situations where a personnel action affects the person's reputation, career prospects, or ability to find employment elsewhere. In *Board of Regents* v. *Roth* (1972), *Perry* v. *Sinderman* (1972), *Arnett* v. *Kennedy* (1974), and *Bishop* v. *Wood* (1976),[32] the Court defined the conditions under which property and liberty interests could exist and what standards of due process applied under specific conditions.

In the area of freedom of expression, the Court set forth a balancing test under which it rejected the proposition that public employment could be subjected to any conditions, no matter how unreasonable. In *Pickering* v. *Board of Education* (1968),[33] the Court ruled that the First Amendment rights of Pickering, an Illinois high school teacher, to publicly criticize the board had been violated. However, while teachers could not constitutionally be compelled to give up a right "they would otherwise enjoy as citizens to comment on matters of public interest," the state did have interests as an "employer in regulating the speech of its employees that differ significantly from those it possesses in connection with regulation of the speech of the citizenry in general." In other words, in each case the interests of the teachers as citizens in regard to their ability to comment openly on matters of public concern were to be balanced against the interests of the public employer in providing services to the public.

Since *Pickering*, the Court has applied this balancing test to a number of cases, often with the minority expressing the opinion that the majority had "tilted" in the wrong direction. Overall, first the Burger and then the Rehnquist Court have tended to uphold the employer's position more often than the employee's. The Court has also been reluctant to entertain anything but cases involving fundamental or sweeping constitutional issues. In practice, this has meant that the present Court is far less likely than the Warren Court to consider cases originating in the employment relationship. This is nonetheless a far cry from the earlier conditions, under which the courts simply refused to recognize *any* First Amendment protections for public employees.

Over the past 30 years, the Court has voided or meaningfully limited public employers' power and discretion in several areas of the employment relationship. Public employees may no longer be required to take vague and overly broad loyalty oaths, and their freedom of political association cannot arbitrarily be limited by blanket prohibitions against membership in the Communist Party, or any other organization for that matter. Likewise, unless the employer can show a rational connection or "nexus" between the personal behavior or appearance of an employee and his or her job performance, dismissals and other serious actions taken against the employee stand a good chance of being overturned by the courts.

RESTRICTIONS ON EMPLOYEES' POLITICAL ACTIVITIES

It has been a long-standing practice for the political activities of millions of public employees to be greatly restricted. Historically, the intentions of federal and state legislation imposing such restrictions were to prevent partisan coercion of public employees, to assure the political neutrality of the civil service, and to protect the merit principle. Restrictions on political activity have been attacked in court on grounds that they are unconstitutional, but they have withstood these challenges. In effect, the federal courts have ruled that current restrictions on the political activity of public employees are matters of legislative discretion.

Passed at least in part because of congressional fears that President Franklin D. Roosevelt was building a powerful political base in the federal bureaucracy, the 1939 Hatch Act limited the political activities of federal employees. It applies to most workers in the executive branch but not to the president and vice president, heads and assistant heads of executive departments, members of the White House staff, and officials who determine national policy and are appointed by the president with Senate confirmation. The principal responsibility for developing and enforcing the rules and regulations to implement the act was assigned to the U.S. Civil Service Commission and now resides in the Office of Personnel Management (OPM).

A second Hatch Act passed in 1940 extended coverage to state or local employees "whose principal employment is in connection with any activity which is financed in whole or in part by loans or grants made by the United States."[34] This act was repealed by the Federal Campaign Act of 1974, and state and local workers are now permitted to engage in certain partisan political activities (e.g., to solicit votes in partisan elections and to serve as delegates to party conventions) if state laws do not prohibit them.

The Hatch Act forbids the "use of official authority or influence for the purpose of interfering with an election or affecting the result thereof" and, in the case of federal employees, taking "any active part in political management or in political campaigns." For federal employees the most severe penalty for violation is removal, and the minimum penalty is suspension without pay for 30 days. In the case of state and local workers, if the OPM finds that a violation has taken place, it decides whether removal is warranted. If it recommends removal but the state or local government employer does not comply, the federal funding agency must withhold from the grant or loan supporting the employee an amount equal to two years' pay.

The constitutionality of the 1939 Hatch Act and the 1940 act covering state and local employees was upheld by decisions in two Supreme Court cases in 1947: *United Public Workers* v. *Mitchell* and *Oklahoma* v. *United States Civil Service Commission.*[35] The Court reaffirmed its position in 1973, overturning a federal district court ruling that the Hatch Act was unconstitutional because it was vague and "capable of sweeping and uneven application." In its decision that year in *United States Civil Service Commission* v. *National Association of Letter Carriers, AFL-CIO,*[36] the Court found there was nothing "fatally overbroad about the statute." The majority went on to say that the CSC's regulations were "set out in terms that the ordinary person exercising ordinary common sense can sufficiently understand and observe, without sacrifice to the public interest," and were not unconstitutionally vague.

Opponents of the Hatch Act then turned to Congress in search of a legislative remedy. In 1976, Congress passed a bill to permit federal employees to take part in political campaigns and to seek nomination or election to any office, but President Gerald Ford vetoed that measure. In 1993, however, the House voted to allow federal workers to run for local office and to manage and raise funds for campaigns on all levels of government. President Bill Clinton has indicated his support for this proposed legislation, agreeing with those who argue that protecting public employees from political coercion should not involve stripping them of important political rights.

Present Policies

Under existing policies, federal employees may not campaign for partisan candidates, work to register voters for one party only, make campaign speeches, or be candidates for partisan offices. Other prohibitions include soliciting and collecting contributions, distributing campaign literature in a partisan election, holding office in a political party or club, and circulating nominating petitions.

Federal workers are permitted to vote, express opinions about candidates and issues, and assist in voter registration drives. They may also participate in nonpartisan campaigns, contribute money to political parties and organizations, and campaign for and against referendum questions, constitutional amendments, and municipal ordinances. Displaying political badges, buttons, and stickers may be allowed, subject to departmental regulations concerning situations where the employee is carrying out official duties.

To varying degrees, most state and local governments also restrict their employees' political activities. A few have laws that are more restrictive than the Hatch Act; for example, they may prohibit voluntary contributions or not allow workers to express their opinions publicly. For the most part, the pattern on the state and local level is to have statutes that parallel the Hatch Act. The numbers and types of employees covered, however, differ from state to state.

CIVIL SERVICE REFORM II: MAKING GOVERNMENT WORK

The first civil service reform movement sought to replace spoils with merit systems and to limit line management's control over many aspects of personnel administration. Now the term *civil service reform* usually refers to efforts to align personnel practices with the day-to-day needs of public managers, to improve the performance of public employees, and to make the bureaucracy more responsive to its political leadership.

In this context, the source of civil service reform is public dissatisfaction with the performance of administrative agencies and the widespread perception that government no longer "works." Business, civic, professional, and other concerned groups argue that the civil service machinery set up in the original reform movement has become outmoded and counterproductive. Line managers complain that they are denied the authority and flexibility needed to manage human resources efficiently and effectively. Workers in departmental personnel offices, trying to be more responsive to agency needs, are frustrated by central personnel organizations that do not delegate the needed authority. Employees see little connection between the quality of their work and promotions, pay raises, and other incentives.

Thus, on one level, the battle cry of the reformers is: "Let managers manage, and set up personnel systems that help them do it." On another level, reformers call for changes that will make civil servants responsive to the policy goals and directives of elected officials. As patronage, once the great engine of political accountability and responsiveness, has steadily declined in scale and importance, political leaders have found no widely accepted functional equivalent. Now they often identify highly protective and semi-independent personnel systems as largely responsible for the problem. In these terms, a goal of today's civil service reform is to design personnel systems that protect the merit principle while allowing elected executives to establish firm policy control over the bureaucracy.

The concerns for managerial effectiveness and political responsiveness have produced two approaches to civil service reform. The management flexibility model seeks to place control of key personnel functions in the hands of chief executives and line managers. The political responsiveness model focuses on measures designed to assure the responsiveness of public employees to political leadership and public opinion.

The Management Flexibility Model

An important feature of the new civil service reform is its emphasis on the need to allow chief executives, department heads, and program administrators greater control over the personnel function. Proponents of the management flexibility model maintain that merit systems have functioned far too independently and have seemed intent on imposing restrictive and cumbersome controls on the discretion of line management in personnel matters. They disagree with the proposition that chief executives and line managers must be kept at arm's length because they cannot be relied upon to protect the merit principle.

According to this line of reasoning, the first civil service reform movement created a separation between general management and personnel administration, despite the fact that personnel, like budgeting and finance, is an integral part of the management function in any public agency. Although it may have "kept the rascals out," critics argue that this approach seriously compromises management's capacity to use human resources effectively. If governments are to satisfy public demands and overcome the difficulties created by fiscal stress, the separation between executive management and the personnel function must be bridged. There is no necessary contradiction between merit and a management-oriented personnel system.

The management flexibility model proposes four specific reforms. First, the traditional civil service commission should be abolished and replaced by an office of personnel management or department of human resources. This organization should be headed by a director who is appointed by and directly accountable to the chief executive of the jurisdiction (the mayor, city manager, governor, or president). This structural change allows the chief executive to establish direct policy control over the personnel function and to use it, through the department of human resources, to support organizational efforts. This arrangement, typical in the corporate world, should not threaten the merit principle if the management hierarchy is made legally responsible for protecting that principle and, equally important, is held strictly accountable for violations. In addition, independent boards or commissions established to hear employee appeals and empowered to conduct investigations of personnel practices would assure fairness and prevent political abuses.

The Civil Service Reform Act (CSRA) of 1978 followed this model on the federal level by providing for an Office of Personnel Management, whose director reports directly to the president, and a

Merit Systems Protection Board responsible for the watchdog function. In state and local governments, civil service commissions with personnel policy-making, appellate, and administrative responsibilities still operate in many jurisdictions. In a growing number, however, the commissions have been either abolished or limited to advisory, appellate, and investigatory roles. The personnel director reports directly to the governor in over half of the states.[37]

The second reform proposed in the management flexibility model is that central personnel agencies and personnel offices in line departments should eliminate the numerous unnecessary rules and regulations they have used to closely control managers' discretion in personnel matters. Procedures should be streamlined and, wherever possible, simplified. Along these lines, in testimony before the Congress in 1978, Alan Campbell, chairman of the Civil Service Commission, argued that the CSRA was needed to reduce "the accumulation of laws, regulations, and policies which have grown up over the last 95 years." He included the following in a list of problems with rules and regulations confronting the federal civil service:

1. Supervisors, employees, political leaders, and others are confused about what they may and may not do without violating essential merit principles.
2. Excessive centralization of personnel authorities takes many types of day-to-day personnel decisions out of the hands of line managers, who nonetheless are held responsible for accomplishment in major program areas. Managers must go through extensive paperwork justifications to obtain Civil Service Commission approval of relatively minor decisions.
3. Overcentralized, restrictive systems for examining and selecting employees make it hard for managers to hire expeditiously the best qualified people and to meet their equal employment opportunity responsibilities.
4. Managers find a confusing array of regulations and procedures standing in their way when they seek to reward good work performance, to discipline employees, or to remove employees whose performance is clearly inadequate and cannot be improved.
5. The jumble of laws, regulations, and special provisions affecting executive positions makes it very difficult for agency heads to utilize their top staff most effectively.[38]

According to Campbell and other supporters of the management flexibility model, problems such as these can be solved only if the personnel system shifts from a *regulatory* to a *service* orientation. In these terms, the proper role of the central personnel agency is to provide general policy guidance and technical assistance to line departments in public agencies in such areas as EEO, performance appraisal, and training. Within the limits set by law and negotiated contracts, control over the details of the personnel function and authority to tailor practices to specific conditions should be left to the line departments. A central agency such as the OPM should conduct research and development programs, exercise quality control through periodic evaluations of departmental policies and practices, and provide leadership across the spectrum of human resources challenges facing the government.

The third reform provides for separate personnel systems for executives. The success of programs depends heavily on the loyalty, expertise, and motivation of career executives, but traditional civil service systems do not make any special provisions to assure strong executive leadership and effective use of administrative talent. Procedural flexibility, appropriate incentives, and well-planned career development systems for executives are needed.

This was the rationale for the Senior Executive Service (SES) that was established in the federal government by the CSRA and is now found in some form in about 20 states. In an SES, rank is in the person, not in the job or position. This arrangement facilitates mobility by preventing the downgrading that is always possible under conventional position-based systems if the classifiers rule that the executive's new duties are of a less responsible nature. In addition to enhanced mobility, SES personnel systems usually allow some discretion in setting the entrance salaries of executives, and they typically use some form of merit pay and bonuses instead of automatic step and inflation increases. SES members are untenured and may be returned to lower-level positions if their performance is less than satisfactory—an element of flexibility for agency management.

The fourth reform in this model is to give management the capacity to reward good performers and to discipline and remove poor performers. This means that sound performance appraisal systems must be developed and competently administered in conjunction with merit pay plans. Under traditional personnel systems, few incentives exist to measure performance carefully, and complex, drawn-out appeals procedures often discourage efforts to remove unsatisfactory employees. While merit pay plans have been instrumental in getting legislative approval of civil service reform packages on the federal and state levels, they have proven to be very difficult to implement, and evaluations of their effects on performance are at best inconclusive. However, this has not dampened enthusiasm for the concept in the states, and in the federal government an extension of merit pay to the entire General Schedule is being considered by Congress.

The Political Responsiveness Model

The other side of the reform coin is the idea that personnel systems should promote, rather than block, responsiveness and accountability to political leadership. A long-standing complaint of presidents, governors, mayors, and other chief executives is that the merit system extends so far up in the hierarchy that there are too few "exempt" positions they can fill with supporters of the administration and its policies. The issue here is not partisan spoils but rather the executive's capacity to be in control of administrative agencies, to carry out electoral mandates, and to be able to overcome "bureaucratic inertia."

Just how many positions, and which ones, should be excluded from the classified civil service or merit system remains a much-argued question. It is clearly not in the public interest to cultivate a civil service that feels it can safely ignore public opinion and elected officials' priorities because it is protected by a dense thicket of merit system laws and regulations. Taken to its extreme, this can produce a center of political power that is at once unresponsive and very difficult to hold accountable for its actions.

In the City of Los Angeles, for example, the position of chief of police is a merit appointment. In theory, this approach greatly minimizes the possibility of partisanship by placing the Los Angeles Police Department (LAPD) under the control of a career professional in law enforcement, in line with the value of neutral competence. In practice, this has allowed the chief to build a powerful political coalition for the department. Mayors, city councils, and police boards have found it difficult to influence departmental policies, and it has been almost impossible to remove chiefs for political reasons until their own coalitions abandon them. Over the years, the LAPD frequently has been accused of being deliberately unresponsive to certain interests and community needs, particularly those of the city's large minority population. The videotaped beating of Rodney King in 1992 exposed what many considered to be a long-standing pattern of brutality for which the department had escaped accountability. Lacking the authority to discipline or fire the LAPD chief, the mayor and city council of Los Angeles had to wait until the recommendations of a special commission and public outcry finally forced the chief to retire.

Advocates of the responsiveness model would say that the LAPD case is simply a dramatic example of a more general problem: Overextended merit system coverage has made it possible for bureaucrats to be unresponsive and less than fully accountable for their performance. Even city managers (who serve at the pleasure of the city council) have said that they could not manage efficiently because incompetent department and assistant department heads were protected by civil service. The solution would be to expand the number of exempt or policy positions, especially at the higher levels where policies are made and programs designed. In Oregon, for example, a substantial number of positions were taken out of the classified service and placed in the exempt category. In many states, up to 25 percent of the work force is exempt, and in the federal service up to 10 percent of the SES positions may be filled with noncareer or political appointments (to a maximum of 25 percent in any single agency). Noncareer appointees may be removed from the government at will, and career executives may be demoted from the SES.

Critics have suggested that the political responsiveness model is nothing more than a smokescreen designed to cover up a return to partisan public administration. They point to a long history of efforts by chief executives to evade merit system requirements. President Franklin Roosevelt used his authority under the Pendleton Act to "cover in" thousands of New Deal appointees who had not been hired through competitive merit procedures. President Dwight Eisenhower, confronted by a bureaucracy dominated by career administrators hired during the Roosevelt and Truman administrations, made an aborted effort to purge some of these employees from their classified positions, and he did succeed in getting legislation passed that expanded the number of exempt policy positions available for presidential appointments. The Nixon White House staff developed and skillfully implemented a calculated strategy for clearing the bureaucracy of officials not considered loyal to the president and replacing them with team players. The so-called Malek Manual set forth a shadow personnel operation intended to evade CSC rules and procedures.[39]

Tactics of this kind did not originate with Nixon; both the Kennedy and Johnson administrations had worked around civil service rules to assure the loyalty of career employees. The Reagan administration adroitly used the CSRA to establish rather firm policy control over federal agencies. In fact, with varying degrees of skill, determination, and success, all presidential administrations have tried to get "their people" into key positions, including positions that are supposed to be filled by career merit appointments.

Suspicions that elected chief executives on all levels of government would sacrifice the merit principle on the altar of political responsiveness if given the chance have encouraged opposition to the entire concept. The national trend over the past ten years, however, has been toward strengthening the executive's position relative to the career civil service through procedures such as the creation of senior executive services. At what point responsiveness becomes narrow partisanship is an important issue, and clashes between the values of neutral competence and political responsiveness will continue as policymakers seek to achieve a reasonable balance between the two.

■

NOTES

1. The classic reference is Carl Russell Fish, *The Civil Service and the Patronage* (Cambridge, MA: Harvard University Press, 1904).
2. See Paul P. Van Riper, *History of the United States Civil Service* (New York: Harper and Row, 1958), p. 44.
3. Ibid., pp. 17–18.
4. Ibid., p. 27.
5. Douglas T. Miller (ed.), *The Nature of Jacksonian Democracy* (New York: John Wiley & Sons, 1972).
6. Van Riper, *History of United States Civil Service*, pp. 27, 33.
7. Frederick C. Mosher, *Democracy and the Public Service* (New York: Oxford University Press, 1968), p. 62.
8. Van Riper, *History of United States Civil Service*, p. 42.
9. William L. Riordon, *Plunkitt of Tammany Hall* (New York: E. P. Dutton, 1963), p. xii.
10. Ibid., pp. 12–13.
11. Martin J. Schiesl, *The Politics of Efficiency* (Berkeley, CA: University of California Press, 1977).
12. 427 U.S. 347, 96 S.Ct., 2673 (1976).
13. *Branti* v. *Finkel*, 445 U.S. 507 (1980) and *Rutan* v. *Republican Party of Illinois*, 58 LW 4872 (1990).
14. O. Glenn Stahl, *Public Personnel Administration*, 5th ed. (New York: Harper & Row, 1962), p. 28. Italics in the original.
15. Albert H. Aronson, "Personnel Administration: The State and Local Picture," *Civil Service Journal*, vol. 13, no. 3 (January–March 1973), p. 38.
16. Herbert A. Simon, Donald W. Smithburg, and Victor A. Thompson, *Public Administration* (New York: Alfred A. Knopf, 1950), p. 312.
17. U.S. Bureau of the Census, *Statistical Abstract of the United States: 1992*, 112th edition (Washington, DC, 1992), Table 672.

18. U.S. Commission on Civil Rights, *For All the People…By All the People: A Report on Equal Opportunity in State and Local Government Employment* (Washington, DC: U.S. Government Printing Office, 1969), pp. 32–37, 64–65.
19. 442 U.S. 256 (1979).
20. 401 U.S. 424 (1971).
21. 98 S.Ct. 2733 (1978).
22. 443 U.S. 193 (1979).
23. U.S. Bureau of the Census, *Statistical Abstract of the United States: 1992*, Table 483.
24. Gregory B. Lewis, "Progress Toward Racial and Sexual Equality in the Federal Civil Service?" *Public Administration Review*, vol. 48, no. 3 (May–June 1988), pp. 701–702.
25. Ibid., p. 705.
26. Rita Mae Kelly et al., "Public Managers in the States: A Comparison of Career Advancement by Sex," *Public Administration Review*, vol. 51, no. 5 (September–October 1991), pp. 402–412.
27. *Patterson* v. *McLean Credit Union*, 109 S.Ct. 2363 (1989); *Wards Cove Packing Co.* v. *Atonio*, 109 S.Ct. 2115 (1989); *Price Waterhouse* v. *Hopkins*, 109 S.Ct. 1775 (1989); *Martin* v. *Wilks*, 109 S.Ct. 2180 (1989).
28. 341 U.S. 918 (1951).
29. *McAuliffe* v. *Mayor of New Bedford*, 155 Mass. 216, 29 N.E. 517 (1892).
30. Arch Dotson, "The Emerging Doctrine of Privilege in Public Employment," *Public Administration Review*, vol. 15, no. 2 (Spring 1955), p. 87.
31. See David H. Rosenbloom, "Some Political Implications of the Drift toward a Liberation of Federal Employees," *Public Administration Review*, vol. 31, no. 4 (July–August 1971), p. 421.
32. *Board of Regents* v. *Roth*, 408 U.S. 564, 92 S.Ct. 2701, 33 L.Ed. 548 (1972); *Perry* v. *Sinderman*, 408 U.S. 593, S.Ct. 2694, 33 L.Ed. 2d 570 (1972); *Arnett* v. *Kennedy*, 416 U.S. 134 (1974); *Bishop* v. *Wood*, 426 U.S. 341 (1976).
33. 391 U.S. 563, 88 S.Ct. 1731, 20 L.Ed. 3d 811 (1968).
34. Ch. 410, 53 Stat. 1147, ch. 640, 54 Stat. 767.
35. *United Public Workers* v. *Mitchell*, 330 U.S. 75, 67 S.Ct. 556, 91 L.Ed. 754 (1947); *Oklahoma* v. *United States Civil Service Commission*, 330 U.S. 127 (1947).
36. 93 S.Ct. 2880, 27 L.Ed. 2d 796 (1973).
37. N. Joseph Cayer, "Merit System Reform in the States," in Steven W. Hays and Richard C. Kearney (eds.), *Public Personnel Administration: Problems & Prospects*, 2nd ed. (Englewood Cliffs, NJ: Prentice-Hall, 1990), pp. 266–267.
38. Alan K. Campbell, "Testimony on Civil Service Reform and Organization," *Civil Service Reform*, Hearings of the U.S. House Committee on Post Office and Civil Service (Washington, DC: U.S. Government Printing Office, 1978).
39. White House Personnel Office, "The Malek Manual," in Thompson (ed.) *Classics of Public Personnel Policy*, pp. 58–81.

Personnel and Organizational Effectiveness

3

Public personnel administration in the United States has undergone a pronounced shift in emphasis over the past 25 years. Efficient administration and enforcement of merit system laws and regulations are still important, but supporting public administrators' efforts to improve performance also has a high priority.[1] The term *human resources management* is often used to distinguish this orientation from the legalistic, regulatory image conveyed by the term *public personnel administration.*[2]

The increased emphasis on the human resources management aspect of the responsibilities of public personnel administration does not mean that other values have been set aside. The degree to which personnel policies and practices promote organizational efficiency and goal achievement is certainly a major concern, but it is not the only standard of evaluation. In the United States, public personnel systems have not been designed to operate only as instruments of line management. Bruce Buchanan and Jeff Millstone observed "numerous structural embodiments of democratic morality" in any agency:

> There are Civil Service grievance procedures and liaison offices whose purpose is to protect the rights of employees who feel unjustly used by superiors or agency procedures. There are Affirmative Action

offices and officers, intent on securing compliance with Civil Service dictums on the hiring of disadvantaged minorities, thereby promoting equal opportunity and representative democracy....Each of these structural instruments for the protection of individual rights is capable of disrupting or slowing program operations, in the interest of securing *priority* attention for the "equal protection" or "procedural due process" rights of individual citizens. This fosters a *de facto* co-equality between program structures and structures aimed at promoting democratic morality.[3]

In this chapter, we will present an overview of the ways in which applications of the human resources management point of view might enhance the performance capabilities of public agencies. Two broad areas of organizational activity are involved: *external extraction*, or the organization's efforts to get the human resources it needs from its environment, and *internal extraction*, or the organization's efforts to obtain needed contributions from its members. Major topics introduced, such as recruitment, compensation, and collective bargaining, are discussed in detail in Section II.

EFFECTIVENESS IN EXTERNAL EXTRACTION

One way of judging the effectiveness of organizations is to compare their "ability... in either relative or absolute terms, to exploit [their] environment in the acquisition of scarce and valued resources."[4] From this perspective, the measure of an organization's effectiveness is its *ability to attract needed human and material resources from its environment*. All human organizations are open systems, which continually interact with their environments. The human and material resources required to carry out the organization's activities must be obtained from the external environment. For many reasons, some organizations and their administrators are more successful than others in influencing outside agents to provide political support, skilled personnel, and money. In other words, they have a relatively well-developed external-extraction capability. Effective organizations perform well in this regard; therefore, they are more likely to achieve their objectives.[5]

For example, during the 1960s and early 1970s, the National Aeronautics and Space Administration (NASA) had a very high external-extraction capability. It had a popular goal, and it met that goal in spectacular fashion: landing astronauts on the moon and getting them back to earth safely before 1970. By 1987, however, NASA was in trouble. After the Apollo lunar program, it had gradually lost its "star" quality, and its budgetary support had eroded. In January 1986, the Challenger shuttle disintegrated in midlaunch, and the subsequent investigation revealed serious management problems and insufficient resources to fully carry out the agency's mission.

At the time of the first lunar landing by Apollo astronauts in July 1969, however, NASA was a highly effective organization working in a supportive environment. It had public approval and strong legislative and executive support, and it was a magnet for the most talented engineers, scientists, pilots, and managers in the United States; the best and the brightest wanted to work for NASA. Under these conditions, NASA did not have to worry very much about getting and keeping the people it needed. Now NASA's external-extraction capability has been considerably diminished. It does not have strong public support, congressional and executive backing is lukewarm, and its ability to recruit and retain topflight talent is not what it used to be. The organization has to work hard to get and keep people with the skills, knowledge, and experience needed to carry out its missions.

With regard to human resources, NASA's external extraction problems are far from unique in the public sector.[6] The quiet crisis in public service described in Chapter 1 has forced public employers to concentrate on developing strategies to allow them to compete successfully for human resources. As an important part of this process, public personnel systems use various kinds of strategies of external extraction, including three approaches that have been identified by students of formal organizations: competition, cooperation, and incorporation.[7] Individually and in combination, these strategies are used to try to build predictable access to human resources for public-sector organizations.

Competitive Strategies

The competitive types of strategies are designed to achieve success in human resources management through superior organizational performance in several key areas. As an employer, the organization must be able to offer competitive financial and social-psychological inducements to prospective as well as current workers. The organization must also maintain its comparative prestige, since positions in highly regarded agencies (e.g., NASA and the FBI) may attract qualified people who could make more money in less-prominent jobs. And the organization must have the internal flexibility needed to adjust to varied and changing labor market conditions. An ability to align recruitment processes, hiring procedures, compensation plans, and job designs with the *available* labor pool is a great advantage. In the final analysis, a competitive strategy is results-oriented. The standard for evaluation is: Has the organization been able to attract and keep the human resources it needs in order to be both effective and efficient?

In the public sector, competitive strategies often do not easily mesh with the norms and practices of traditional merit systems. Although the current wave of civil service reforms has increased agency flexibility in areas such as position classification and selection and strengthened line management's hand in pay administration in some governments, many public personnel systems are still centralized and heavily rules-oriented.[8] Thus, while some public employers, such as the federal government, are making efforts to encourage a competitive orientation on the agency level, in other jurisdictions standardization and conformance to formal procedures are given greater weight than competitiveness. Often this is done because it is the way things have "always" been done.

Political, legal, and ethical considerations set limits on the degree to which competitive advantage can be the overriding goal of public personnel policies and practices. Equal employment opportunity laws and affirmative action programs, for example, require recruitment and hiring procedures that may limit an agency's discretion and hence its capacity to act quickly and conclusively. Classification standards, negotiated contracts, and statute-based wage and salary schedules may greatly restrict management's ability to offer pay and benefits that are competitive.

Unlike their private counterparts, public employers are subject to constant scrutiny by many groups that are intensely interested in all phases of personnel administration, from recruitment to retirement. These influential groups, including public employees, are at times inclined to resist policies intended to increase competitiveness because they see them as threatening other values such as pay equity, equal opportunity, and political neutrality. For broad public-interest and more narrow partisan reasons, legislators and elected executives are often reluctant to relinquish control over key aspects of personnel policy. It is therefore highly unlikely that the competitive strategies used by public employers can ever be as organization-centered as those generally used in business.

Competitive Pay and Working Conditions

Pay, benefits, working conditions, and career opportunities are key elements of a public agency's competitive position as an employer. In the long term, the attractiveness of the pay and benefits offered by public employers typically varies in relation to the condition of the national or local economy. A slow or recessionary economy usually makes it easier to attract and retain high-quality employees. During periods of expansion, when business profits are high and jobs are plentiful, public-sector recruitment suffers, and mobile employees are more likely to leave for better-paying jobs in the private sector.

Historically, legislatively set pay schedules and benefits have tended to adjust slowly and often inadequately to changes in the labor market. Accurate blanket statements about the competitiveness of government employment are difficult to make, however. For some categories of scientists, professionals, and technicians, comparatively low salaries have made the public sector an unattractive place to work, but many public employers have been consistently able to offer prevailing rates of pay and relatively good benefits (e.g., insurance programs, pensions plans, and job security) that have made them highly competitive for other categories of workers. Nevertheless, during the 1980s the competitive position of public employers deteriorated across a wide range of jobs as fiscal stresses took their toll.[9] Governments rely on legislative and executive support for the money needed to compete for human resources successfully, but widespread public opposition to increasing taxes to fund pay raises or improved benefits has greatly limited this support. There has been increasing pressure on public personnel systems to use their limited funds to maximum effect, rather than depending on general increases to keep pace with the wages and salaries offered by private employers.[10]

Pay increases and enhanced benefit plans in the public sector traditionally have been implemented across the board, without much attention to whether they are needed to maintain an agency's ability to compete effectively for specific kinds of workers. At best, in competitive terms, across-the-board increases have been blunt instruments. For example, for some positions or locations the new salary or wage will not be sufficient to keep the agency competitive, but for others it will be higher than required. A federal employee making $40,000 in Iowa City may be able to live very comfortably; in New York City, the same salary would provide a far lower standard of living. The same can apply to benefits.[11] (Across-the-board cuts in personnel budgets are similarly insensitive to competitiveness issues.) Contemporary approaches stress careful analyses of market factors in relation to the public employer's specific needs and competitive position (see Chapter 7).

Another significant threat posed by fiscal stress and the low prestige of public employment is a deterioration of working conditions. The severe limits imposed on funds for new equipment, facilities construction and maintenance, and supplies inevitably make the public sector less attractive to prospective employees. Over the long haul, they will also affect employee productivity. Drab and uncomfortable working conditions, combined with low public esteem, are difficult handicaps to overcome in the competition for qualified workers.

The Prestige of Public Employment

As important as pay and working conditions are to government's ability to attract and retain qualified personnel, equally important may be the status or prestige of the civil service. The Volcker Commission pointed out in its 1989 report (see Chapter 9) that attitudes about government work and beliefs about the career opportunities it offers contribute significantly to the competitive position of public-sector employers. As Bruce Adams observes:

> Inevitably, negative rhetoric about our public servants becomes a self-fulfilling prophecy, making it difficult to recruit and maintain high quality people in government. The cumulative impact of the negative aspects of the lives of government officials at all levels—negative attitudes about government, demanding interest groups, unrelenting news media, time consuming and rigid decision making procedures, and financial sacrifice—is making government service unnecessarily frustrating and unattractive to many.[12]

The problems created by negative attitudes toward the public service are not restricted to their impact on people considering where to work; relations with influential actors in the organization's environment are affected as well. A vicious circle develops. Politicians, civic leaders, corporate executives, clientele groups, and voters may be hostile or at best noncommittal about the talent, commitment, or responsiveness of civil servants. As a consequence, financial resources and political support are withheld, and the competitiveness of public employers is further reduced. In the long run, the quality of the public service actually declines, attitudes about it become even more negative, and levels of support continue to fall.

Changing the public's image of how public personnel systems operate must be part of any effort to break this vicious circle. A public service with a strong reputation for merit staffing, equal employment opportunity, competence, pay for performance, integrity, and responsiveness to political leadership is most likely to be held in high esteem. According to Alan Campbell, the first director of the Office of Personnel Management, one of the purposes of the Civil

Service Reform Act of 1978 was to improve the reputation of the federal civil service.[13]

Adapting to Conditions in the Labor Market

Being able to adapt to labor market conditions is the third strategy for maintaining government employers' competitive position in human resources management. An employer must be able to respond to conditions in the environment in an effective and timely manner, a challenge that often can be met only if it is capable of making needed adjustments in jobs, technologies, and administrative arrangements. For example, public employers may find that they are competing for skills or experience that are in short supply because of the labor market's limited capacity to respond to the demand for qualified workers. Even if an agency can offer competitive pay and benefits, it will have difficulty locating and attracting enough candidates for jobs with these requirements. Such inelastic supply conditions are due to a number of factors, including limited capabilities of suppliers such as universities and technical schools, long training or apprenticeship periods, policies of regulatory or licensing bodies, demographic trends, and social biases against certain kinds of work.

Eventually, the market probably will respond, but matching supply with demand may take several years or more. As school teachers, aerospace engineers, and others working in fields requiring extensive education and experience can testify, achieving such a balance is not easy. In contrast, the unskilled and semiskilled component of the labor market responds rather quickly, because these workers do not need a great deal of education, training, or experience. As the public sector becomes increasingly professionalized, however, its skill requirements are constantly rising. A passive approach that fails to monitor organizational needs and to anticipate labor market conditions leaves the public employer open to a potentially disruptive situation: a chronic inability to fill certain key positions, and an oversupply of candidates for other jobs.

One way to improve the match between agency needs and available workers is to make adjustments in internal task structures and technologies. Personnel specialists are in a position to make major contributions to this effort. Often they can redesign jobs, restructure relationships among jobs, or alter supervisory patterns in ways to improve the organization's capacity to make good use of those human resources that are available to it. Some positions can be simplified or broken down into less-complex sets of tasks, while others can be enlarged or enriched to take better advantage of employees' abilities. Paraprofessionals may be used to reduce the numbers of highly trained, expensive, and scarce professionals such as doctors, registered nurses, lawyers, and engineers an agency might otherwise need, and with paraprofessional support, the professional personnel may be used differently and more efficiently. Mechanized, automated, or computerized systems can be installed to replace or supplement human resources and thereby reduce labor costs, lower or redistribute skills requirements, and increase overall productivity. Minimum position requirements and job progression may be altered to accommodate employees' upgrading and retraining, and on-the-job training or education can be provided to make it possible for positions to be filled through promotions and transfers.

Public personnel systems have long had the reputation of being unimaginative human resources planners. They have been charged with legalistic rigidity in their approach to job design and position classification and an inclination to assume that the labor market will respond readily to their staffing needs. To the extent that this reputation is deserved, it signals a serious competitive disability, an organizational weakness that is most evident when human resources are limited or a sellers' market for personnel exists. In today's labor market, public employers cannot afford to be internally inflexible or passive in the face of stiff competition and an imperfect balance between supply and demand.

Administrative Designs and Competitiveness

Historically, personnel systems on all levels of government have employed bureaucratic arrangements that stress control and standardization. Centralization of both policy and rule-making authority is typical of merit systems with roots in the original civil service reform movement. While these administrative arrangements may be effective in keeping the "rascals" out and protecting merit principles by limiting managerial discretion, they are notoriously slow in identifying or responding to changes in the organization's social and economic environment. Increasingly complex and volatile environments have made it difficult for agencies with these stability-oriented administrative designs to compete successfully for human resources.

The conclusions of contemporary thinking and research on organization-environment relationships suggest that effective organizations use administrative structures that are well-adapted to their specific environments. In other words, from a competitive standpoint, an administrative structure should be a strategic response to a particular set of environmental conditions. For example, organizations that successfully deal with dynamic, diverse, and highly competitive conditions tend to rely on decentralized decision making, within broad policy guidelines, and to emphasize managerial flexibility and discretion.

Highly centralized personnel systems seem to work relatively well when human resources are readily available through routinized recruitment and selection procedures. Likewise, relying on generalized rules that standardize recruitment, testing, selection, compensation, and other personnel functions normally is effective when the range of likely situations is known, and tested ways of dealing with them have been established. Under these conditions, it is not inappropriate to centralize authority and to house responsibility for personnel administration in specialized units separated from line management.

When time and material resources are limited, competition is intense, or environmental conditions are rapidly changing, however, personnel systems often need a structurally supported capacity to "read" or monitor the environment and to tailor organizational responses accordingly. In practice, this means that the authority, expertise, and other resources necessary for diagnosing situations, making decisions, and implementing personnel strategies must be decentralized, or diffused throughout the organization. One way of accomplishing this objective is to deploy personnel generalists as consultants to (and resources for) line managers who have the authority to make personnel decisions such as hiring, as long as they adhere to general rules and regulations. Another structural option is to have a central personnel office for overall policy-making, evaluation, and audit purposes but delegate day-to-day personnel operations to agency offices with extensive authority to develop policies and methods that are best suited to local conditions.

Cooperative Strategies

Like competition, cooperation is a type of external-extraction strategy designed to maintain the organization's access to essential human resources. Basically, cooperation means entering into more-or-less formal agreements with other organizations and resource-controlling agents in the environment. These agreements, which may be bilateral or multilateral, involve commitments intended to reduce the levels of uncertainty and risk faced by the parties to the agreement.[14] Cooperative strategies seek to identify and implement arrangements that make it possible for all parties to benefit in some way. We will focus on three common forms of cooperation that have direct relevance for public personnel administration: intergovernmental joint ventures and contracts; contracting-out with private producers of goods and services; and negotiated labor agreements with public employee organizations.

Intergovernmental Joint Ventures

One cooperative strategy for improving the ability of public-sector organizations to extract human resources from their external environments is for several public agencies to pool or share workers in order to address common concerns. In addition to increasing organizational effectiveness, such negotiated arrangements may also improve efficiency by lowering overall personnel costs. In some cases, competition among levels of government and public agencies for qualified personnel has been supplemented by cooperative recruitment, testing, and placement services. Since the 1970s, for example, the federal government has been authorized to join with states and localities in cooperative recruiting and testing programs, with the costs to be shared by the participating employers. States may also sponsor joint ventures among their local governments; such cooperation is likely to become increasingly significant to state and local governments as federal aid continues to decline.

Another type of intergovernmental cooperation is joint ventures to provide training for personnel. Some state and local workers are able to attend federal training sessions dealing with problems or policy issues requiring intergovernmental action, such as those offered by the Federal Bureau of Investigation, the U.S. Internal Revenue Service, and the Federal Executive Institute. User-funded statewide or multistate regional training centers for police and fire fighters provide services well beyond the individual capacities of the public employers who send their personnel to these centers for basic or advanced training.

Direct sharing of personnel also is possible under agreements negotiated among jurisdictions on the same or different levels of government. Cities may agree to share police and fire personnel under emergency or other special conditions. Costs are shared, and the participating jurisdictions usually retain recall rights. The emphasis is on recognizing interdependency and dealing with it through mutual support, as opposed to expensive, and perhaps futile, efforts to become self-sufficient. Interagency joint ventures are also feasible within governmental units; an interesting example is the cross-training of workers in two or more organizations (e.g., police and fire departments) so they are able to back each other up and, if need be, move from one job to another.

Governments also contract with one another for services in functional areas such as law enforcement, fire protection, sanitation, streets and roads, and administration.[15] Under these intergovernmental contracts, one government undertakes to provide services to another for a fee. For example, Los Angeles County "sells" police services to many of the incorporated municipalities within the county. Other services commonly contracted for are water supply, sewage treatment, tax collection, and libraries.

Intergovernmental contracting is used by small jurisdictions because it is usually less expensive than building an in-house capacity to deliver a full range of services. It gives the user immediate access to an established personnel system and the equipment and skills of the supplier. Intergovernmental contracting also may reduce operating costs to smaller communities, mainly because of the economies of scale that larger contractors enjoy. From the suppliers' point of view, contracting provides a way to sell unused or underutilized capacity and to generate profits that can be used to support and expand their own operations. Thus, in economic terms, the intergovernmental contract is a winning proposition for both parties.

Contracting-Out with Private Suppliers

Privatization is currently a "hot topic" in the public sector, and governments on all levels are scrutinizing their operations to determine which ones might be more productively handled by outside contractors. Fiscal stress and changing philosophies of government have generated considerable interest in extending the scope of contracting-out for goods and services ordinarily provided by public employees. Parks and recreation, building inspection and maintenance, sanitation, fire and police services, prisons, and even general administration are among the many functions now considered possibilities for contracting-out to the private sector.

Although competition among rival contractors is supposed to lower costs to the taxpayer, contracting-out creates a basically cooperative relationship between supplier and consumer.[16] According to James D. Thompson, contracting-out involves the negotiation of "an agreement for the exchange of performances in the future."[17] It is an alternative to the direct delivery of services, not a device for eliminating administrative responsibilities. Contracts must be negotiated and administered, and contractor performance must be evaluated in political as well as technical and economic terms.

Contracting-out offers potential advantages in human resources management for several reasons. Under certain conditions, primarily the existence of active, genuine competition among alternative suppliers, it can lower the per-unit cost of public services. Private contractors are frequently in a position to keep labor costs below those of the public employer. In a study of local government responses to the approval of Proposition 13 by California voters in 1978, which cut property taxes to the extent that public-sector revenues were severely limited, Anne Cowden found that "Contracting out is considerably cheaper when wage rates are lower in the private sector, when fringe benefits are less, or when private parties have internal labor and organizational arrangements which permit increased economies."[18]

The second reason for contracting-out is that it increases administrative flexibility. Rather than build expensive in-house capabilities involving long-term investments or sunk costs, public agencies can "rent" the human and other resources of the contractor. This is particularly important when agencies are asked to adopt programs or assume responsibilities requiring skills or technologies that are not readily available on an in-house basis, or when the activity is of a temporary nature. A state department of transportation, for example, contracts for the actual construction of new highways with private businesses that hire the needed personnel and provide the necessary equipment, and the department and the contractor part company when the highways are finished, unless they have negotiated separate contracts for maintenance services. The department focuses on continuing activities such as project design and specifications, contract negotiation and administration, and fiscal management. Another interesting (and controversial) example is the use of private contractors by the federal government to operate its nuclear weapons production facilities.

Contracting-out allows agencies to terminate, reorient, or scale back programs without having to go through the demoralizing, costly, and protracted reduction-in-force procedures that are required by merit systems. The contractor takes on these risks and problems. Also, where private enterprises are able to offer compensation packages superior to those authorized by public personnel systems, using contracting to tap these resources allows public agencies to avoid personnel ceilings, inflexible wage and salary schedules, and often-cumbersome staffing procedures. Moreover, shifting responsibility for day-to-day management to contractors allows governments to reduce or at least slow the growth of administrative overhead costs. It may also be possible to escape having to add supervisory personnel as new programs are acquired or existing ones are expanded.

A third reason for contracting-out has to do with political considerations. As the U.S. Department of Defense illustrates, an extensive web of contractual relationships provides the foundation for a strong supportive coalition. Private corporations and labor unions often come to rely heavily on the money and jobs they get through government contracts, so they develop a vested interest in the political and budgetary "health" of public agencies that use such contracting services. From an agency point of view, the active support of concerned (if self-interested) contractors and other clientele groups is vitally important when budgets have to be defended against proposed cuts or efforts are being made to expand or add programs.

A related value of contracting-out is to protect public employers from criticism that they are overgrown, inefficient, and encroaching on the proper domain of private enterprise. Since public attention is easily drawn to the size of the public service, significant expansion is more than likely to produce attacks from those fearing increased taxes, "creeping socialism," or "big government." In very practical terms, while contracting-out does not necessarily mean smaller budgets or even higher productivity, it is a way of acquiring the use of facilities and human resources without running the political risks associated with having to request more money for more "bureaucrats."

Negotiated Agreements with Employee Organizations

Public attention to collective bargaining usually centers on conflicts such as strikes, but when it is successful it actually is a cooperative process because it reduces uncertainty for both labor and management. A negotiated contract is a legally binding document detailing the terms under which management and the employee organization or union will jointly administer key elements of the personnel system. It also specifies how each side will supply the other with some of the inputs it needs to operate effectively.

Management typically agrees to pay clearly stipulated wages and salaries, to provide fringe benefits such as health care and pension plans, and to maintain safe working conditions. Management may also reduce uncertainty for the employee organization by agreeing to various forms of union security, such as dues checkoff or an agency or union shop. For its part, the employee organization or union agrees to deliver human resources and to participate in good-faith administration and enforcement of the rules of the workplace, as set forth in the contract. It also agrees to follow contractually established appeals procedures for resolving conflicts between management and workers. In effect, the union and the employer become partners in an effort to minimize the possibility that unresolved conflicts will disrupt the workplace or lower productivity.

Collective bargaining is a way of identifying, formulating, and implementing cooperative solutions to problems that arise from the interdependence of management and labor organizations.[19] Where employee organizations or unions are forces in their environments, public employers must be equipped to deal with them effectively; in most cases, this means being able to work out mutually beneficial relationships. Because win-lose confrontations involving job actions, strikes, court sanctions, or firings are almost always costly to both sides, considerable attention is now being paid to the development of effective labor relations programs in government. Labor relations offices have been created in many jurisdictions in order to provide the expertise necessary to organize and carry out negotiations and to assist line management in the administration of contracts. Chapter 8 focuses on collective bargaining in the public sector.

The Incorporation Strategy

Competition and cooperation are external-extraction strategies that will work if the organization's environment can reliably generate the needed human resources. If an agency faces an economy or labor market that is unpredictable in these terms or is chronically incapable of supplying appropriately trained and educated people in sufficient numbers, a more appropriate strategy may be creating an *internal* source of personnel with the needed qualifications. The incorporation strategy reduces or eliminates uncertainty not by cooperation with an external source but by expanding or restructuring the organization to allow direct administrative control over the supplier of human resources.

In a country such as the United States, with an extensive system for education and training, public as well as private employers are often able to obtain from their external environments sufficient personnel with the needed skills and experience. Nevertheless, it may be necessary for employers to set up training departments or centers in order to develop the specific skills workers must have to carry out their duties and responsibilities. Over the past ten years or so, both sectors have complained that the system of public education is not reliably producing graduates who are able to read, write, and compute at the levels required by today's organizational processes and technologies. The response has sometimes been to incorporate in the organization a capacity to provide education in basic communications and mathematics skills, rather than relying on the public schools.

In some cases, no external organization may be equipped to provide highly specialized or advanced skills needed by government. Since there is little or no capacity to train qualified military officers outside of government, for example, the military academies (through incorporation) and the Reserve Officers' Training Corps (through cooperation with universities) are used to meet these nation's special requirements. Police and fire-fighter training academies are another example of the incorporation strategy.

On the federal level, a good illustration of the incorporation strategy is in the field of civilian training and development. The Federal Executive Institute (FEI), an OPM facility, offers broad-gauged administrative training for high-ranking executives. Established in 1968, the FEI was designed to fill what was seen to be a serious gap in the federal system for developing senior career executives. It caps an extensive training and career development system that gives the federal government a valuable internal complement to external suppliers of personnel. Because the system is financed, staffed, and administered by the OPM and federal agencies, the content and methods of training can be closely controlled and designed to meet specific needs. This internal resource reduces uncertainty because it increases the probability that federal agencies will have access to a steady stream of qualified managers and executives.

Government in the United States has grown since World War II in response to continuing public demands for new or expanded services. Where governmental effectiveness is crucial and a capacity to perform services such as police and fire protection, air traffic control, national defense, or public health is essential, long-term investments in an internal capacity to train and develop the necessary human resources may be justified. While the issue of *what* services government will or should provide is always on the political agenda of a democracy, as an *organizational* function public personnel administration is more directly concerned with *how* to acquire the human resources needed to provide public services. Incorporation, like competition and cooperation, is an option available to public policymakers.

EFFECTIVENESS IN INTERNAL EXTRACTION

Internal extraction is concerned with the ability of personnel specialists to participate in the design and operation of social-psychological and technical systems to encourage workers to make the contributions needed to accomplish organizational goals. From a human resources management perspective, personnel policies are key elements of the organization's internal-extraction strategies. To be effective in this sense, personnel practices must elicit from employees certain behaviors, including the following:

1. Regular attendance and participation in organizational tasks and activities (low absenteeism).
2. Staying with the organization as long as it needs their skills, knowledge, and experience (low turnover).
3. Reliably good performance of the technical and social requirements of their positions or jobs.
4. A consistent willingness to carry out more than formal role requirements by actively cooperating with others, helping to promote and protect the organization, developing innovative ways to solve problems, and working to keep skills current and to acquire new abilities.[20]

Achieving and sustaining these behavioral patterns is not easy, and the organization's efforts to do so require substantial outlays of human and material resources. From the internal-extraction perspective of the organization, these outlays should be treated as investments in organizationally profitable *transactions,* or exchanges with employees.

The Inducements-Contributions Transaction

The inducements-contributions transaction involves an exchange of values between the organization and the individual that yields a material or psychological profit for both sides. The terms *inducement* and *incentive* are often used interchangeably in this context. William G. Scott defines incentive as "any inducement, material or nonmaterial, which impels, encourages, or forces a person to perform a task to accomplish a goal."[21] A major challenge facing management is to identify what inducements (e.g., health insurance) will influence specific categories of workers to make needed behavioral contributions (e.g., staying with the organization).

Applying the Inducements-Contributions Concept
A clear understanding by management of the needs and expectations of workers is the basis for efficient administration of organizationally effective incentives. Unfortunately, existing knowledge about human motivation in organizational settings is far from complete.

Research on the connections among technological, social, and psychological factors in the workplace and such employee-contribution variables as morale, job satisfaction, and productivity has revealed a very complicated and confusing picture. Lyman Porter and R. P. Miles describe the situation in the following terms:

Of all the problems that are faced by management, motivation must be ranked as one of the most intractable. For years, organizations—both business and non-business types—have attempted to find better ways of motivating employees or at least better ways of understanding how they are motivated.... we still have at best only a hazy and far from firm grasp of motivation. In our opinion, there is no single theory relating to motivation that can be completely and unqualifiedly accepted as accounting for all the known facts, and there is no definite set of prescriptions that are unequivocally supported by the research data.[22]

Simplistic and overgeneralized assumptions about human nature have been largely discredited, but they have not been replaced by any broadly accepted or empirically confirmed alternatives. It is unlikely, therefore, that the near future will bring anything resembling a set of principles that tells public managers how to design and operate a universally effective system of organizational inducements or incentives. This does not mean that no progress has been made. Today's public managers, as a group, are far more likely to be sensitive to the social and psychological dimensions of motivation than earlier generations were, and many success stories about employee motivation can be found in the management literature.

Another problem has to do with assumptions about the personnel management function that are implicit in bureaucratic structures and administrative procedures. Existing theory and research on motivation suggest the need to gear incentives to specific conditions and to the traits of small groups or individuals. Bureaucracies, however, are designed to handle people in large groups or categories and to deal with them in largely depersonalized ways. Centralization and standardization, hallmarks of bureaucracy, have become typical of the approach taken to incentives in public personnel systems. In other words, control over the day-to-day administration of incentives is at best only partially in the hands of managers and supervisors. Much of the argument for management-centered personnel systems hinges on the proposition that meaningful increases in productivity will come only when supervisors have the capacity to manage performance by manipulating incentives to fit the conditions and the people with which they must deal.[23]

Extrinsic and Intrinsic Inducements

The traditional division of the spectrum of inducements available to organizations is into the two categories of extrinsic and intrinsic. Extrinsic inducements offer rewards that are "external to the job itself."[24] Pay, working conditions, and benefits are examples of material extrinsic inducements; promotions in rank, professional honors, and prestige are nonmaterial extrinsic rewards that may serve as inducements. The majority of organizations today rely primarily on material extrinsic inducements administered through their personnel systems.

Intrinsic inducements, in contrast, are properties of the work itself. An intrinsically motivated person does something because it yields rewards in the form of feelings of competence, personal worth, self-determination, or solidarity with coworkers. The reward flows from doing the work. The available evidence strongly suggests that much of the effort people put into their jobs is related to how interesting, challenging, or personally meaningful they find them.[25] Varied work activities, influence over how the job is done, and autonomy or self-direction are important to many employees. While people differ in the degree to which they value such work characteristics, the overall pattern is for job satisfaction to be higher in jobs that offer these types of intrinsic rewards.

Against this background, there has been growing support for the idea that job designs and supervisory behaviors should expressly take into account factors related to job satisfaction and motivation. Frederick Herzberg's job enrichment concepts, Rensis Likert's participative group system, Abraham Maslow's humanistic psychology, and a wide variety of other approaches to enhancing the intrinsic rewards of work in complex organizations (e.g., quality circles, total quality management, or TQM) have been influential in this regard.[26] There is considerable debate, however, over the degree to which the application of any of these concepts or techniques may be expected to increase an organization's ability to offer intrinsically rewarding jobs.

One conclusion does seem justified: Job content, operating technologies, and working relationships are at least potential sources of organizational inducement. Public managers and personnel specialists should therefore pay close attention to the social-psychological implications of how jobs are designed and interrelated, as well as to the impact of supervisory styles and group dynamics on employee attitudes and behavior. In both cases, it may be possible to create conditions under which employees are likely to be more productive and committed than they would be if management limited its attention to external inducements such as pay and benefits.

Membership-Based and Individualized Inducements

Extrinsic as well as intrinsic inducements may be subdivided into two further types, depending on how they are administered. Under membership-based systems, incentives are keyed to functional units, job classifications, hierarchical levels, or some other grouping of employees. Satisfactory performance enables all employees to keep their membership in the group and receive the same rewards. Organizational efforts to relate inducements to contributions are focused on identifying those who have met a standard of acceptable performance.

Individualized inducement systems, in contrast, attempt to tie employee rewards *directly* to the individual worker's job performance or output. Rewards such as pay increases or bonuses are allocated on the basis of differences among individuals. For example, each person in a work group (e.g., secretarial pool, nursing staff) is paid according to performance in one or more task area, which means that individual rates of pay could vary widely within a group where everybody is doing at least acceptable work.

Membership-based systems are the dominant type in the public sector. Currently there is widespread criticism, however, that they encourage mediocre performance while offering no positive incentive to do work that is above average or superior in quantity or quality. Some critics who have associated individualized incentives with American culture attribute what they see as declining productivity in the U.S. work force to management's current disregard for performance. Daniel Yankelovich and J. Immerwahr call the widespread use of membership-based inducements "a sharp departure from the traditional American value of individualism," maintaining that:

> A central theme of our cultural heritage supports the idea that individuals will fail or succeed through their own efforts and hard work. When people receive equal rewards regardless of effort or achievement, the implicit message from management is: "We don't care about extra effort, so why should you?"[27]

While membership-based inducements have not been particularly successful as devices for promoting above-average performance by *individuals*, organizations may be able to achieve high levels of *overall* productivity by requiring high standards for maintenance of membership. There is also evidence to suggest that gainsharing, or group incentives systems, can raise productivity and increase job satisfaction. Since organizations are seldom merely collections of competing individuals, membership-based inducements may be appropriate.[28]

The practice of combining membership-based with individualized incentives is gaining support in the public sector. While most of the attention has been focused on pay-for-performance or merit pay systems, other individualized inducements are available. These include time off, educational opportunities or sabbaticals, payment for unused sick leave, honors and commendations, and cash awards for cost-saving suggestions. In the merit pay area, there has been renewed interest in using within-grade salary increases as rewards for better-than-average to superior performance, instead of the common practice of giving increases to workers who achieve "satisfactory" ratings. Federal supervisors and managers are in a merit pay system (Performance Management and Recognition System), and high-performing members of the Senior Executive Service are eligible for cash bonuses. Many localities and about half of the states have experimented with some kind of merit pay, pay-for-performance, or bonus system.[29] Chapter 13 offers a closer look at the merit pay concept, particularly in the federal experience.

Structuring the Relationship between Inducements and Contributions

Despite the saying that "a happy employee is a productive employee," there is little evidence to suggest that meeting the material, social, and psychological needs of people will by itself somehow make them work harder or be more productive. Actually, a large body of research has not supported the idea that job satisfaction necessarily leads to greater effort or better performance. There is, in fact, no logical reason why it should. As William Scott and T. R. Mitchell put it:

> ... there is no reason to believe that liking the job will prompt one to higher levels of effort. People are attracted to jobs for various reasons (the work conditions, the friendships, the supervision, and so on). They may find that all of these things can be obtained without extra effort, and indeed, this is the case in many organizations. It is true that some rewards may be lost such as a bonus or a promotion, but in many cases these incentives are not of utmost importance. The other incentives are typically not related to effort, and it should not be surprising, therefore, that overall job satisfaction is only slightly related to output.[30]

Expectancy Theory

From an organizational point of view, the problem is to identify and "manage" inducements in a manner explicitly designed to elicit desired contributions. One approach to solving this problem is offered by expectancy theory, which proposes that a person's motivation to behave in a particular way is a function of three conditions:

1. Expectancy, or the extent to which the individual believes that a certain behavior (e.g., getting to work on time) is possible.
2. Instrumentality, or the degree to which the behavior in question is seen to be likely to result in a specific outcome (e.g., getting a pay raise).
3. Valence, or the worth or value attributed to that outcome by the individual.

Expectancy theory predicts, for example, that an employee's level of effort to get to work on time will be a function of the behavior's perceived expectancy and instrumentality, plus the value given to the expected outcome—in this case, a pay raise. Actual performance, of course, will depend on effort *and* the objective ability of the person to perform the behavior.[31] The assumption is that people have needs they want to satisfy, are able to calculate expectancies and instrumentalities rationally, and will behave accordingly. Management must know what outcomes the employees value and must be able to motivate them by setting up conditions wherein expectancy is high and the instrumentalities of behaviors such as getting to work on time are clearly defined and highly predictable in their outcomes.

To illustrate, assume that an agency has found its productivity is suffering because employees habitually arrive a few minutes after the start of the work day. Rather than engaging in a series of punishment-centered responses that might depress morale and encourage various forms of evasion, management decides to set up a system of positive incentives designed to significantly increase their effort to be at work on time. It must first consider the extent to which employees believe they can routinely get to work on time (expectancy). The organization may need to address reasons why people are late, such as transportation problems and child-care needs. Then if expectancy is or can be made to be high, management is in a position to develop an incentive plan that connects certain rewards with coming to work on time. In addition to offering rewards that are valued (valence), the plan must be administered in a manner that consistently and clearly relates the rewards to attendance behavior (instrumentality). If these goals are met, expectancy theory predicts that employees will make a strong effort to come to work on time.

Studies of motivation and performance in organizational settings tend to support the general outlines of expectancy theory. It does have some practical limitations, however. It requires management to have a great deal of information about values and perceptions on the individual level. It also assumes that everybody engages in rational, quasi-economic calculations before choosing a course of action. It has been observed that "critics suggest that expectancy theory defers too much to the nineteenth century ideal of the economic man...[and] employees cannot be as knowledgeable about outcomes as the model assumes."[32]

Nevertheless, expectancy theory does offer some useful guidelines for structuring and managing relationships between inducements and contributions for employees in public agencies. First, it stresses the importance of clearly communicating in advance the linkages between certain behaviors and rewards such as pay raises, promotions, or honors. Second, it reminds policymakers and supervisors that the personnel system must be administered in a manner that firmly establishes these connections in the eyes of employees. Third, management must make an effort to understand, at least in general terms, the values placed on specific material and nonmaterial rewards by different groups and types of employees. Information of this kind is necessary if an agency's inducements strategy is to be reasonably well aligned with the values and needs of large segments of its work force.

The fourth guideline is to take into account how the perceived and real abilities of employees affect their effort and performance. Perceptually, ability is a factor in expectancy; the person must believe that effort will result in performance. Objectively, it sets limits; no amount of effort will yield performance if ability does not exist, as many aspiring professional athletes have discovered. Employees' physical and intellectual capacities must therefore be taken into account. Equally important are the technical and other resources the organization makes available to the work force. No matter how much effort they make, skilled carpenters wielding hand saws are not likely to be as productive as those using power saws.

It is, of course, possible to improve the objective ability of a public agency's human resource base, in addition to increasing the effort the members exert. Interventions of this type include:

1. Upgrading recruitment and selection standards in such key areas as education, experience, and physical abilities.
2. Making available training and other developmental opportunities so that employees are able to increase their skills and knowledge.
3. Designing jobs and career paths that take full advantage of employees' abilities.

Investments in technological aids (e.g., computers, communications equipment, automated machines) are frequently justified by their capacity to raise productivity for the individual as well as the organization.

The fifth guideline expectancy theory offers is to appreciate the significance of perceived as well as actual equity and fairness in the allocation of rewards. If employees believe that rewards are not actually given on the basis of accurate and unbiased measures of performance, any incentive plan can be undermined. Employees must trust their supervisors, who are in large measure responsible for the administration of the plan, to implement it competently and impartially. Perceived equity also depends on the existence of clearly defined performance objectives and standards and broadly accepted, trusted procedures for performance evaluation. Chapter 5 focuses on performance appraisals in the public sector.

HUMAN RESOURCES MANAGEMENT AND THE ROLE OF THE PERSONNEL SPECIALIST

The distinguishing mark of the human resources management perspective, compared to the orientation of traditional public personnel administration, is that personnel specialists must take an organizational as opposed to personnel department point of view. In the area of external extraction, they should have the diagnostic skills and information needed to help agency administrators formulate successful competitive and cooperative strategies. They must be prepared to help implement personnel policies and programs that reach well beyond their organization's formal boundaries and to establish or maintain productive relationships with other public and private agencies.

With regard to internal extraction, there are at least five areas of activity in which personnel specialists can make important contributions to the implementation of human resources management concepts in public agencies.

First, they can help in the design, implementation, and administration of incentives plans that reflect the current state of knowledge about human motivation and behavior in organizations. They should also play a key role in the systematic evaluation of these plans in light of agency needs and goals.

Second, they can develop ways of more clearly defining and describing the technical and behavioral content of positions. Traditional job evaluation is a good example of how the formal aspects of positions (tasks performed and technical skills required) may be clarified. Techniques for identifying behavioral requirements that are not captured by job evaluation are less well developed but probably no less important to the overall design of an incentives system.

Third, they have an important role to play in the design of systems to attract, select, and place employees who are most likely to respond favorably to the inducements an organization is able to offer. Today's public personnel administration" is far more advanced in its capacity to screen applicants on the basis of their technical qualifications than it is in predicting responses to social and psychological variables.

Fourth, they can take the lead in developing ways of monitoring employee perceptions and attitudes. Management needs accurate, up-to-date information on how workers feel about their jobs, organizational processes, supervisory behavior, and personnel policies and practices. Periodic audits of how workers are perceiving and responding to these and other conditions might help management identify problem areas that need to be addressed.

Fifth, they should be prepared to support management's efforts to increase productivity through ongoing evaluations of the human resources management programs of the organization, including incentives, employee training and development, and performance evaluation. Well-done evaluations of this kind provide a solid foundation for changes designed to improve performance on one or more levels of the organization.

In a recent review of the research on the personnel function, Steven Hays found that "the central theme of much of the relevant literature is that the personnel office must become more closely integrated with line management." Personnel specialists can give managers the input they need on such matters as incentive systems, job design, productivity measurement, and employee attitude assessment, as well as the formulation of operational plans.[33]

■

NOTES

1. Steven W. Hays, "Environmental Change and the Personnel Function: A Review of the Research," *Public Personnel Management*, vol. 18, no. 2 (Summer 1989), pp. 113–114.
2. David E. Bowen and Larry E. Greiner, "Moving from Production to Service in Human Resources Management," in John Matzer, Jr. (ed.), *Person-*

nel Practices for the '90s (Washington, DC: International City Management Association, 1988), pp. 3–14.

3. Bruce Buchanan and Jeff Millstone, "Public Organizations: A Value-Conflict View," *International Journal of Public Administration*, vol. 1, no. 3 (1979), pp. 273–274.

4. Stanley Seashore and Ephraim Yuchtman, "A System Resource Approach to Organizational Effectiveness," *American Sociological Review*, vol. 32, no. 6 (December 1967), p. 898.

5. Daniel Katz and Robert Kahn, *The Social Psychology of Organizations*, 2nd ed. (New York: John Wiley & Sons, 1978).

6. Larry M. Lane and James F. Wolf, *The Human Resource Crisis in the Public Sector* (New York: Quorum Books, 1990), pp. 27–59.

7. James D. Thompson, *Organizations in Action* (New York: McGraw-Hill, 1967), pp. 25–38.

8. Hays, "Environmental Change and the Personnel Function," pp. 115–117.

9. Charles H. Levine, "The Federal Government in the Year 2000: Administrative Legacies of the Reagan Years," *Public Administration Review*, vol. 46 (May–June, 1986), pp. 195–206.

10. John Matzer, Jr. (ed.), *Pay and Benefits: New Ideas for Local Government* (Washington, DC: International City Management Association, 1988), pp. ix–xxiv.

11. The Hudson Institute, *Civil Service 2000* (Washington, DC: U.S. Office of Personnel Management, 1986), p. 6.

12. Bruce Adams, "The Frustrations of Government Service," *Public Administration Review*, vol. 44 (January–February 1984), p. 5.

13. Alan K. Campbell, "The Institution and Its Problems," in Eugene B. McGregor, Jr. (ed.), "Symposium: The Public Service as Institution," *Public Administration Review*, vol. 42 (July–August 1982), pp. 305–308.

14. Thompson, *Organizations in Action*, pp. 34–36.

15. Sidney Sonenblum, John J. Kirlin, and John C. Ries, *How Cities Provide Services: An Evaluation of Alternative Delivery Structures* (Cambridge, MA: Balinger Publishing, 1977).

16. Thompson, *Organizations in Action*, pp. 34–35.

17. Ibid.

18. Anne C. Cowden, "California Local Government Contracting after Proposition 13," *International Journal of Public Administration*, vol. 4, no. 4 (1982), p. 405.

19. Richard E. Walton and Robert B. McKersie, *A Behavioral Theory of Labor Negotiations* (New York: McGraw-Hill, 1965), p. 3.

20. Katz and Kahn, *Social Psychology of Organizations*, p. 403.

21. William G. Scott, *Organization Theory: A Behavioral Analysis for Management* (Homewood, IL: Richard D. Irwin, 1967), pp. 284–285.

22. Lyman W. Porter and R. P. Miles, "Motivation and Management," in J. W. McGwire (ed.), *Contemporary Management: Issues and Viewpoints* (Englewood Cliffs, NJ: Prentice-Hall, 1974), p. 545.

23. Gerald T. Gabris, "Can Merit Pay Systems Avoid Creating Discord between Supervisors and Subordinates? Another Uneasy Look at Perfor-

mance Appraisal," *Review of Public Personnel Administration*, vol. 7 (Fall 1986), pp. 70–89.

24. Debra W. Stewart and G. David Garson, *Organizational Behavior and Public Management* (New York: Marcel Dekker, 1983), p. 33.
25. Edward Deci, *Intrinsic Motivation* (New York: Plenum Press, 1975).
26. A. H. Maslow, *Eupsychian Management* (Homewood, IL: Richard D. Irwin, 1965); Rensis Likert, *The Human Organization* (New York: McGraw-Hill, 1967); Frederick Herzberg, *Work and the Nature of Man* (Cleveland, OH: World Publishing, 1966); James S. Bowman, "Quality Circles: Promise, Problems, and Prospects in Florida," *Public Personnel Management*, vol. 18, no. 4 (Winter 1989), pp. 375–403.
27. Daniel Yankelovich and J. Immerwahr, *Putting the Work Ethic to Work* (New York: Public Agenda Foundation, 1983), p. 26.
28. G. Ronald Gilbert and Ardel E. Nelson, "The Pacer Share Demonstration Project: Implications for Organizational Management and Performance Evaluation," *Public Personnel Management*, vol. 18, no. 2 (Summer 1989), pp. 209–225.
29. James L. Perry, "Compensation, Merit Pay, and Motivation," in Steven W. Hays and Richard C. Kearney (eds.), *Public Personnel Administration: Problems and Prospects*, 2nd ed. (Englewood Cliffs, NJ: Prentice-Hall, 1990), pp. 104–115.
30. William G. Scott and T. R. Mitchell, *Organization Theory: A Structural and Behavioral Analysis*, 3rd ed. (Homewood, IL: Richard D. Irwin, 1976), p. 159.
31. V. H. Vroom, *Work and Motivation* (New York: John Wiley & Sons, 1964), p. 18; L. W. Porter and E. E. Lawler III, Managerial Attitudes and Performance (Homewood, IL: Richard D. Irwin, 1968); E. E. Lawler III, "The Strategic Design of Reward Systems," in R. Steers and L. Porter (eds.), *Motivation and Work Behavior*, 4th ed. (New York: McGraw-Hill, 1987), pp. 210–228.
32. Stewart and Garson, *Organizational Behavior and Public Management*, pp. 25–26.
33. Hays, "Environmental Change and Personnel Function," p. 114.

Public Personnel Systems: Problems and Policy Responses

II

Recruiting and Selecting a Quality Work Force

4

Public employers are finding it increasingly difficult to compete effectively for workers qualified to handle the technical and administrative challenges of modern government. Inadequate pay and benefits, deteriorating working conditions, and hostile public attitudes have done much to make careers in the public service unattractive to many potential applicants. But these are not the only problems. Historically, the public sector has not invested heavily in recruitment, often settling for a passive, announce-and-wait approach. Selection methods are notoriously cumbersome and of dubious validity in many instances. Moreover, the procedural rigidities imposed on public employers by merit systems are a disadvantage in competing with the more flexible personnel systems of private enterprises.

A major task confronting the public sector today is to develop recruitment and selection techniques and processes that not only conform to the merit principle and the standard of equal employment opportunity but actively support the overall effort to build and sustain the human resources base of an effective public service.[1] The federal government, as well as some states, has begun to develop systems for monitoring the quality of applicant pools and the existing work force.[2] The standards for merit and EEO are set on the federal level by the requirement of the Civil Service Reform Act of 1978 that recruitment "should be from qualified individuals from appropriate sources in an endeavor to achieve a work force from all segments of society, and selection and advancement should be determined solely on the basis of relative ability, knowledge, and skills, after fair and open competition which assures that all receive equal opportunity."

Although recruitment and selection are conceptually discrete steps in the process of filling government jobs, in practice they are often inseparable. As the Volcker Commission noted in its 1989 report (see Chapter 1), complicated, slow selection procedures undermine recruitment efforts because potential candidates may see getting government jobs as "an exercise in frustration."[3] For the employer, ineffective recruitment may make it necessary to select employees from among a pool of applicants who are less than fully qualified. Weak recruitment programs also may produce candidate pools that underrepresent women and minorities and therefore make it difficult to achieve affirmative action goals, and the questionable validity of selection tests may be a basis for legal challenges and a suspicion among minorities and women that public employers really do not want to hire them.

RECRUITMENT PROBLEMS AND RESPONSES

In countries such as England and France, government jobs—particularly in the central government—have historically been accorded status and prestige. Highly qualified candidates are more often than not willing to accept lower pay in exchange for the status, respect, and authority that comes with public service careers. Public attitudes and social traditions in these nations thus allow governments to pick and choose from candidate pools that offer some of the most talented and educated people in these societies. With rare exceptions, however, this has not been the case in the United States. Governments on all levels have had to struggle to overcome the society's inclination to value careers in the private sector over those in the public service.

In contrast to countries where the public service enjoys elevated status and prestige, in the United States high socioeconomic status is *negatively* associated with positive attitudes about civil service careers. From a recruitment perspective, this means that government's competitive position currently is strongest with minorities and women, groups that have experienced a long history of active discrimination by corporate employers. This particular advantage is likely to be temporary, due to the effects of changing attitudes, antidiscrimination laws, and the realities of the labor market. Public employers in the United States have rarely been able to "cream" the pool of available talent, and the future promises intensifying across-the-board competition for workers with all but the lowest levels of skills.

Recent thinking about recruitment stresses three strategies. The first involves taking advantage of government's potential to successfully recruit minorities and women. The second concentrates on lessening public employers' dependence on recruitment from outside sources (external extraction) and upgrading existing employees to meet changing or new skills requirements. This strategy requires substantial investments in training and formal education.[4] The third strategy consists of initiatives designed to improve the overall image of the public service and to make the public sector an effective competitor across all segments of the labor market, particularly in technical and professional occupations.[5]

Recruiting Minorities and Women

The public sector has been the leader in breaking down barriers to the employment and promotion of women and minorities, though its record is far from perfect. To the degree that these groups associate public employment with equality of opportunity and career mobility, government has a potential advantage over private businesses in the competition for human resources. The Hudson Institute expressed this view in *Civil Service 2000*, a report prepared in 1988 for the Office of Personnel Management (OPM) Career Entry Group:

> As an employer with a demonstrated record of unbiased hiring and upward mobility, and with a set of programs designed to enhance the quality of worklife for women and minorities, the Federal government may be perceived as a particularly attractive employer by these groups. Thus, the best qualified women and minorities may be predisposed to accept Federal job offers. Because the Federal government has a greater proportion of women and minorities in top jobs, new recruits are likely to see Federal employers in a more favorable light compared to private companies where advancement opportunities have been more limited.[6]

The Hudson Institute recommended that the federal government should take advantage of this strength by developing personnel policies that recognize the changing demographics of the labor force and of American society as a whole (see Chapter 14). The rapidly growing proportion of women in the work force creates an opportunity *if* innovations such as flexible work schedules, extended-leave policies, and child-care benefits are "pursued aggressively." The institute's comments, which refer to the federal government, appear equally relevant to the states and localities:

> Few employers have been able to satisfy the desires of two-earner families for more time away from work to care for children and aging family members. Organizations that are able to offer more flexible work schedules...are more likely to have their pick of the available candidates for hard-to-fill jobs....[E]very agency should be seeking to find cost-effective ways to assist parents in providing high-quality child care. The Federal government should not allow itself to lag behind other employers...if it wishes to hire and keep large numbers of mothers (and fathers) during the 1990s.[7]

Investments in Training and Education

Rapid social and technological change places great pressure on organizations to maintain work forces with the skills, knowledge, and abilities needed to handle new responsibilities and job tasks. It is no longer safe to assume that a high school or college education, once completed, will equip workers to handle their jobs until they retire. Historically, when government needed personnel with new or different skills it recruited them from outside sources, rather than retraining existing staff to fill new positions. However, as the Hudson Institute points out:

> This historic pattern is likely to be unworkable for many Federal agencies by the year 2000. The disparity between the salaries, perquisites, and advancement opportunities available to workers in the Federal service and those in the private sector is likely to make it increasingly difficult for Federal agencies to hire talented employees with advanced educations, particularly in such high-growth fields as medicine, engineering, and computer science.[8]

One obvious way to reduce the pressure on external recruitment efforts is to invest the resources necessary to upgrade and change the skills profiles of those currently working for public agencies. This applies to situations where skills are already in short supply or will be in the foreseeable future. Skills-upgrading programs such as tuition reimbursement, sabbaticals, and advanced training opportunities could be focused in areas and specific agencies where they are most needed and where they can provide cost-effective leverage in recruitment and retention. Education and training of this kind also could be designed to help employees work their way up a career ladder, from paraprofessional to professional positions, for example. Another goal might be to improve the basic skills of potential employees who would not otherwise be qualified for lower-level jobs.

Interest in retraining and skills upgrading has been spurred by growing concern about work-force quality. Walter Broadnax, a commissioner of the New York State Department of Civil Service, stated at the 1989 Conference on Workforce Quality Assessment sponsored by the U.S. Merit Systems Protection Board (MSPB) and the OPM that New York State had decided it was going to have to "grow a lot of our own talent," due to the difficulty of trying to compete with the private sector. His description of the state's initiatives in this area included Project Reach, a literacy program designed to raise the reading level of state employees to a minimum of eighth grade; a Basic Skills Video Training Method; and a School-to-Work Program, in which high school students are actively recruited to enter state government with summer training programs in which they can begin to learn skills and workplace values. Those who complete the bridge program are placed in a variety of paraprofessional jobs such as mental health therapy aides.[9]

At the same conference, Sally K. Marshall, director of personnel for the U.S. General Services Administration, reported a growing governmentwide interest in retraining. The GSA had increased its investment in training from 1 percent to 3 percent of salary expenditures, in response to the need to develop high-tech skills adaptable to rapid changes in the telecommunications industry, electronic data processing, and procurement practices. Marshall also recognized a need for substantial investments in remedial training, in light of "huge turnover rates" among clerical staff and high failure rates among high school graduates taking exams for clerical jobs. While some turnover, especially among low performers, is functional, she disagreed strongly with the idea it should be designed into the system:

> I would suggest that it is a very dangerous theory when we look out at "Workforce 2000" and the shortage categories. . . . With many of our job occupations, we have a need to start growing and nurturing our own. There is going to be hell to pay with the labor-market shortage that is on the horizon if we do not take care of our own.[10]

An OPM report published in June 1992 announced a series of policy initiatives intended to strengthen human resources development in the federal government by attention to such areas as: (1) probationary training for new employees, (2) basic skills and literacy training, (3) continuing technical/professional education and training, (4) retraining for occupational changes, (5) participation in professional associations, and (6) academic-degree training. Training and development programs for supervisors and managers were to be encouraged and supported. The OPM also was to develop regulations and guidance to promote efforts to assess training needs and to offer agencies technical assistance in planning, research, and evaluation for human resources development.[11]

Recruiting College Graduates

While the number of public-sector jobs requiring college degrees can be expected to increase during the 1990s, the number of new graduates with bachelor's and master's degrees will actually decline somewhat, and about one-third of all new jobs in the United States will be filled by college graduates by the year 2000. It can be expected, therefore, that public, private, and nonprofit organizations will all have to compete for a limited pool of college-educated employees.[12] Although the problem is expected to be particularly acute on the federal employment level, state and local governments will also find it difficult to recruit the college graduates they need to fill technical and professional positions. Even under the best of conditions, the competition for such talent will be intense. Public employers can improve their prospects for securing qualified personnel by paying greater attention to campus recruitment and student-hiring programs.

Improving Campus Recruitment Efforts

In comparison to large private companies, public employers do not invest heavily in campus recruitment programs. In the language of a 1991 report by the Illinois Commission on the Future of Public Service, government's recruiting efforts "remain staid." Astrid Merget, Dean of the Ohio State University School of Business, observes in this report that "students may not even know what choices of career await them in the public sector...the passivity [of government] probably deflects many who would otherwise apply." The following examples of weak and ineffective recruiting by public agencies in Illinois are cited:

> Recruiters representing more than 200 [private-sector] employers flood the University of Chicago Graduate School of Business each fall and conduct 13,000 on-campus interviews a year—more than 10 interviews per student. At the same university's Graduate School of Public Policy Studies, only six employers recruited last year and conducted 61

interviews—less than one interview per student. Four of these six were from government, and of these, only one was from Illinois.[13]

The national government faces a similar situation. Most federal agencies have shown a lack of commitment to campus recruitment. When asked about federal recruitment efforts, many college students reported that they were not getting enough information about job opportunities and how to apply for positions. They also had the feeling that jobs were unavailable or that "the agencies do not value students as potential employees." College placement offices, well stocked with recruiting literature from private employers, seldom had much up-to-date material on jobs and careers in federal agencies. Nor were students disposed to contact agencies directly, believing as they did that "contacting the government is a burdensome and lengthy process." One undergraduate public administration student told the GAO, "Obtaining information on employment is very hard. It takes forever to get the forms. You write them a letter saying you want the information, and about four months later you'll get the information, and then you're wondering who it is from. You forget by then."[14]

In an effort to respond to these kinds of problems, the OPM has launched several recruitment initiatives intended to help federal agencies attract desirable candidates. Among these is Career America, a collection of sophisticated brochures available to all federal agencies at relatively low cost which describe career opportunities and highlight the attractive features of federal service. Other informational resources include automated telephone systems that provide job information, assistance in completing applications, and status reports on applications that have been submitted. Computer systems are also being used, including software that allows college students to make job searches and "user friendly" computers at Federal Job Information Centers which make it easy for visitors to get job information. Recruitment videos are available, and a career directory has been developed.[15]

The GAO reported in 1990 that college students in general prefer personal contacts with employer representatives to other recruitment methods. Campus interviews and presentations to classes or student groups are given high marks for effectiveness because they allow face-to-face meetings with knowledgeable employees. Brochures such as the Career America portfolio attract interest but do not substitute for personal contacts. Recruiting videos are not considered particularly effective, and many students believe they fail to provide a balanced description of work and careers in government agencies. The impersonality of prerecorded telephone messages and computer information systems also does not please college students. Along similar lines, career fairs, at which public employers set up booths on university campuses and collect resumés, are not likely to attract top candidates. Most graduates do not go to job fairs or wait to be processed through OPM registers; they are "courted by the private sector and skimmed off like cream."[16]

The GAO recommends that federal agencies provide employment contact persons to college placement centers to channel information and answer questions quickly and accurately. OPM staff and federal managers also should become familiar with college campuses, where motivated students and career counselors are to be found. In the GAO's opinion, if campus recruiters are able to provide clear information about career opportunities and application procedures, "they will be able to hire some top talent."[17] These observations should be equally relevant to the recruitment efforts of state and local governments.

Enhancing Student Hiring Programs

Another way public employers can introduce college students to jobs and career opportunities in the public service is to hire them as part-time workers or interns. The OPM has recently moved to enhance existing part-time programs, such as the Cooperative Education Program (Co-op), the Federal Junior Fellowship Program, and the Stay-in-School Program. It has simplified the process through which Co-op participants may be converted to permanent positions (about 68 percent are hired), and both the Co-op and Stay-in-School programs have been streamlined to permit agencies to hire students under these programs more easily. The Junior Fellowship Program has been expanded.

The size of the Presidential Management Intern (PMI) Program, designed to attract highly qualified graduate students, was doubled in 1989, from 200 to 400 positions. Students are nominated by their schools and undergo a competitive selection process. Once they graduate, those selected are given an opportunity for challenging assignments, including rotational responsibilities, mentoring, and development seminars. Those who successfully complete the program are eligible for permanent positions, and many PMIs have achieved top-level management jobs over the years.

In addition to expanding the size of the PMI program, the OPM has increased the number of graduate schools where it recruits applicants and has changed the training curriculum. Agencies assume responsibility for technical training, while the OPM provides training in the management areas of communication, interpersonal skills, group behavior, planning, and organizational culture.[18] On the state level, also, programs for internship and cooperative education are being expanded. The Illinois Commission on the Future of Public Service, for example, recommended expansion because it believes these programs "provide the greatest potential for increasing the pool of undergraduate and graduate students interested in public service."[19]

Changing the Image of Public Employment

For many potential employees, the image of what it is like to work in government compounds already negative feelings about pay and benefits in the public sector. Job applicants may see government as a setting in which it is next to impossible to get anything done. It seems to offer careers that are unlikely to allow them to use their talents, to be infested with specialists in red tape, and to offer dreary working conditions. Encouraged by political rhetoric, media depictions, and the American tendency to ascribe all manner of evils to the bureaucracy, this image of public service is a serious liability in government's effort to recruit the "best and the brightest."[20]

A GAO study found that about 40 percent of applicants for federal entry-level professional and administrative positions who *declined* job offers over a six-month period in 1990 cited lack of opportunity as an important factor in their decisions (close to 70 percent cited economic factors). More specifically, they thought the positions lacked opportunities to apply their education and skills, advance in their careers, or receive challenging job assignments. In contrast, 70 percent or more of those who *accepted* offers during this period anticipated that the federal service would offer these important opportunities, and they were less sensitive to financial considerations than those who declined offers.[21]

The available evidence suggests that a generally negative image of work in the public service is indeed a major contributor to government's recruitment problems among highly qualified college students. Illinois, for example, found that image was more important than noncompetitive pay to potential employees. In that state, government salaries often compare favorably with those in the nonprofit sector, which, in contrast to the public sector, "enjoys a positive public image and receives applications from a very competitive pool of candidates."[22] The GAO study found that many students saw federal employment as "rife with bureaucracy, paperwork, and inefficiency."

They were unwilling to work under such conditions, even if they re-garded benefits and job security as comparatively good.

To the degree that such perceptions are factually inaccurate, public employers need to devise strategies for countering them and changing their image. Information and education programs describ-ing the challenges, rewards, and opportunities associated with pub-lic service and careers in particular agencies could be effective, particularly if recruiters are prepared to follow up in terms of specif-ic jobs and career lines of interest to applicants. Systematically build-ing direct contacts with the public service through internship and co-op programs also should be helpful. More broadly, as the Volcker Commission noted, the nation's political leadership must be willing to describe the public service and its functions in positive terms *and* to back its words with supportive policies and needed resources.

Efforts to improve the image of public service are unlikely to succeed, however, if financial incentives are not competitive and working conditions are actually substandard. While federal agencies were impressed with the Career America materials and said that they went a long way in breaking the stereotypical image of govern-ment, most did not think they would strengthen their recruitment ef-forts. The Department of the Treasury stated this conclusion forcefully: "Slick packages do not make the government more attrac-tive to high quality candidates. Money, profit-sharing, child-care centers, etc., are factors in career shopping for today's quality job market. [The] private sector provides these for the most part; we do not."[23]

The GAO reported a case in which naval officials said they dis-couraged applicants from visiting their offices because they were concerned that the candidates would decline job offers after seeing the poor working conditions.[24] In Illinois, efforts to recruit profes-sionals are undermined by limited opportunities for career advance-ment and the state's extensive use of patronage appointments.[25] No amount of image-making will erase these hard realities.

Administration of Recruitment Programs

On all levels of government, complaints are commonplace about re-cruiting programs' procedural rigidities, overcentralized and unre-sponsive personnel offices, and a widespread lack of organizational attention to recruitment. Studies of the recruitment process reveal that relatively successful programs share certain characteristics. Probably most important, top-level agency management actively supports and participates in the planning, implementation, and evaluation phases. Line managers are directly involved, and they have been delegated considerable authority to plan and carry out recruiting initiatives and, under some conditions, to offer jobs to qualified candidates. Line managers also work closely with personnel specialists in the design and execution of recruitment strategies keyed to specific agency needs and conditions. Those actually doing the recruitment in the field are well trained and fully informed about agency requirements, job and career opportunities, and the resources that are available from central personnel agencies.[26]

Extensive delegation of recruitment and hiring authority to line managers often raises concerns that pressures for competitive success in the job market will undermine the merit principle and EEO goals. These issues, as well as questions of administrative organization, inevitably involve selection procedures as well as recruitment processes.

SELECTION PROCEDURES

A hallmark of the first civil service reform movement (see Chapter 2) was its focus on the methods used to decide who should be selected for civil service jobs. Intensive concentration on selection was a direct result of the movement's efforts to eliminate patronage or spoils as an organizing principle of public personnel administration. Merit systems universally emphasize both the value of neutral competence and objective selection procedures designed and controlled by personnel specialists. Selection thus is at the technological heart of the conventional merit system.

Traditional selection procedures attempt to measure a candidate's ability to perform a specific job satisfactorily. In order to make this determination, one or more tests are used. Technically, all measurements of capacity are considered tests, although all do not involve written examinations. The combination of tests used varies, depending on the requirements of the job being filled. Tests applied by public employers with merit systems usually involve some combination of the following components: (1) minimum qualifications requirements, (2) evaluations of training and experience, (3) written tests, (4) performance tests, (5) oral examinations, and (6) background investigations.

For every position or category of positions, applicants are evaluated and ranked according to their scores or outcomes on one or more of these tests. Each test is weighted in accordance with the civil service agency's determination of the relative importance of the qualifications it is supposed to measure. For example, mathematical skills may be very important to an accountant but relatively unimportant for a file clerk or secretary. Minimum qualifications are not weighted, since the applicant must meet them in order to receive further consideration. The same rule applies to background checks or investigations.

Tests are sequenced, with minimum qualifications coming as the first hurdle. An applicant who satisfies the minimum qualifications then undergoes one or more of the following procedures: an evaluation of training and experience, a written test, or a performance test. Oral examinations may come next, followed by a background investigation. This sequence is economical in the sense that it places the most expensive and time-consuming tests at the end of the process, where the fewest number of candidates need to be considered. It would make little sense, for example, to administer physical agility tests to everybody who applies for a fire fighter position before determining if they meet a minimum requirement such as a high school diploma.

Eligibility Lists and Certification

A distinctive feature of civil service systems in the United States is that the names of candidates who pass entrance or promotional examinations are placed on eligibility lists, ranked in order of composite scores. When hiring officials in agencies have openings to fill, they request the civil service agency to certify names of eligibles from these lists in the order specified in the civil service law and regulations.

Until recently, the "rule of three" (the three highest ranking eligibles) was by far the most common standard for certification of candidates from eligibility lists. Historically, this rule emerged as a device for protecting the merit system and, at the same time, allowing some discretion to appointing officers. The assumptions were that examination scores would reflect real differences in ability to do the work, and three was a reasonable number of names to certify for each opening. To certify more names or the entire list of those passing the examination would increase the risk that appointments would be made on a partisan basis. Some jurisdictions were so concerned about political "contamination" that they adopted the "rule of one," and a few state and local governments still operate on that basis. As questions about test validity have increased and EEO concerns have mounted, public employers have moved to liberalize the process by certifying more names.

Minimum Qualifications

The reason for imposing minimum qualifications such as extent and type of education, training, physical abilities, and experience is to screen out applicants who are realistically not likely to be able to carry out the responsibilities associated with a position. Examples would be requiring applicants for legal positions to have a degree from an accredited school of law, requiring fire fighters to be able to lift and carry a certain weight, and requiring applicants for senior administrative positions to have prior experience in equivalent or related positions.

The key standard for minimum qualifications is that they are actually *essential* to job performance and do not arbitrarily deny persons who might be able to do the job a chance to compete for it. Until recently, little attention was paid to establishing the validity of minimum qualifications as an accurate measure of a candidate's ability to do the job, and the personnel technicians' best judgment sufficed. A minimum qualification such as requiring a high school diploma of janitors, truck drivers, or machine operators is at best a questionable way to predict job performance.[27] Public employers must be prepared to offer convincing evidence of validity, because the courts are striking down minimum qualifications that cannot be shown to be logically related to the demands of a particular job. The trend is to remove minimum requirements that cannot be validated and to allow the substitution of education for experience up to a certain point (and vice versa). The catch-all phrase "or any equivalent combination of training and experience" is often added in position requirements.

Some minimum qualifications may be imposed as a matter of law or social policy. Residence, age, and citizenship status requirements, while not necessarily related to job performance, may serve wider political, social, or economic purposes. It is not unusual for police departments to require that officers reside in the city or county where they work in order to build community relations. National child labor laws were passed to protect children from exploitation by employers; even the most talented 13-year-old computer whiz is not eligible for a computer programmer position in government. The Supreme Court ruled in 1978 that New York State could make U.S. citizenship a requirement for police positions, on the grounds that policy-making is the exclusive responsibility of citizens, and the exercise of discretion by police officers is a form of policy-making.[28] Since these types of requirements are fixed by federal, state, or local laws, the personnel agency has no discretion in their application, beyond determining whether or not to argue for changes in the law.

Evaluation of Training and Experience

Evaluations of training and experience may be used in combination with written or oral examinations in order to generate a more complete evaluation of applicants' skills, knowledge, and abilities (SKAs). In other cases, written and oral examinations may not be practical, and the evaluation of training and experience constitutes the entire examination. This is called an *unassembled examination* because candidates do not gather in one place to sit for a written test. Suitable written tests may not exist, or tests may be redundant because the applicants have already passed examinations for licenses or degrees needed to practice their profession (e.g., law, medicine, engineering, social work).

Experience has shown that many highly qualified persons will not apply for government jobs if they have to take a written test, because they believe their academic degrees, professional credentials and licenses, and experience should be enough to demonstrate their competence. Unassembled examinations are often used in the federal service, in some cases for entry-level professional positions, and some use is made of them in state and local governments. The combination of evaluation of training and experience, plus an oral examination, is found at all levels of government.

The evaluation of training and experience is based on a more-or-less thorough understanding of the SKAs required by a position. Applicants are ranked by trained examiners according to the extent to which they have these SKAs, a process that is inevitably judgmental. Many personnel experts believe that the most effective way of minimizing subjectivity in the evaluation process is to use the job-element method. Job elements are SKAs that have been determined through job analysis to be significant requirements for successful performance. Using this method, candidates are ranked using various "evidences" determined to be acceptable for showing relative competence in the different job elements. For example, ratings of the job element "knowledge of the theory of electronics" are based on such evidence as "verified experience in mathematical analysis requiring electronic theory *or* outstanding record in advanced theory courses *or* score of 85-100 on theory test."[29]

The rating of training and experience often is a cooperative undertaking of personnel specialists and subject-matter experts. Personnel specialists contribute knowledge of rating techniques and career-staffing concepts and methods, and subject-matter experts assess the relative value of certain types of experience for particular jobs.[30]

Written Tests

Written tests are extensively used in the public sector to measure job knowledge or skills. Personnel agencies may construct tests or purchase them from consulting or other organizations such as the International Personnel Management Association. Small jurisdictions typically do not have the expertise or financial resources needed to develop and validate their own written tests.

Multiple-choice tests are most commonly used. Essay-type examinations are rare, primarily because they are difficult to construct, take a long time to score, and are open to the interpretations and biases of the evaluators. Despite problems associated with test validity and adverse or disparate impact on minority groups, written tests are likely to continue as the dominant way of rating applicants for a large variety of civil service positions, primarily because they are administratively convenient and provide a quantitative basis for ranking candidates. Commenting on the OPM's new written tests for entry-level professional and administrative positions (see the final section of this chapter), the MSPB concluded that they have "the potential to be among the most efficient and least expensive ways of making selections, at least when hiring a large number of employees from among a large number of applicants."[31]

Performance Tests

A performance test simulates major facets of the job and asks the applicant to perform essential tasks related to job performance. Theoretically, all kinds of SKAs could be tested using performance tests, but they are most likely to be used to evaluate skills such as typing (speed and accuracy), operating vehicles and machinery, and doing computational tasks. Simulating complex jobs and situations is technically difficult and expensive. As more sophisticated computer technologies and software become available, however, it will probably be possible to evaluate complex mixes of SKAs using performance tests such as those now being used in simulators to test pilots' responses to a range of situations they might face in actual flight.

In comparison to other kinds of tests, performance tests yield very direct measures of how candidates perform on a series of job elements. Accordingly, these tests are said to have high face validity. From the perspective of the test taker, the tests are concrete and likely to be seen as fair and objective if they are clearly job-related. For these reasons, many jurisdictions are switching to performance tests for manual jobs. The major limitation is cost: Equipment must be acquired and maintained, and related personnel costs can be high. To keep costs down, written tests are often used if they are available. Moreover, validated performance tests do not exist for many jobs.

Oral Examinations

The terms *oral examination* and *interview* are often used synonymously. *Interview* may also refer to the conversation a hiring official has with applicants whose names have been certified from a list of eligibles. These applicants have already passed the battery of tests, and the official is given a choice from among a certain number of names, ranked according to scores. *Oral examination* refers more generally to a *weighted* part of the entire combination of tests.[32] The weight assigned varies with the importance given to the worker traits the oral is designed to measure. Orals are often used to measure applicants' abilities to communicate ideas and to interact effectively with others, which are important for managerial positions. For technical or manual jobs, these abilities have relatively less impact on overall examination scores, and oral examinations are not ordinarily used. In addition to extensive use for managerial and administrative positions, orals often are a part of test batteries for entry-level professional positions.

Oral examinations are used to evaluate candidates' SKAs or illuminate job-related personality traits that are not reliably probed by written or performance tests. Many experts on selection believe that the best use for the oral is for the latter purpose, because the accuracy of written personality tests is at best doubtful. Other, less subjective measures of SKAs are available.

The results of oral examinations are inherently open to distortion by interviewer bias or a poorly structured interview in terms of content or process. To deal with these problems, the behaviors and responses to be observed, the evaluation standards to be applied, and the procedures for conducting the examination must be well planned.[33]

An interview of an individual candidate by a panel is the most common form of oral examination. In order to assure test reliability, or comparability and consistency of results, the examiners record their observations according to a standardized format. Well-trained examiners are essential because their expertise is the foundation for confidence in the validity as well as the reliability of the ratings. Including women and minorities on interview panels minimizes the possibility of discrimination in selection and may also increase the probability that they will perceive the process as fair.

The Group Oral Performance Test

In group oral performance tests, candidates are assembled in small groups, and a topic is assigned for discussion. Civil service examiners evaluate how the candidates *perform* during the discussion, particularly how they interact with the other members of the group.

Advocates of the group oral test argue that it shows how well candidates "think on their feet," and, since the examiners only listen, more careful observation is possible. Critics point out, however, that since group orals are staged, the participants may not behave as they would in a normal administrative situation. The attention of examiners also can be disrupted, so they may have less time to size up each person than they would in a panel interview. Because examiners may tend to rate each participant in terms of how the group performs rather than the actual requirements of the position in question, use of the group oral raises significant concerns about validity and reliability. As a way of compensating for these liabilities, in some jurisdictions both a panel-type interview and a group oral are used, and the candidates' scores on both are averaged.

Background Investigations

Background investigations of applicants are used for a variety of purposes. For most civil service jobs, they consist of routine reference checks through mail and telephone inquiries. For some categories of positions, investigators employed by a central personnel agency visit and interview former employers and others who have direct knowledge of the applicants' educational preparation, work experience, abilities, and personal qualities. On the state and local levels, the most intensive and comprehensive background checks are done for law enforcement positions. For federal jobs where access to sensitive or secret information is involved, detailed, comprehensive loyalty and security checks are conducted by the FBI.

Due to limited resources and time, public employers do not conduct thorough background investigations for most positions. The relative neglect of this phase of the selection process is regrettable, because people who have worked with or supervised candidates on previous jobs often can supply far more information about them than any interview can produce. The findings of careful background investigations are often good predictors of performance.[34]

The Probationary Period

While the probationary period is not technically a test or examination, it is the last stage in the selection process. No matter how much effort is put into making preemployment tests valid, they may not screen out some applicants who lack the ability or motivation to perform satisfactorily in particular jobs. The probationary period (usually six months to a year) gives supervisors a chance to evaluate new employees and to approve for permanent status only those who have done satisfactory work. Probationary employees usually do not have appeal rights. If unsatisfactory workers are not separated at this point, it is almost always much more difficult to fire them later.

Management typically does not act as if the probationary period were an important part of the selection process. In practice, only a tiny percentage of appointees is removed during or at the end of the probationary period. Schemes such as requiring the appointing officer to certify in writing that the employee's services have been satisfactory or all salary payments will be suspended have not been very effective. Needless to say, the practice of routinely moving probationary employees to permanent status without a careful performance evaluation undermines the selection process.

THE TEST VALIDITY PROBLEM: MERIT AND EQUAL EMPLOYMENT OPPORTUNITY

In civil service selection, the goal is to determine if an applicant has the knowledge, skills, abilities, and other traits deemed necessary or important to successful performance in a particular job. The content of most selection tests is supposed to be based on the results of careful job analysis.[35] Although most civil service tests in the United States are geared to the requirements of *positions,* some are intended to assess the likelihood that an applicant will have a successful career in a variety of *occupations* or *administrative roles.* Because these types of tests are most often used for entry-level professional positions, the questions do not require knowledge or experience that can only be acquired on the job.[36] Instead they emphasize general traits, such as verbal skills and reasoning abilities, which are believed to be closely linked to performance.

From a technical standpoint, the purpose of selection tests is to provide the employer with a reasonably accurate prediction of how applicants are likely to perform in specific jobs; in other words, the tests must be valid. In Norma Riccucci's words, "test validation continues to be relied on to conceptualize and operationalize merit."[37] A valid test measures only what it is intended to measure, such as knowledge of labor law or accounting principles. Tests must also be reliable, or consistent in their results. All other things being equal, as determined by statistical tests that control for other potential sources of variation, if the same person takes the test twice (or a hundred times), the scores should be roughly the same. If the scores are significantly different, the test is unreliable and unlikely to be valid.[38]

Three types of validation methods are generally accepted by specialists in testing: criterion-related validity, content validity, and construct validity. These three validation strategies are described by the American Psychological Association in its *Standards for Educational and Psychological Tests and Manuals*.[39] The term *test* includes all selection methods used to make employment decisions, such as interviews, written tests, and evaluations of training and experience.

To establish the criterion-related validity of a test, the test scores of some applicants who have been hired are correlated with subsequent measures of their performance. Assuming that these performance ratings are accurate, a valid test should produce scores that are positively correlated with performance, so they can be used as standard scores to predict the performance of future applicants. An important limitation of this approach is that the performance of those who do not pass the test (or who receive a passing score but are not hired) is not included in the standard scores. Another method, called concurrent validity, has been devised to deal with this limitation. A proposed new test is given to incumbent employees, and their scores are compared with existing measures of their job performance. Although the goal is to develop a test that can be used to predict how well job applicants are likely to do, some critics argue that with concurrent validation, selection tests favor the SKAs of incumbent workers over the actual requirements of positions, as determined by job analysis.[40]

In establishing content validity, the goal is to develop a test that closely matches the content (the SKAs) of a job. Two examples are written job knowledge tests and performance tests in which the actual duties are carried out, as in typing, driving, or welding. A content-validity approach is attractive to public employers for a variety of reasons and is often used to validate performance tests. It may raise questions, however, about how scores are interpreted in hiring decisions and the extent to which job analyses accurately reflect conditions faced by those holding the positions in question.[41]

In a construct-validity approach to test validation, attempts are made to establish strong theoretical or empirical connections between certain general traits or constructs, such as intelligence or creativity, and satisfactory job performance. If these connections can be shown to exist, a validated measure of the construct can be used in a selection test. A test for a legal position provides an example of the difference between content and construct validity. Such a test would have content validity if it asked questions about specific provisions of the law with which the incumbent must be familiar (e.g., the tax status of municipal bonds). If an ability to comprehend complex written material is needed for successful job performance, the test would have construct validity if it could be shown to accurately measure this aspect of human intelligence.[42] Since construct validity relies on hard-to-measure constructs such as intelligence and often depends on largely theoretical connections between them and job elements, it is a controversial strategy.

The Controversy over Direct Hire Based on GPA

An interesting illustration of the issues raised by a contruct-validity approach concerns recent proposals by the OPM to give federal agencies the authority to directly hire college graduates on the basis of their grade point averages (GPAs). In order to expedite the process of recruiting high-quality college graduates, the OPM recommended an expansion of the "outstanding scholar" provisions of the consent decree entered into by the Carter administration to settle a legal challenge to the validity of the Professional and Administrative Career Examination (PACE) (discussed in the final section of this chapter). These provisions originally authorized agencies to directly hire students having GPAs of 3.5 or better (on a 4.0 scale) without OPM certification. In 1988, 972 persons were hired under this authority.

The OPM's proposed new procedures would allow agencies to directly hire any college graduate with at least a bachelor's degree and an overall average of 3.0 or above. Applicants meeting these criteria could be hired on the spot; they would not have to take any of the normally required written tests or receive OPM certification. The intent is to lessen the time required to hire applicants, while providing a tool for merit-based selections. On the recruitment side, the OPM believes that this direct-hire authority would make federal agencies more competitive in the market for highly qualified college students. On the selection side, it argues that GPA is a valid and fair selection test. The office proposed that because "GPA is assumed to be a reflection of overall accomplishment and achievement,... its use will afford closer assessment of the total person including such factors as self-discipline, perseverance, and ability to work cooperatively with others." According to the OPM, the expanded use of GPA should help ensure equitable hiring among minority and majority groups, since both groups have typically been well represented among graduates with high GPAs.[43]

This proposal has not been implemented because of concerns about validity, EEO, and the potential impact on work-force quality. The MSPB, which has statutory responsibility for protecting the merit principle, has challenged OPM's position. In a 1990 report, it questioned the validity of GPAs as a selection test and raised concerns about the impact on the hiring of minorities and women. With regard to validity, it attacked the OPM's assumption "that persons with higher GPAs are more likely to be successful employees than persons with lower GPAs." In fact, the MSPB noted, research has consistently shown that the correlation between GPA and job performance is "quite small":

> Taken in total, what the research shows is that while there is a statistical relationship between GPA and job success, the usefulness of GPA as a predictor of job success is minimal. In effect, using GPA as a basis for selection will only slightly improve the quality of those selections over what would have been obtained if applicants were chosen at random.[44]

In the MSPB's opinion, agencies relying on GPAs to select employees would be running a serious risk of lowering the quality of the federal work force.

In addition to its reservations about GPAs, the MSPB also expressed doubts about the OPM argument that direct hire based on GPA would eliminate the adverse impact associated with PACE. It found nothing in the results of the outstanding-scholar program to indicate that minority hiring would be improved. In fact, only 8 percent (81) of the 972 hires in the program in 1988 were African-American, and only 4 percent (35) were Hispanic, but African Americans and Hispanics made up 25 percent of all entry-level hires during that year.[45] The Schedule B hiring authority federal agencies used after the demise of PACE was more successful than the program, primarily because all college graduates could be considered (see the final section). Under the new OPM proposal, only those students with GPAs of 3.0 or greater could be hired without having to take the written tests. As the MSPB pointed out, this means that students with GPAs of 3.0 or higher would be much more likely to be hired, despite the fact that the relationship between GPA and job success is small. It concluded that "If there is a difference between minorities and nonminorities in terms of the likelihood of obtaining a high GPA [3.0 or higher], OPM's proposal could actually result in the establishment of a new barrier to the hiring of minorities."[46]

The MSPB did acknowledge in its report that agencies may need direct-hire authority when they have a high number of vacancies in relation to the number of qualified applicants. In 1989, about 30 percent of hires into the competitive service were made under direct-hire authority delegated to agencies by the OPM, and tests of lesser validity such as GPA might reasonably be used in such circumstances. However, the MSPB stressed that "it is doubtful that GPA should ever be the sole criterion for selection."

Test Validity and Equal Employment Opportunity Guidelines

In *Griggs* v. *Duke Power Company* (1971), the U.S. Supreme Court ruled that if a selection test has an adverse impact with regard to race, sex, religion, or national origin, *and if its validity has not been established*, its use constitutes unlawful discrimination under Title VII of the Civil Rights Act of 1964 (see Chapter 2). Under the Equal Employment Opportunity Act of 1972, coverage was extended to governments, governmental agencies, and political subdivisions. If a selection test cannot be validated, it must be discarded and replaced with one that can be validated using an approved methodology.

During the late 1960s and early 1970s, the Equal Employment Opportunity Commission, the U.S. Department of Labor, and the Civil Service Commission each issued guidelines on selection procedures. Their guidelines concerning how to demonstrate the job-relatedness of selection methods were not the same, and efforts to get uniform guidelines failed. The principal issue was a disagreement between the EEOC and the Civil Rights Commission on the one hand and the Civil Service Commission and the Departments of Labor and Justice on the other. In late 1976, the latter agencies agreed upon and adopted what was called the Federal Executive Agency (FEA) Guidelines, but the Civil Rights Commission and the EEOC were opposed, and the EEOC retained the guidelines it had adopted in 1970. The EEOC guidelines were more difficult to satisfy. The principal points of disagreement between the EEOC guidelines[47] and the FEA guidelines[48] are described below.

First, the EEOC guidelines did not offer a concrete definition of the term *adverse impact* but indicated that its existence would be determined by comparing the "rates at which different applicant groups pass a particular selection procedure." The FEA guidelines did set forth a definition of sorts: a "substantially different selection rate...which works to the disadvantage of members of a racial, sex, or ethnic group." A rule of thumb for determining if selection rates were substantially different was provided. This "80 percent rule" stated that if the selection rate for a group was within 80 percent of the rate for the group with the highest rate, "the enforcement agency will generally not consider adverse impact to exist."

Second, the EEOC guidelines required validation of every component of the selection process used to fill a position. In practice, this meant making investigations of disparate or adverse impact for all examination components, even when the examination as a whole did not have an adverse impact. In contrast, the FEA guidelines stated that adverse impact was to be determined for the "overall selection process for each job category." If no overall adverse impact was found, there was no obligation to validate the various selection components. If it was found, then each component would have to be analyzed, and any having adverse impact would have to be validated if the employer wanted to continue using them.

Third, whereas the EEOC expressed a preference for criterion-related validity, the FEA pointed out that "generally accepted principles of the psychological profession do not recognize such preference, but contemplate the use of criterion-related, content, or construct validity strategies as appropriate." Criterion-related validity studies are often difficult to conduct because small jurisdictions do not test or hire enough people in single job classifications to give a statistical sample large enough for meaningful analyses comparing test scores and performance measures. In large jurisdictions, the sample is usually big enough only in a few classifications.[49]

Fourth, the EEOC required that an employer, while in the process of validating a selection procedure, must be able to show that an alternative procedure with less adverse impact does not exist. The main objection to this standard was that it could mean an endless, "cosmic" search for alternatives with less adverse impact. The FEA guidelines stated that in the course of a validity study the employer should try to find and use procedures that have as little adverse impact as possible. Once a good-faith effort had been made and the chosen procedure had been shown to be valid, the employer did not have to search further for alternatives.

Fifth, the EEOC guidelines required that tests be validated for each minority group in order to assure that differential validity did not exist. In a test with differential validity, there are significantly different validity coefficients (measures) for different groups. Clearly, to use a test that routinely overestimates or underestimates job performance for one group or another would be unfair. The FEA guidelines were less demanding; they recommended that data be compiled separately for all groups to determine "test fairness."

After extensive negotiations, Uniform Guidelines for Employee Selection Procedures were agreed on in 1978.[50] In general, they follow the FEA guidelines closely. The Uniform Guidelines are not regulations, but they have had a major impact because the Supreme Court has said that as the administrative interpretations of the enforcing agencies they are entitled to "great deference." Nonetheless, when legal disputes arise, the final determinations as to test validity requirements and whether or not an employer has met them are made by the courts. In fact, the federal courts have not followed the Uniform Guidelines slavishly; for example, a Supreme Court decision required establishment of the fairness of a written test to *individuals*, regardless of adverse impact on African Americans as a *group*. The dissenting justices warned that the majority's opinion could discourage financially pressed local governments from validating any tests at all and might encourage them to adopt quotas. Also, the data the courts have accepted on what constitutes a "substantially different rate of selection" has varied.[51]

Apart from the question of costs to employers, the Uniform Guidelines have been criticized as technically unsound in some respects, unclear in many others, and requiring excessive record keeping. Efforts to change them, however, have met strong political opposition. The reality is that after a long history of relatively little pressure for test validation, public personnel agencies were suddenly placed in the position of having to validate a wide variety of selection tests for EEO reasons. With the exception of court rulings requiring rapid and comprehensive validation of tests having adverse impact, public policy (as expressed by the Uniform Guidelines) makes it clear that decisions about whether to take action against employers will reflect the degree to which the employer has made a sincere effort to develop and implement an affirmative action plan (see Chapter 9).

It will be many years before public employers can meet the full requirements of the uniform selection guidelines. The technical, organizational, and political barriers to achieving this aspect of the merit principle are formidable. But however distant the ideal may be, test validation is now fully established as an important objective for public personnel systems.

THE UNEASY RELATIONSHIP AMONG
COMPETITIVENESS, VALIDITY, EEO, AND MERIT

For those who believe in the merit principle, the best of all possible worlds might be one in which public employers would use highly competitive recruitment processes based on valid selection tests that produce no adverse impact whatsoever. Unfortunately, such harmony among personnel functions and goals is indeed difficult to achieve. The federal government's experience with the Professional and Administrative Career Examination (PACE) is an instructive example.

A chronic complaint about public-sector recruitment is that it is slow—so slow, in fact, that many highly qualified applicants become frustrated and accept job offers elsewhere. For many years, lengthy delays could be anticipated by applicants for entry-level administrative positions in the federal service, due to the centralized control over the ranking and certification of applicants for positions that had been publicly offered by agencies. The rationale was that this procedure was the most reliable way to assure that quality candidates were referred to the agencies for selection, and it would protect the merit principle from potential abuses on the agency level. The Civil Service Commission and the OPM used PACE, a nationwide written examination, to rank applicants for entry-level professional and administrative career positions; thousands of college graduates sat for this test every year. In 1981, the latest version of the examination was derailed by a class action suit challenging its validity. In response, a consent decree was negotiated with the Carter administration under which the OPM was required to replace PACE with job-specific written tests that had no adverse impact on minorities.

Challenges to the Validity of PACE

Prior to the consent decree, the OPM had gone to great lengths to establish the validity of PACE. The first step had been to identify the abilities or constructs important for successful performance in PACE jobs and to decide how they would be measured. Twenty-seven PACE occupations accounting for about 70 percent of PACE hires during the early 1970s were chosen for intensive analysis. Senior-level supervisors in these occupations prepared lists of the duties of the jobs in these 27 occupations, assessed the relative importance of these duties, and rated the required SKAs according to their importance to successful job performance. These ratings created one basis for identifying the abilities to be measured on the written test. The other basis was a comprehensive review of hundreds of tests whose construct validity had been evaluated.

The OPM analysts matched the SKAs and other traits identified in the 27 PACE occupations with those found in earlier tests and then wrote examination questions similar to those in the earlier tests. After this PACE was administered, the OPM made criterion-related validity studies that revealed a positive relationship between test scores and job performance scores of persons already in PACE positions, such as social security claims examiners. This is an example of concurrent-validity research.

The general abilities found necessary for successful job performance in PACE jobs included:

1. Verbal skills, the ability to understand and interpret complex technical reading materials and to communicate effectively orally and in writing.
2. Judgment, the capacity to make decisions or to take actions in the absence of complete information and to solve problems by inferring missing facts or events to arrive at the most logical conclusion.
3. Induction, the ability to discover underlying relations or principles in specific data by the formulation and testing of hypotheses.
4. Deduction, skill at discovering implications of facts and logically applying general principles to specific situations.
5. Numbers-related abilities, such as performing arithmetic operations and solving quantitative problems when a specific approach or formula is not specified.

The results of test measuring such abilities or constructs indicated that PACE did have a disparate or adverse impact on African Americans and Hispanics. Data compiled by the OPM on the April 1978 administration of PACE showed that 8.5 percent of whites taking the test received unaugmented scores (not including veterans' preference points) of 90 or higher, but the percentages of African Americans and Hispanics who received such scores were 0.3 and 1.5 percent, respectively. In practice, very few appointments were made of applicants who scored lower than 90. Other administrations of PACE produced similar results. Clearly, PACE was not an effective means of increasing the representation of minorities in the professional and administrative career lines of the federal service.

Those who brought the class action suit challenging the validity of PACE argued that the five constructs upon which the test was based were far too general in nature to measure the ability to succeed in all of the 118 occupations covered. They also questioned the technical soundness of the OPM's validity research. For better or worse, however, the courts did not have the opportunity to rule on the examination's validity. Two weeks before Ronald Reagan assumed office, the Carter administration entered into the consent decree that settled the suit.

Opponents of "preferential hiring" interpreted Carter's action as a politically motivated response to minority-group pressures. The new administration strongly opposed the decree and was able to negotiate modifications, including elimination of a requirement that the government was to continue affirmative action efforts until African Americans and Hispanics comprised at least 20 percent of all employees at the GS-5 and higher grade levels in the job categories covered by PACE. As OPM Director Donald Devine later said, the Reagan administration wanted to withdraw from the terms of the decree but had regretfully concluded that the matter was in the "hands of the court, beyond the power of the government unilaterally to bar."[52]

The main terms of the modified decree (*Luevano* v. *Devine*) were:

1. OPM was to phase out PACE as a selection test by 1985.
2. Applicants for PACE occupations were to be selected through alternative examination procedures based on the requirements of the particular occupation.
3. If the alternative procedures had adverse impact, their validity had to be established.
4. Federal agencies were to make "all practicable efforts" to eliminate adverse impact from the interim use of PACE or from alternative procedures, through recruiting and other special programs.
5. The U.S. district court for the District of Columbia was to retain jurisdiction for five years after the implementation of an alternative examination procedure for each occupation.

Schedule B Appointments

The OPM announced on May 11, 1982, that PACE was to be abolished and replaced by a new Schedule B appointment authority applicable to positions for which it is not practical to hold competitive examinations. Under Schedule B authority, agencies were allowed to hire applicants for entry-level professional and administrative positions without competitive examinations if they could show that no qualified internal candidates were available. Employees selected in this manner were placed in the excepted (noncompetitive) service.

Until 1987, such employees were required to compete for competitive positions in order to advance to the GS–9 level, and those who were selected for positions at this level were converted to the competitive service.[53] In 1987, however, President Reagan issued Executive Order 12596, which authorized noncompetitive conversions of Schedule B appointments based on "proven performance."

The Reagan administration offered several explanations for ending PACE and turning to Schedule B appointments. First, no alternative written tests or other merit selection procedures were available. Second, projected reductions in federal hiring rates would result in substantially fewer appointments from outside the service. Third, the cost of developing validated competitive examinations consistent with the decree would be prohibitive. In fact, at the time, the OPM showed little interest in a serious effort to develop alternative selection procedures, and its general counsel was quoted as saying that the intention "was to allow *Luevano* to sink of its own weight."[54] By 1987, the OPM had developed 16 tests which covered only about 60 percent of the positions involved.[55]

Whatever the motivation, the use of Schedule B appointments did much to decentralize hiring for professional and administrative positions. Under Schedule B, agencies developed and used their own recruitment and selection procedures. Federal line agencies, long frustrated by centralized, slow-moving hiring processes that undermined their recruitment efforts, were generally pleased with the Schedule B authority for professional and administrative career (PAC) positions.[56]

Less enthusiastic were organizations concerned about protecting the merit principle, maintaining quality control over agency hiring practices, and assuring that potential applicants could access the system from outside the government. The OPM's monitoring and evaluation efforts were minimal, and it was very difficult for agencies to get approval to fill entry-level PAC positions from outside. College placement offices were given little information about job opportunities for specific entry-level positions in the excepted service, and because of the delays and frustrations involved in attempting to locate and apply for positions, well-qualified candidates followed other career paths. Both the GAO and the MSPB were critical, calling for more-effective OPM oversight and guidance.

Occupationally Specific Tests

The end of the OPM's slow movement toward alternative selection procedures was signalled by a suit brought by the National Treasury

Employees Union in early 1987. The District of Columbia district court ruled that the OPM had acted improperly in deciding to place in the excepted service all job categories formerly covered by PACE and abolish PACE ahead of schedule when no alternative examinations were available. The judge also ruled that the OPM had not made a convincing case about the prohibitive costs connected with developing and validating alternative tests. The original order gave the OPM only six months to produce a competitive examination, and it ordered the agency to stop using Schedule B authority to fill PACE positions. Although a stay was granted, the need to implement a legally as well as technically viable alternative was obvious.

In response, the OPM produced in 1988 a two-pronged strategy for replacing PACE. First, it proposed the policy of expanded direct hire based on GPA described earlier in this chapter. Second, it announced the development of six new written tests designed to cover all the professional and administrative occupations of concern: (1) health and environment, (2) writing and information, (3) business and program management, (4) human resources and administration, (5) examining and adjudicating, and (6) investigation and inspection. A seventh category includes some 16 occupations with specific educational or experience requirements (e.g., economist, international relations, museum curator). Applicants for positions in this category are rated on the basis of their training and experience.

All applicants for PAC positions are also required to answer a series of questions intended to generate information on the self-discipline, leadership qualities, and problem-solving abilities of applicants.[57] This component, the Individual Achievement Record (IAR), includes questions about a person's experience and achievement in academic, employment, organizational, and interpersonal activities. The IAR asks questions that are similar to those that might be used in a personal interview, but it uses a multiple-choice format and is machine-scored.[58]

Under the OPM plan, applicants' scores on occupationally specific examinations are combined with their IAR scores. Each score has the same weight, and veterans' preference points are added to the total score. Candidates' names are then placed on a list of eligibles, ranked according to scores. The new examinations were first given in June 1990, and Schedule B authority was revoked by the OPM effective July 1, 1990.

Clearly, the OPM's strategy is to balance agency-level demands for flexible, streamlined recruitment and selection against pressures for central oversight and control. Although federal agencies applauded the idea that they should be given direct-hire authority for students with GPAs of 3.0 or higher, this proposal (as we have already noted) has not been approved. The new examinations have been generally well-received, despite some questions about their effects on recruitment.

As the GAO has observed, OPM procedures for applying for these Administrative Careers with America (ACWA) positions are potentially slow-moving and frustrating to agencies as well as applicants. The OPM brochure specifies the following procedure for applicants:

1. Call the menu-driven college hotline.
2. Schedule an examination by completing OPM Form 5000AB and return it to the OPM office closest to where you want to take the exam.
3. Travel to the nearest available location where the examination is being given.
4. Complete the examination and wait up to four weeks for the results.

A complicating factor is uncertainty as to where the examination will be given, because applicants must wait for OPM notification. Further, since applicants must take an examination and complete an IAR for each occupational category, taking more than one exam can require considerable time, effort, and expense, especially if the examinations are not given at the same location. Finally, applicants for ACWA positions who pass the tests may have to wait for some time before they know if they will be offered positions. Test scores, demand for new employees, and the pace at which individual agencies operate are all factors that may create long delays.

The ACWA program may also create difficulties for agencies, especially those with active recruiting programs. The GAO has noted that the program "effectively breaks the link between recruiting and hiring. Unless a student interested in an ACWA occupation can be employed through the Outstanding Scholar provision, there is no guarantee that agencies can hire the candidates they meet and interview on college campuses."[59] A recruiter can advise students with GPAs under 3.5 to take one or more of the occupationally specific examinations, but agencies may not be able to hire applicants who are "blocked by higher scoring candidates." Also, as was the case with PACE and other centrally administered PAC examinations, applicants may get job offers from agencies where they do not want to work. Thus, in the GAO's opinion, while the ACWA program is intended to support the goal of merit-based, nondiscriminatory hiring, its impact on federal agencies' ability to compete in the labor market is uncertain.[60]

The federal personnel system seems to have gone through a decade of turbulence with regard to PAC hiring, only to find itself still trying to balance the values of competitiveness, EEO, and merit within the framework of its PAC examination process. The validity of the new examinations may also be challenged; the National Federation of Federal Employees (NFFE) has already questioned the validity of the IAR, and the MSPB has expressed misgivings about its capacity to predict job performance. Given the inherent tensions among these values, it is unreasonable to expect that any single recruiting and hiring system can be fully satisfactory under all conditions. There is a continuing need for flexibility and adaptiveness in the system, which will allow such strategies as the delegation of examining and hiring authority to agencies under certain conditions.

■

NOTES

1. U.S. General Accounting Office, *Federal Recruiting and Hiring: Making Government Jobs Attractive to Prospective Employees*, (Washington, DC, August 1990).
2. U. S. General Accounting Office, *Federal Workforce: A Framework for Studying Its Quality over Time* (Washington, DC, August 1988); U.S. Merit Systems Protection Board and U.S. Office of Personnel Management, *A Report of the Conference on Workforce Quality Assessment* (Washington, DC, September 1989); Advisory Committee on Federal Workforce Quality Assessment, *Federal Workforce Quality: Measurement and Improvement* (Washington, DC, August 1992); U.S. Merit Systems Protection Board, *Federal First-Line Supervisors: How Good Are They?* (Washington, DC, March 1992).
3. National Commission on the Public Service, *Leadership for America: Rebuilding the Public Service* (Washington, DC, 1989).
4. The Hudson Institute, *Civil Service 2000*, report prepared for the OPM Career Entry Group (Washington, DC, June 1988), pp. 38–41.
5. National Academy of Public Administration, Panel on the Public Service, *A Statement Concerning Professional Career Entry into the Federal Service* (Washington, DC, April 1987).
6. Hudson Institute, *Civil Service 2000*, p. 39.
7. Ibid.

8. Ibid., p. 40.
9. U.S. Merit Systems Protection Board and U.S. Office of Personnel Management, *Report on Workforce Quality Assessment*, pp. 29–30.
10. Ibid., p. 45. Also see William B. Johnston, *Workforce 2000: Work and Workers for the 21st Century* (Indianapolis: Hudson Institute, June 1987).
11. U.S. Office of Personnel Management, *OPM HRD Policy Initiatives* (Washington, DC, June 1992).
12. U.S. General Accounting Office, *Letter to The Honorable David Pryor, Chairman, Subcommittee on Federal Services, Post Office and Civil Service Committee on Governmental Affairs, United States Senate* (Washington, DC, September 27, 1990), p. 5.
13. Illinois Commission on the Future of the Public Service, *Excellence in Public Service: Illinois' Challenge for the '90s* (Chicago: Chicago Community Trust/Government Assistance Project, January 1991), p. 32.
14. U.S. General Accounting Office, *Federal Recruitment and Hiring*, pp. 53–54.
15. U.S. Merit Systems Protection Board, *Attracting and Selecting Quality Applicants for Federal Employment* (Washington, DC, April 1990), pp. 9–10.
16. U.S. General Accounting Office, *Letter to the Honorable David Pryor*, p. 19.
17. Ibid.
18. U.S. Merit Systems Protection Board, *Attracting and Selecting Quality Applicants*, pp. 8–9.
19. Illinois Commission on the Future of Public Service, *Excellence in Public Service*, pp. 28–30.
20. Marc Holzer, "Attracting the Best and the Brightest to Government Service," in Carolyn Ban and Norman Riccucci (eds.), *Public Personnel Management: Current Concerns—Future Challenges* (New York: Longman, 1991), pp. 3–16.
21. U.S. General Accounting Office, *Federal Recruiting: Comparison of Those Who Accepted or Declined Federal Job Offers* (Washington, DC, March 1992), pp. 8–9.
22. Illinois Commission on the Future of Public Service, *Excellence in Public Service*, p. 39.
23. U.S. Merit Systems Protection Board, *Attracting and Selecting Quality Applicants*, p. 11.
24. U.S. General Accounting Office, *Federal Recruiting and Hiring*, p. 56.
25. Illinois Commission on the Future of Public Service, *Excellence in Public Service*, pp. 7 and 35.
26. U.S. General Accounting Office, *Federal Recruiting and Hiring*, pp. 61–68.
27. John W. Gibson and Erick P. Prien, "Validation of Minimum Qualifications," *Public Personnel Management*, vol. 6, no. 6 (November–December, 1977), p. 447.
28. *Foley* v. *Connelie*, 98 S.Ct. 1067 (1978).
29. Albert P. Maslow, "Evaluating Training and Experience," in J. J. Donovan, *Recruitment and Selection in the Public Service* (Washington, DC: International Personnel Management Association, 1968), p. 253.

30. U.S. Office of Personnel Management, Federal Personnel Manual Letter 335–13, *Guidelines for Evaluation of Employees for Promotion and Internal Placement* (Washington, DC, December 31, 1979), p. 6.
31. U.S. Merit Systems Protection Board, *Attracting and Selecting Quality Applicants*, p. 24.
32. Mary K. Stohr-Gillmore and Michael W. Stohr-Gillmore, "Improving Selection Outcomes with the Use of Situational Interviews: Empirical Evidence from a Study of Correctional Officers for New Generation Jails," *Review of Public Personnel Administration*, vol. 10, no. 2 (Spring 1990), pp. 1–18.
33. U.S. Office of Personnel Management, *Guidelines for Evaluation of Employees*, p. 8.
34. Bernard Cohen and Jan M. Chaiken, *Police Background Characteristics and Performance* (Lexington, MA: D. C. Heath, 1973).
35. U.S. Office of Personnel Management, Personnel Research and Development Center, *Job Analysis for Selection: An Overview* (Washington, DC, August 1979).
36. U.S. Merit Systems Protection Board, *Attracting and Selecting Quality Applicants*, p. 21.
37. Norma M. Riccucci, "Merit, Equity, and Test Validity," *Administration and Society*, vol. 23, no. 1 (May 1991), p. 80.
38. Vernon R. Taylor, *Test Validity in Public Personnel Selection* (Chicago: International Personnel Management Association, n.d.), p. 2.
39. American Psychological Association, *Standards for Educational and Psychological Tests and Manuals* (Washington, DC, 1966), pp. 12–24.
40. Riccucci, "Merit, Equity, and Test Validity," pp. 82–83.
41. Ibid., pp. 81–82.
42. Taylor, *Test Validity in Public Personnel Selection*, p. 5.
43. See U.S. Merit Systems Protection Board, *Attracting and Selecting Quality Applicants*, pp. 20–21.
44. Ibid., pp. 25–26.
45. Ibid., p. 28.
46. Ibid.
47. Equal Employment Opportunity Commission, "Guidelines on Employee Selection Procedures," *Federal Register*, vol. 35, no. 149 (August 1, 1970).
48. "Questions and Answers on the Federal Executive Agency Guidelines on Employee Selection Procedures," Part VI, *Federal Register*, vol. 42, no. 14 (January 21, 1977).
49. Taylor, *Test Validity in Public Personnel Selection*, p. 10.
50. "Adoption of Questions and Answers to Clarify and Provide a Common Interpretation of the Uniform Guidelines for Employee Selection Procedures," *Federal Register* vol. 44, no. 43 (March 2, 1979).
51. See Albert P. Maslow, *Staffing the Public Service* (Cranbury, N.J.: Basswood Plaza, 1983), pp. 52–53.
52. William C. Valdes, *The Selection of College Graduates for the Federal Civil Service: The Problem of the "PACE" Examination and the Consent Decree*

(Washington, DC: National Academy of Public Administration, n.d.), p. 12.

53. U.S. Merit Systems Protection Board, *Attracting and Selecting Quality Applicants*, p. 18.

54. Valdes, *Selection of College Graduates*, p. 31.

55. U.S. Merit Systems Protection Board, *In Search of Merit: Hiring Entry-Level Federal Employees* (Washington, DC, September 15, 1987).

56. U.S. General Accounting Office, *Federal Recruiting and Hiring*, pp. 34–37.

57. Statement by Constance Horner, Director of OPM, before Subcommittee on Civil Service, Committee on Post Office and Civil Service, U.S. House of Representatives, hearing on OPM's Alternative Hiring Proposal, July 12, 1988, p. 16.

58. U.S. Merit Systems Protection Board, *Attracting and Selecting Quality Applicants*, p. 22.

59. U.S. General Accounting Office, *Letter to the Honorable David Pryor*, p. 22.

60. Ibid., p. 21.

Performance Appraisal   5

A striking feature of public personnel administration today is its preoccupation with employee performance appraisals as managerial or organizational instruments and the accompanying trend toward efforts to relate *individual* performance to that of the *organization* and its *programs*. In these terms, the criteria and procedures used to evaluate performance should be explicitly related to the goals and policies of the public agency and its administrative leadership. In current thinking, then, the emphasis is on the *managerial* uses of performance appraisal systems.

Interest in performance appraisals was renewed by passage of the Civil Service Reform Act (CSRA) of 1978, which was prompted by intensifying public sentiment for improved productivity in the public sector. Americans were more than willing to accept the proposition that government services and programs were not meeting their expectations because public employees were chronically inefficient and unresponsive. It was widely believed that to improve productivity, it was essential to have in place measurement systems that could accurately discriminate among different levels of job performance. Removing unproductive workers or improving their job performance, and appropriately rewarding excellence, became popular public policy goals—as well as mandatory campaign promises.

This orientation is clearly expressed in the Georgia State Merit System manual for supervisors, which describes a good employee performance appraisal system as:

> ...a powerful management tool which can positively affect employee motivation, commitment to organizational goals, and potentially improve employee performance....First, performance feedback can guide the employee in making career choices....Second, managers can use this information to base their decisions concerning promotions, transfers, pay increases, or disciplinary actions on job-related criteria. Third, performance evaluations also provide an objective basis for deciding the order of layoffs that may be required by budgetary constraints.[1]

Two sets of factors converged during the late 1970s and the 1980s to bring about the new approach to performance appraisal. First, the traditional systems were in disrepute on all levels of government; they simply were not doing what they were supposed to. Second, the pressures for greater bureaucratic productivity, accountability, and responsiveness had created a political climate that was supportive of major reforms. The result was a pronounced shift toward executive control and a management-centered philosophy.

TRADITIONAL APPRAISAL SYSTEMS: SCIENTIFIC MANAGERS AND CIVIL SERVICE REFORMERS

Under conventional merit systems, the discretion of management in personnel matters is limited. Employees' appraisals or service ratings concentrate on how well they are carrying out the tasks associated with particular jobs or positions, and the supervisor's role in evaluation is largely to provide answers to trait- and task-related questions derived from job analyses done by personnel specialists. The results of such evaluations are supposed to be of help in making a variety of decisions regarding personnel actions such as retention, training, compensation, and promotion. Technical questions regarding appraisal focus on how to identify or rank job elements and measure performance along these dimensions accurately. Thus in practice, the traditional appraisal process operates in virtual isolation from the planning, program implementation, and management-control functions of public agencies.

The methods used in the context of many merit systems had their origins in the ideas of scientific management and the aims of the first civil service reform movement in the late 19th and early 20th centuries (see Chapter 2). From scientific management came the concepts of job design and analysis, empirical observation, and quantification. Management's job was to design and interrelate jobs in a manner that would generate the highest possible levels of technical efficiency. This required careful study of what workers were doing, the identification and combination of tasks into efficient packages or jobs, and the measurement of worker performance against key job elements. These performance data could then be used objectively to make decisions about retaining or dismissing workers, reassignments, training, and compensation. Scientific managers such as Frederick Taylor firmly believed that appraisals keyed to specific jobs were essential if the work force was to be managed efficiently and harmoniously. For the most part, however, they did not extend their thinking on this matter beyond the "shop" level, nor did they systematically consider how appraisals might be linked to the broader concerns of upper management.

The civil service reformers had a different agenda in mind. Based on their experience with spoils, they did not trust managers to administer a personnel system impartially. They were intent on removing partisan considerations from virtually all aspects of the personnel process, including performance appraisals. Neutral competence was to be the normative foundation of public personnel administration. In order to assure that public employees would not be rewarded or punished for partisan reasons, the reformers worked hard to establish merit systems under which supervisory discretion was severely limited and closely policed by nonpartisan civil service commissions that had been empowered to defend merit principles.

The ideal advanced by the reformers was rigorously objective performance appraisals formulated by disinterested specialists using scientific methods. This was particularly attractive because it meshed nicely with the American values of individualism and egalitarianism. The scientific approach promised accurate job-related measures free from subjective biases of all kinds, and merit systems were supposed to provide the nonpartisan and professional environment required to create and administer valid, objective evaluations of individuals' work. Such appraisals, it was assumed, would guarantee fair and equitable treatment of all workers. Performance, and performance alone, would determine pay and status. These norms were very much in line with the merit principles advocated by the reformers, and they were embodied in civil service laws on all levels of government.

As merit systems were established and expanded, the design and operation of performance appraisal systems came to be dominated by technical specialists working for civil service commissions or their functional equivalents. At their best, the methods used to construct appraisal instruments rather closely followed those recommended by the scientific managers. Line management's role was limited to providing the job-related information needed by these specialists to formulate rating schemes, keep necessary records, and fill in rating forms. In a 1991 report on the research on pay for performance, the National Research Council described the "measurement tradition" that dominated the field of performance appraisal until the late 1970s. This tradition, based in psychometrics and testing, stressed accurate measurement as a precondition for establishing performance standards and producing accurate evaluation. The report noted that "By and large, researchers in measurement have made the assumption that if the tools and procedures are accurate (e.g., valid and reliable), then the functional goals of organizations using tests or performance appraisals will be met."[2]

It is difficult to conceive of a true merit system without a valid, fully implemented system for appraising individual performance. Nevertheless, while the majority of states and localities have had some kind of rating system on the books for many years, and the federal government has been in the business since the establishment of the old Civil Service Commission in 1883, performance appraisals have been a notoriously weak link in the chain of techniques needed to firmly connect merit principles with merit practices.

Problems with Traditional Appraisals

In the late 1950s, Felix Nigro described service ratings as a "dark area" in public personnel administration because the results with the systems in use had been so dismal. Generally, there was much skepticism and even a feeling of futility; employees and supervisors alike expressed serious doubts about even the possibility of developing effective evaluation plans. At least three kinds of problems—technical, managerial, and organizational—plagued efforts to realize the goals of the scientific managers and civil service reformers.

Technical Problems

For all but the most routine and mechanical kinds of work, identifying and clearly defining the performance dimensions of civil service positions was not easy. Under the Performance Rating Act of 1950, appraisal systems were to have three summary ratings: outstanding, satisfactory, and unsatisfactory (see Chapter 13). But professional and administrative jobs are often complex and variable, and static, necessarily general position descriptions seldom provided a meaningful picture of what these people were actually doing. Moreover, even if agreement on performance dimensions could be reached, developing administratively feasible methods for accurately measuring performance on the job turned out to be an equally difficult technical problem. The scientific managers had developed their concepts and tested their methods in industrial settings for the most part, and their interest in shop-level work had not been extended in any systematic way to supervisory, professional, or administrative jobs. Since few government jobs are industrial in nature, scientific management techniques were of limited value in the public sector.

The technical problems were considerable. Furthermore, attempting to solve them was expensive; developing performance measurement plans based on job standards required expertise and time. Administering and maintaining these plans was also costly. Predictably, with increasing claims on limited resources came waning interest in performance appraisals. Funding was minimal, so relatively little staff effort was devoted to appraisals. Training programs for supervisors were nonexistent or superficial, and supervisors did not invest much time in the process; typically, they delayed completing evaluation forms until the last minute. As they sought to avoid conflict and accusations of unfairness, they inevitably arrived at ratings that were skewed at the high end of the scale. It was not unusual for over 95 percent of the ratings to be in the satisfactory or higher categories. In effect, there was very little discrimination among levels of performance.

Managerial Problems

The scant attention paid to performance appraisals by supervisors was not only a reflection of technical problems, it was also a response to the largely peripheral role played by line management in the design and use of the systems. Investing heavily in these systems did not make much sense for management. Supervisors were not rewarded for doing so by their bosses, and any negative ratings they gave often yielded nothing more than stressful interpersonal conflict and time-consuming appeals by resentful workers to suspicious civil service boards.

Public managers are asked to accomplish, effectively and efficiently, objectives established under law and by the policy initiatives of their superiors. From this perspective, performance appraisals are useful only to the extent that they promote managers' efforts to control, guide, and coordinate the actions of subordinates. Did existing performance appraisal systems help managers manage? Overall, the answer was that they did not. At best, they were not very relevant, and therefore they were appropriately treated as required formalities or annual rituals. At worst, they erected barriers to successful management by stimulating cynicism and distrust of supervisors, by stripping managers of any meaningful control over incentives such as pay, and, most important, by greatly constraining the supervisor's role in defining performance goals and standards. Under these conditions, veteran managers could not have been expected to take performance appraisals very seriously.

Organizational Problems

Performance appraisals were not connected to mainline organizational activities such as planning and budgeting. Neither were they used in the efforts of higher-level administrators to control programmatic activities. Appraisal methods and procedures did little to promote administrative efforts to set goals, monitor organizational performance, or allocate human as well as material resources effectively. From the standpoint of managers trying to get work done on the organizational and program levels, appraisals were *administratively* irrelevant. Accordingly, like supervisors down the line, higher-level public executives were not inclined to expend their limited resources on efforts to enhance performance appraisals. From an organizational point of view, these appraisals were done largely to satisfy the demands of civil service statutes and merit system rules.

A Victory of Form over Substance

As might be expected under these conditions, performance appraisals became just forms to be filled out, signed-off on, complained about, and forgotten. Various kinds of plans were used, the most common being trait rating. Typically, a graphic rating scale was used on which the supervisor marked on a continuum the degree to which particular factors (mostly personality traits such as initiative, courtesy, cooperativeness, and enthusiasm) could be said to describe the employee. The supervisor could rate subordinates rapidly by making check marks in the spaces indicated at various points on the continuum with labels such as "unsatisfactory" at one end and "fully satisfactory" at the other. This method does have the virtue of being easy to administer, and it is largely for this reason that trait rating was widely adopted. However, the connection between the rater's analysis of the employee's traits and that employee's job performance could only be assumed. It was not unusual for these rating forms to include some very generally stated items about the quantity or quality of work, but this was usually the extent of inquiry into actual job performance. Factors were seldom clearly defined, and those doing the rating normally were given no specific guidance as to how to measure the degree to which a factor described the employee being rated.

Rating work-related traits was the common method of employee evaluation in state and local jurisdictions. The system used in the Overland Park, Kansas, police department before 1980 was described by Lawrence O'Leary and Myron Schafe as "generic performance appraisal, used throughout the city." It involved an evaluation by supervisors that was focused on work-related traits. Not only was there no connection between performance ratings and pay, but the Overland Park system had basic weaknesses that were not unusual, including the following:

1. The rating form was not job-related or specifically applicable to many positions within the department.
2. The system allowed so much subjectivity that ratings varied widely among supervisors, and some employees believed that another supervisor would have rated them higher for the same level of performance.
3. With the traits format and ample room for subjectivity, there were grounds for suspicion that favoritism was distorting ratings.
4. Performance evaluations were implemented inconsistently; some supervisors took them seriously while others did not.
5. There were growing numbers of minority and female officers, but management was unable to demonstrate that appraisals were in fact free of discriminatory biases.[3]

The attitudes of supervisors toward performance appraisal in Overland Park were representative of those held around the country. O'Leary and Scafe identified two types of resulting behaviors under the trait-rating approach. First, there was only occasional notation by the supervisor of very bad performance or, even less frequently, of very good performance. Second, shortly before a semiannual interview, there was "a mad scramble to create some approximation of a performance appraisal while moaning and groaning about the silliness and ineffectiveness of this process."[4] In 1981, the Urban Institute concluded that "evidence currently available indicates that systems utilizing supervisor ratings of personal traits and focusing on nonspecific aspects of performance are not valid or effective enough to be worthwhile."[5]

The situation was very similar in the federal government. The General Accounting Office (GAO) recommended in a 1978 report to

Congress "fundamental changes" in the performance rating systems being used, noting that "about every third employee at five of six agencies indicated insufficient job knowledge and feedback on their performance." Often, performance requirements were nonexistent or so vague as to be useless, and many position descriptions were outdated. A Civil Service Commission regional director stated, "Supervisors are often unable to furnish statements on what is actually required on the job, beyond performing the duties listed in the position description. This leads us to believe that performance requirements appear only when they are needed to document an outstanding or unsatisfactory rating." Although the Performance Rating Act of 1950 and agency rules required supervisors to establish performance standards and discuss them with their subordinates, many supervisors stated that they had not done so. The GAO study also revealed that up to half of all supervisors had never received training in the major elements of performance evaluation, and some who had did not think it was very useful.[6]

Federal managers' efforts to use the existing system were also frustrated by poorly conceived legislation and restrictive court decisions. Despite the 1950 act's requirements for summary-adjective ratings of overall performance (outstanding, satisfactory, or unsatisfactory), in practice over 95 percent of federal workers received satisfactory ratings. The law provided that outstanding ratings could be given "only when *all* aspects of performance not only exceed normal requirements, but are outstanding and deserve special commendation" (italics ours). This is a very demanding standard to meet, and from a supervisory point of view, a heavy investment in time and effort was required to justify an outstanding rating. Thus the system encouraged giving satisfactory ratings to the vast majority of employees who were doing acceptable work or better.

For marginal or unproductive employees, the 1950 act provided that a rating of unsatisfactory was grounds for "removal from the position in which the performance was unsatisfactory." However, in 1960, a court of claims ruled that the Lloyd-LaFollette Act of 1912 and the Veterans' Preference Act of 1944 took precedence. In short, dismissal could not be automatic because the ruling was interpreted as establishing two statutory appeals rights—the first after receipt of the notice of unsatisfactory performance and the second after initiation of dismissal action by management. Under these conditions, federal managers usually bypassed giving unsatisfactory ratings and went directly to adverse-action proceedings. This strategy saved both time and money, but it meant that virtually all federal employees were rated as satisfactory. Between 1954 and 1978, the GAO calculated, 99 percent of ratings had fallen into this category.

To make matters worse, the Federal Salary Reform Act of 1962 contained a provision eliminating an automatic within-grade increase for everybody rated satisfactory or better. Instead, the basis for granting the increases would be an independent determination by the agency head that the employee had met an "acceptable level of competence." The rationale was that supervisors were not critically rating performance because they did not want to deprive employees of within-grade increases or otherwise damage their status. Instead of encouraging and supporting genuine efforts by supervisors to discriminate among levels of accomplishment, the 1962 act simply forced agency heads to routinely give certifications of acceptable performance because they were in no position to do otherwise.

Surveys of federal workers conducted by the Office of Personnel Management shortly after passage of the CSRA in 1978 revealed widespread dissatisfaction with the performance appraisal system and, at least by implication, potentially strong support for reform. Supervisors, long frustrated by their inability to use personnel policies to establish effective linkages between performance, pay, and status, were more than ready for change.

THE NEW PERFORMANCE APPRAISAL

In practice, performance appraisal languished as a backwater of public personnel administration until the late 1970s, though its importance to merit systems and management effectiveness was recognized in theory. After World War II, at all levels of government, there was a period of interest in developing *performance* rating plans, that is, evaluation of the facts of the employee's performance rather than impressions of the employee's personality traits. While efforts to define and accurately measure performance met with minimal success in the public sector, the concept became firmly entrenched in the professional and research literature on public administration. Debate over the relative merits of a variety of techniques for measuring performance surfaced on a fairly regular basis, and research focused on alternatives to the trait-rating approach such as behaviorally anchored rating scales, evaluation by objectives, and narrative evaluation models.[7] Proposals to overhaul performance appraisal policies and practices in the public sector had relatively little effect, however, until public dissatisfaction with government and intense political pressures for civil service reform forced the issue (see Chapter 2). The late 1970s and early 1980s were marked by enthusiastic, often overly optimistic efforts to place appraisals at the center of this second civil service reform movement.

Alan K. Campbell, the first director of the OPM, noted some ten years after passage of the CSRA that the federal reforms were intended to respond to what were seen to be very real problems in a personnel system that "had developed into a protective negative system primarily designed to prevent patronage, favoritism, and other personnel abuses." According to Campbell, the emphasis on performance appraisals in the 1978 legislation was in part a response to the widespread popular belief that many public employees were inefficient, incompetent, and largely immune from any logical connections among job security, compensation, and performance. In fact, many public employees shared this perception. The legislation was also intended to respond to the concerns of federal managers, who indicated in attitude surveys that they were as disillusioned about how well the system worked as the general public was. They had little confidence in their ability to manage the system and believed that the restrictions and regulations imposed by the oversight agencies had made it impossible for them to be effective.[8]

Campbell's recollections of the background of the CSRA and his admonition that performance evaluation systems will not work unless they are "based on a carefully drawn plan for the organization's activities over [its] planning cycle" neatly summarize the approach taken to appraisals during the 1980s.[9] In addition to the federal government, many state and local agencies have been pressed to develop appraisal instruments that require supervisors to evaluate performance in terms of specific job responsibilities and objectives. Ratings are to be connected, in form and substance, with personnel actions such as dismissals, training assignments, pay increases, promotions, and retention under reduction-in-force situations. Administrative control over evaluation formats and processes has been expanded in response to the argument that organizational performance will be improved if managers have the discretion they need to manage their human resources effectively.[10]

According to the National Research Council study of research on pay for performance, the current emphasis is "less with questions of validity and reliability than with the workability of the performance appraisal system within the organization, its ability to communicate organizational standards to employees, to reward good performers, and to identify employees who require training and other development activities." Within the framework of this "management tradition" (in contrast to the "measurement tradition" of earlier appraisal efforts), performance appraisals have been added to the inventory of resources executives can use to encourage greater responsiveness and accountability in the work force. Extensive delegation of the authority to design and administer appraisal systems, within broad policy guidelines, has received strong support from many personnel specialists as well as line managers. Evaluation methods based on management-by-objectives concepts have become popular elements of efforts to make agency goals and plans the basis of the performance measures used throughout the organization.[11]

With regard to accuracy, attention has shifted from the properties of rating scales to factors affecting the ability of those doing the rating to provide accurate judgments of performance. Because employee acceptance and organizational utility are central objectives of the management tradition, the organizational setting (social, psychological, and technical) within which the appraisal process takes place is a major consideration. The rating technology also has an effect on accuracy, but the focus is on "the conditions that encourage raters to use the performance appraisal systems in the way that they were intended to be used."[12]

The regulatory concerns of Civil Service Reform I faded into the background as the executive and managerial uses of performance appraisals proposed in Civil Service Reform II assumed center stage. In the 1990s, these uses are, in the words of Charles J. Fox, "ubiquitous in the public sector." The widespread enthusiasm for systematic performance evaluation may be explained by its appeal to managers, personnel specialists, and employees alike. According to Fox,

> The ubiquity of performance appraisal is no accident. On first blush, it appeals to virtually all legitimate standpoints in organizational life. To some managers it offers direct control. To other managers, it offers the capacity to coordinate individual aspirations to organizational objectives. To personnelists it offers rationality, consistency, and litigation avoidance. To employees it offers recognition and just deserts. It seems to be a "win, win, win, win" proposition. And it comports well with, indeed flows from, deeply held American cultural norms.[13]

However, the high expectations generated by reform initiatives such as the CSRA are seldom fully realized. Failures like those experienced with the appraisal systems that were derived from Civil Service Reform I could lead to widespread cynicism and pessimism that *any* approach will work in government.[14] The federal effort to achieve the goals set by the CSRA has met with at best mixed results, leading some critics to warn that the "new" performance appraisal systems are losing credibility and support throughout the work force.[15] The conclusion drawn from the findings of a survey of some 16,000 federal employees reported in 1990 by the Merit Systems Protection Board was hardly reassuring: "The components of the Federal Government's performance management program are not creating an atmosphere that strongly encourages quality performance.... performance appraisal systems, which are the heart of the performance management program, are not doing well."[16] The following section offers a closer look at the recent federal experience with performance appraisal under the provisions of the CSRA. A 1981 review of state and local government initiatives in appraisals found essentially the same problems and issues, but the federal experience has been much more intensively studied.[17]

THE FEDERAL EXPERIENCE WITH PERFORMANCE APPRAISAL UNDER THE CSRA

The CSRA contains two sections on performance appraisal systems: one for the Senior Executive Service (SES) and the other for most other executive-branch employees. Title II (Chapter 43) of the act applies to most federal workers and Title IV to the Senior Executive Service.

CSRA Provisions for Most Federal Workers

The CSRA requires each agency to develop one or more systems for the periodic evaluation of employee performance. The OPM is instructed to issue regulations for the establishment of performance standards that, to the maximum extent possible, provide for evaluations based on objective criteria. Agencies must encourage the participation of employees in the development of performance standards, and they are to use the ratings employees receive as a basis for decisions regarding training, rewarding, reassigning, promoting, reducing in grade, retaining, or removing them from service. Agencies are also to assist federal workers who receive less than satisfactory ratings with efforts to improve their performance. No one may be reassigned, demoted, or fired without first having the opportunity to demonstrate acceptable performance (30 to 60 days is the usual agency time frame).

Under the CSRA, employee appraisals must be based on elements of the job to be performed, not on traits such as courtesy and adaptability. A performance standard is defined as "the statement of the quality, quantity, etc., required for the performance of a component of an employee's job." Standards are to be prepared for every aspect of a job, but certain factors are identified as *critical elements*. A critical element is any job requirement that is so important that inadequate performance in this respect outweighs acceptable or better performance in other, "noncritical" areas. The CSRA definition of unacceptable performance is that which "fails to meet established performance standards in one or more critical elements of each employee's position."

Shortly after enactment of the CSRA, the employee unions, in a submission to the Federal Labor Relations Authority (FLRA), maintained that the language of the act meant that performance standards are subject to negotiation. This contention was strongly opposed by the OPM and the Carter and Reagan administrations, and the FLRA ruled that standards themselves are not negotiable. However, it also ruled that the procedures used to set standards and the manner in which employees participate *are* negotiable. The standards must be "fair and equitable," and if a union is convinced that they are not, it may take the issue to arbitration.

An employee whose work is rated unacceptable, and whom management proposes to reduce in grade or remove, is entitled to a written 30-day advance notice that identifies the specific instances of unacceptable performance on which the proposed action is based. Critical elements involved in each instance of unacceptable performance must be specified. Employees have the right to be represented by an attorney or other advocate, and they must be given a reasonable amount of time to respond orally or in writing. Management must make a decision within 30 days after expiration of the notice period. For nonprobationary employees, a reduction-in-grade or removal decision may be challenged through a negotiated grievance procedure (if available) or by appeal to the Merit Systems Protection Board.

In considering such an appeal, arbitrators and the MSPB are to apply the standard that the agency must show "substantial" evidence to support its action. The previous standard in adverse actions for alleged incompetence had been a "preponderance" of evidence. In other words, the CSRA makes it easier for agencies to defend their actions in the appeal process, though not as easy as those who drafted the legislation wanted it to be. The original provisions of the bill proposed by the Carter administration would have put the burden of proof on the employee to show why a dismissal was not justified, but opposition from federal employee unions forced the compromise in the legislation that was enacted.

CSRA Provisions for the Senior Executive Service

Title IV of the CSRA, which deals with performance appraisal in the Senior Executive Service (SES), states that each agency shall, in accordance with OPM standards, implement one or more appraisal system based on "criteria which are related to the position and which specify the critical elements of the position." The act states that appraisals are to reflect individual and organizational performance, taking into account the following factors:

1. Improvements in efficiency, productivity, and quality of work or service, including any significant reduction in paperwork.
2. Cost efficiency.
3. Timeliness of performance.
4. Other indications of the effectiveness, productivity, and performance quality of the employees for whom the senior executive is responsible.
5. Meeting affirmative action goals and achievement of equal employment opportunity requirements.

For the SES, agency appraisal systems must provide for annual summary ratings: (1) one or more levels of successful performance, (2) a minimally satisfactory level, and (3) an unsatisfactory level. Under the CSRA, the OPM requires that agencies establish one or more performance review board with the responsibility for assuring that the initial evaluations by senior executives' supervisors are fair and consistent throughout the organization. The boards review these evaluations and any responses by senior executives, conduct further reviews as deemed necessary, and make recommendations on the ratings to the agency head.

Career executives earning a rating at any of the fully successful levels are eligible for bonuses. In the case of an unsatisfactory rating, the executive must be reassigned or transferred and may be removed from the SES. Members of the SES *must* be removed if they receive two unsatisfactory ratings during a period of five consecutive years *or* two less-than-satisfactory ratings in any period of three consecutive years. Appraisals may be challenged before a final decision is made, but removal from the SES for performance is not considered an adverse action, so senior executives have no appeal rights after the decision has been made. A senior executive who believes a personnel action is discriminatory may appeal to the Equal Employment Opportunity Commission, and appeals based on charges of political partisanship or retaliation against "whistle-blowing" may be taken to the MSPB and the Office of the Special Counsel.

Putting the CSRA into Practice

The CSRA set a deadline of October 1, 1981, for agencies to complete the tasks of identifying critical elements of positions and establishing performance standards and communicating them to their employees. Given the complexity and scale of this activity, it is surprising that most federal agencies had new performance appraisal plans in place by this date. It is *not* surprising that implementation of the plans did not go smoothly during these early years of the reform effort. The General Accounting Office was among the first to point out that the deadlines for implementation were unrealistically short. It noted that most federal agencies had little or no experience with performance-based appraisal systems, and experience in the private sector suggested that several years of pretesting and evaluating such plans were necessary. The federal implementation schedule was so tight that virtually no pretesting took place. Moreover, the agencies were required to implement these new systems in the midst of the turbulent transition from the Carter to the Reagan administrations. As Alan Campbell put it, the situation "could hardly have been less conducive to smooth implementation of the major initiatives laid out in the Civil Service reform legislation."[18]

In early evaluations of agency success in implementing appraisal systems that satisfied the goals of the CSRA, mixed results were reported. Probably the most positive finding was what the GAO identified in a 1983 report as the major benefit—better communication between employees and supervisors. As a result, the report said, "Employees who helped prepare their performance standards have gained a better understanding of their responsibilities and of their supervisors' expectations. Supervisors, in turn, have had to define job requirements more clearly and explicitly." The same report cited serious shortcomings in the nine agency systems studied. These included the following failures to satisfy CSRA criteria:

1. Employees often did not actively participate in the development of the performance standards for their jobs.
2. In some cases, workers were not informed of the performance standards at the beginning of the appraisal period.
3. Performance standards often were not clearly stated in measurable terms, failed to distinguish levels of accomplishment, or did not clearly define unacceptable performance.
4. Agencies' procedures for linking ratings with personnel actions were often vague, and employees could not see a direct connection between appraisals and these actions.

5. Few agency and OPM evaluations of appraisal systems had been done to identify problems and design improvements.[19]

While these findings indicated that there was much room for improvement, they also pointed to inherent difficulties in designing and administering appraisal plans. Developments in performance appraisal since the mid-1980s suggest such continuing problems as poor communication, unclear performance standards, failure to systematically connect appraisals with other facets of the personnel system, and resistance to investments in regular program evaluation.

In a 1989 report highly critical of the OPM's leadership of the federal personnel system, the GAO cited the findings of a 1987 study in which over half of the personnel officers queried reported difficulty in developing clear, measurable, and objective performance standards. The study also found:

1. Lack of consistency among raters.
2. Supervisory complaints that procedures were too cumbersome and time-consuming.
3. Difficulties with employee counseling, providing performance feedback, and other interpersonal processes.
4. Inconsistent levels of management support for appraisal systems.[20]

The OPM has provided some technical assistance to agencies through its plan development and approval process, guidance in the *Federal Personnel Manual*, and informational booklets. The GAO found in its 1989 report, however, that many personnel officers felt they needed more help. At the end of the first decade after passage of the CSRA, about half of these officers reported that their organizations needed support from the OPM in a wide variety of problem areas, including:

1. Developing more timely and efficient evaluation processes.
2. Helping managers accurately describe employees' performance.
3. Developing performance elements and standards.
4. Connecting performance appraisals to organizational performance.
5. Building managerial and employee support for the appraisal process.
6. Obtaining information on what innovations are being used by other agencies.[21]

Obviously stung by the GAO's conclusion that it was not exercising enough leadership, the OPM responded in terms not designed to build confidence in the ultimate success of the reform effort. It stated: "Difficulties with performance appraisal and pay-for-performance are in fact pandemic throughout the public and private sectors."[22] The GAO agreed.

Developing and Using Performance Standards

An observation commonly made in studies of federal performance appraisals is that formulating relevant and clearly job-specific performance standards has often been a challenge for supervisors. Employees have complained about their agencies' use of "generic" standards that provide little information relevant to their specific jobs. For many positions, output cannot be measured by counting units of production, and judging quality is frequently a matter of the supervisor's opinion. To further complicate the issue, measures based solely on the quantity or quality of an individual's work may not capture equally important social-psychological factors in group and organizational performance.

As John Nalbandian points out, group skills, informal leadership qualities, values, and loyalty are among the variables that establish and maintain the productivity, cohesion, and sociability of a work group. If performance standards are restricted to "hard" or quantifiable output, supervisors may be placed in the position of having to recognize intangible contributions informally, and they may be accused of bias (or backsliding into a trait approach) by employees who score high on the hard measures. The alternative is to use only formally established "objective" standards, which may discourage informal contributions and encourage employees "to perform in accordance with only the criteria upon which they can be formally evaluated."[23] Since few public employees work in isolation at mechanical production tasks, where output can be easily measured in quantitative terms, problems tied to the development of standards that are satisfactory in all respects should be anticipated.

Standards for Blue-Collar Workers

There are also concerns about performance standards in the methods used to evaluate performance in the Federal Wage System (FWS), which covers some 450,000 blue-collar workers (trades, crafts, and laborers). In a 1987 report, the seemingly tireless GAO cited many examples of performance standards for blue-collar workers that were not clearly stated, were trait- as opposed to performance-based, were difficult to measure, or were tied to "uncontrollable external factors."[24]

The *Federal Personnel Manual* requires that performance standards "clearly state expected job performance." Among the examples of failures to meet this criterion for blue-collar workers found by the GAO was the following critical element for performing journeyman electrical work: "The performance standard at the outstanding or highest level was 'acceptable failures per year to perform work at journeyman level.' The standard is incomplete in that it does not indicate the number of failures that are acceptable."[25]

The *Manual* also states that using personal traits to assess performance does not meet statutory requirements unless these traits can be directly connected to performance, can be documented, and are measurable. Applying this rule, the GAO cited the following example of a standard based "inappropriately" on personal traits:

> The standard for a heavy mobile equipment mechanic: "No more than 1–2 occasions per year when...a subjourneyman has to be counselled for not functioning diligently, cooperatively, and communicating as a team member." It appears that a supervisor would find it difficult to define or objectively measure performance using such traits as diligence, cooperativeness, and communication as a team member.[26]

Here, the GAO illustrates Nalbandian's point about forcing supervisors to disregard potentially important social-psychological factors.

According to the OPM's guidance to federal agencies, standards should be written in a manner that allows supervisors to determine if an employee's performance has exceeded, satisfied, or not met the standards. The GAO blue-collar study found standards that did not clearly distinguish among all the levels of performance, and it cited the following example for a boiler plant mechanic's position:

> The standard for the far exceeded level was "zero failures to perform necessary emergency repairs on the boiler plant and auxiliary equipment." The standard for the satisfactory performance level was "one failure to perform." As written, the performance level between these two levels (i.e., highly satisfactory) cannot be achieved.[27]

The OPM also requires that the capacity to achieve performance standards should be within the employee's control. If factors beyond workers' control affect their ability to meet a standard, it is impossible to measure performance accurately on the individual level. The GAO found examples of standards for supervisors of blue-collar workers that contain these kinds of external factors. One standard calls for presenting performance awards to three or four employees, and another requires achieving a sick-leave usage rate of 60 or fewer hours by the end of the rating period. In the first instance, the supervisor may not have three subordinates who deserve an award, and, in the second, supervisors have only limited control over how much sick leave employees use.[28]

Even if standards are correctly formulated, the OPM emphasis on objectivity and quantification has created predictable technical problems. Standards that contain quantitative criteria (numbers and percentages) require reliable methods for accurately tracking and measuring performance. The GAO's look at blue-collar workers revealed that performance standards that appear to be objective and quantifiable often are not used by supervisors. Such measurement may have been too burdensome or simply not possible because no feasible, cost-effective methods had been developed. In other words, writing appropriate standards has been only part of the task facing federal agencies under the policies of the CSRA and the OPM. An equally imposing challenge has been securing the supervisory commitment, information systems, and material resources needed to track and measure performance against those standards.

Other difficulties associated with performance standards that have surfaced in a variety of contexts include failure to inform employees of expectations in a timely manner and not providing midyear feedback. Reports about supervisors who developed standards for their subordinates without consulting them have not been unusual. Also fairly common are complaints that supervisors do not communicate effectively during the standards-setting process. As the GAO's study of blue-collar workers suggests, at least some agencies are not regularly reviewing and revising standards in order to keep them current.

Dealing with Poor Performers

An important provision of the CSRA requires agencies to take actions to improve the performance of employees with less-than-satisfactory ratings. Agency policies and procedures require supervisors to provide assistance to workers who are performing at the minimally successful or unacceptable levels. Supervisors are asked first to make interventions (e.g., informal counseling and closer supervision) calculated to raise performance to the fully successful level. If they do not succeed within a reasonable period, they must take appropriate action against such employees.

The OPM recommends that a supervisor first discuss poor performance with the employee and document in writing the problems and the assistance offered. According to a 1990 report on performance management by the GAO, if poor performance continues, the supervisor must notify the employee of "an opportunity period to improve performance." Agency policies typically state that the supervisor should allow a poor performer "a reasonable period" (normally from one to two months), depending on the circumstances in each case. If performance has not improved after the opportunity period, the supervisor is to identify the deficiencies, specify the actions that should be taken in order to improve performance, and describe the assistance to be provided.[29]

At least in terms of ratings given, poor performance is not a huge problem in the federal government. In 1988, for example, only some 6 percent of employees fell below the fully successful level, and 83 percent of these employees received a rating of minimally successful. However, there may be more poor performers than these statistics suggest; supervisors can work with poor performers informally, and some positions are vacated before formal appraisals are done.

The 1990 GAO report found that most, but not all, supervisors were willing to work with poor performers. Apparently, some give fully successful ratings in order to avoid having to use the process required to deal with poor performers. The main reasons cited were that the process is too time-consuming, some supervisors wanted to avoid confrontation, and management is not seen as being supportive. Around 20 percent of supervisors reported that they had not received adequate training in using performance standards and assisting poor performers. Also, a fair number said they were reluctant to go through the appeal and arbitration processes that might result if they gave less than fully successful ratings.[30] One supervisor summarized the reasons for this attitude in the following comment to the GAO:

> The balance with respect to documenting and dealing with poor performers is on the side of the employee. The burden of proof rests almost exclusively with the supervisor, requiring much time and an incredible amount of documentation before appropriate action can be taken by the supervisor. Many first-line supervisors are reluctant to take action for this reason. The grievance/appeals/arbitration process often assumes the supervisor to be "guilty" and the problem employee "innocent."[31]

Another problem federal supervisors face in their dealings with poor performers is a lack of consistent options for handling employees who have been rated minimally successful. For the SES and those covered by the current merit pay plan, the Performance Management and Recognition System (PMRS), the alternatives include removal, demotion, and denial of merit pay increases. However, these groups compose a relatively small percentage of the work force. Supervisors of General Schedule (GS) and blue-collar Wage Grade (WG) personnel are limited to reassignments and denials of within-grade increases. Since many are near the top of their grade and are due increases only once every two or three years, supervisors do not have a great deal of leverage in trying to motivate poor performers to improve. Minimally successful workers can hang on for years under these conditions. One frustrated supervisor lamented: "I have seen people that are minimal that are dead ended in jobs they never leave... and they are poor performers for years and years."[32]

The GAO report on performance management estimates that up to 25 percent of minimally successful employees stay at that level for a year or more. It has therefore recommended that Congress consider giving supervisors the options of demoting or removing GS and WG workers who stay at the minimally satisfactory level after having been given an opportunity to improve. The OPM agrees with this recommendation, and it has suggested that some federal agencies might want to eliminate the minimally successful rating option for critical performance elements. Many state and local governments, as well as private corporations, do allow demotion and removal actions against those who do not raise their performance above the minimum level.

In addition, agency management could provide better oversight and support. The GAO report found that most personnel officials

> ...did not receive or maintain statistics on the number of poor performers given opportunities to improve, how poor performance cases were being resolved, or how long it took to deal with performance problems. Moreover, most of the program managers...did not believe they had any responsibility for managing and monitoring the process for dealing with poor performers."[33]

Without attention from management, problems such as difficulty in using performance standards effectively and excessive demands on supervisory time and resources may seriously undermine supervisors' commitment to the goal of improving performance. Since about 75 percent of supervisors were found to be making sincere and often successful efforts to work with poor performers, the GAO concluded that strong management oversight and support are needed to sustain and enhance their efforts.

Performance Appraisal in the SES

In general, experience with CSRA appraisal systems in the SES has paralleled that in the rest of the federal work force. Evaluations done in the mid-1980s revealed general satisfaction with performance plans and the accuracy of appraisals. However, many executives said they were not convinced that the appraisal systems used in their agencies had much of an effect on performance or the quality of communication between superiors and subordinates.[34]

A GAO report to Congress in 1984 pointed out the weaknesses in the administration of the SES performance appraisal systems. The plans seldom expressed CSRA appraisal criteria, typically contained standards stated only in general terms, were not prepared for all executives, and were not ready on time or revised as job responsibilities changed. As might be expected, relating individual accomplishments to the attainment of organizational goals had proven to be extremely difficult, since needed data were seldom available. Moreover, performance review board members indicated that performance measurement data were not used in the appraisal process. Ratings often reflected judgments regarding job difficulty and "importance" or personal knowledge about the executive's performance.[35] Some of these difficulties may be traced to the challenge of formulating specific and quantifiable performance standards for executive-level positions. Also, the authors of the CSRA had put great emphasis on tying appraisals to the individual's contribution toward the accomplishment of organizational goals. In retrospect, they were probably far too optimistic about the agencies' ability to measure organizational performance objectively or to identify an executive's contributions clearly.

The Merit Systems Protection Board concluded from a 1989 survey of federal personnel officials that while the SES performance appraisal program was conceptually sound, its effectiveness was greatly diminished by administrative problems. An MSPB study in 1988 had found that a large percentage of federal workers, including executives, see little if any connection between existing appraisal systems and organizational performance, and the board concluded that "these performance management systems have failed to meet the original high expectations for them."[36] Only 25 percent of the personnel specialists participating in the 1988 study believed that the SES appraisal system had greatly or somewhat improved organizational effectiveness. Over 50 percent saw no impact, and fully 20 percent described it as having had a negative effect.[37]

Among members of the SES, evaluations of agency success in establishing appraisal systems that accomplish CSRA objectives have been at best mixed, and the trend is not encouraging. For example, in 1986, 48 percent of SES members responding to an MSPB survey said they believed that their agencies had been successful in basing compensation, retention, and tenure on executive success, measured in terms of individual and organizational performance. In 1989, 35 percent described their agencies as being completely or somewhat successful. Between 1986 and 1989, the number of those saying that their agencies were completely or somewhat *unsuccessful* in this regard increased from 32 to 39 percent.[38] There has also been a corresponding decline in the percentage of SES members who believe that their agencies are able to recognize exceptional performance. As to improving organizational effectiveness, SES members were even less supportive than the personnel specialists participating in the 1988 MSPB study. Only 15 percent of SES respondents agreed that the performance appraisal process had improved organizational effectiveness, and 62 percent disagreed.[39]

LESSONS FROM THE FEDERAL EXPERIENCE

Like many of their state and local counterparts, federal administrators and personnel specialists have found that the concept of a valid, management-centered, performance appraisal process is not easily translated into practice. Defining, measuring, and rating performance in terms that are generally acceptable to all of those who have a stake in the process has proven to be extremely difficult. To a certain degree, this is a technical problem. However, it is also a reflection of less-than-complete trust or confidence in the intentions of political leaders and executives. Major innovations, such as the installation of a new performance evaluation system, are likely to be resisted—even actively sabotaged—if workers see them as attacks on their integrity and competence.

Over the past 15 years or so, surveys of federal employees have rather consistently revealed a pattern of suspicion about the motives and attitudes of those at the top of the executive hierarchy. One member of the SES expressed this sentiment bluntly:

> The combined image of Federal Employees (including federal employee "bashing" by prior administrations) coupled with low executive pay comparability make staying in Federal Service very difficult for mission-oriented executives. This is the only employer I have had whose basic philosophy towards employees demonstrates a conviction that all employees are motivated by a desire to cheat the employer.[40]

Federal workers had reason to be doubtful about the implementation of CSRA appraisals, even if they generally approved of the concept. The campaign to get the CSRA through Congress was liberally peppered with media descriptions of it as "get rid of the incompetents" reform, and the pay-for-performance provisions of the bill were often explained in terms designed to convince the public that they would force "lazy" public employees out of their sinecures. President Ronald Reagan showed little if any confidence in the abilities and motivation of federal employees, and many of the executives he appointed shared this point of view. The leadership of the OPM, the government's central personnel management agency, cultivated this "philosophy" in its policies and programs during most of the Reagan administration. It has only recently shown any consistent interest in helping agencies design and administer effective performance appraisal systems.

Although confidence in the fairness and competence of immediate supervisors has remained relatively high throughout the federal work force, what supervisors actually do depends greatly on the administrative climate of an agency. If top management does not strongly support the appraisal plan or creates the impression that it will be used punitively, supervisors will be placed in an untenable position. In a climate of fear and suspicion, they will be very reluctant to make frank judgments. They know those being rated will be likely to see them as biased and unfair, and they fear that top management will not consistently back them if they identify and take action against unsatisfactory performers.

A management not fully committed to an appraisal program is unlikely to support the training programs needed to develop supervisory evaluation skills. Setting up and administering a performance appraisal system that conforms to CSRA criteria inevitably places heavy demands on employees, supervisors, the personnel office, and higher executives. (Federal supervisors report spending up to five hours a week working with low performers.) If higher management shows little interest in making and supporting such investments in performance appraisals, supervisors respond accordingly. Administrative leadership is critical. For example, Peter Allan and Stephen Rosenberg describe how an appraisal plan for managers in New York City failed because it was not supported by agency leadership or the mayor. A new plan with their backing was accepted.[41]

Prospects for Success

Despite such gloomy assessments of the current situation, there is some reason to believe that the prospects for federal performance appraisal are improving. The OPM has revitalized its technical assistance efforts, authorized the expanded delegation of personnel authority to agencies, and begun to encourage experimentation and demonstration projects to test alternative approaches. Each of these initiatives would seem to be in line with what the National Research Council found in its analysis of the existing research on performance appraisal in the public and private sectors. Its report to the OPM in 1991 set forth the following general conclusions:

> *First*, in the applied setting of personnel management, heavy investments in measurement precision are not "economically viable" because they are unlikely to improve the overall quality or usefulness of performance appraisals. *Second*, the committee recommends that OPM's policies emphasize and support "informed managerial judgment and not aspire to the degree of standardization, precision, and empirical support that would be required of, for example, selection tests." [42]

In the context of these conclusions, the council advanced several summary observations concerning the measurement side of appraisals.

First, job analysis and specification of performance standards are not substitutes for supervisory judgment, but they may help focus the appraisal process. In other words, the supervisor must be willing and able to implement the concepts and goals of the appraisal system, rather than simply filling in the blanks.

Second, the research evidence reveals that supervisors are able to form "reasonably reliable estimates" of their employees' overall performance levels. However, consistency is not a guarantee of accuracy; systematic error and bias are still possible. For example, some supervisors may consistently undervalue the performance of women or members of racial and ethnic minorities.

Third, although there are many types and formats of rating scales, the council concluded they will yield similar results if "the dimensions to be rated are well chosen and the scale anchors are clearly defined." The council found no convincing evidence to support arguments that distinguishing between behaviors and traits has much effect on rating outcomes. It found that psychologically, supervisors form generalized evaluations which strongly color "memory for and evaluation of actual work behaviors." It also found that there is little evidence to suggest that rating systems based on highly job-specific dimensions produce results that are much different from those using global or general dimensions. [43]

All of these findings imply that the extent to which an appraisal system promotes organizational goals and purposes depends heavily on the extent to which those who administer it are competent and motivated to use the system as intended. In these terms, the council noted that successful performance appraisal systems in the private sector have certain characteristics, including being "firmly imbedded in the context of management and personnel systems that provide incentives for managers to use performance appraisal ratings as the organization intends." These incentives would give public managers discretion in rewarding top performers or dismissing those who continually perform below standard, and managers themselves would be evaluated on the results of their performance appraisal activities. Unfortunately, in the council's judgment, *disincentives* currently prevail in the federal environment. It recommends, therefore, that federal personnel policies encourage decentralization within broad policy guidelines, and it supports experimentation with alternatives through carefully designed pilot studies. Finally, the council stresses that the process of performance appraisal cannot be understood or improved in isolation from the larger organizational and personnel systems of the public sector.[44]

Overall, the federal experience does not imply that efforts to implement credible and managerially useful appraisal systems are necessarily doomed to failure. On the national level, the rapid, sweeping improvements on the technical, managerial, and organizational levels that were promised by some advocates of the CSRA have not materialized. The experience of state and local governments has been essentially similar. In retrospect, of course, this is not a surprising outcome. As George Downs and Patrick Larkey point out, the

> ...benefits of the reform strategies must be greatly overstated at the outset in order to "sell" the strategy to the politicians.... As a result, these strategies leave in their wake a cynicism that makes it more difficult to implement more "tactical" reforms that promise to achieve genuine—if more modest—results."[45]

One example of at least partial success is the Naval Laboratories Demonstration Project, first implemented in 1980. The project introduced a simplified participative approach to setting performance objectives in which employees and their supervisors develop a performance plan that sets objectives and measurement standards. Overall, the response from laboratory personnel has been favorable; they can see a stronger connection between performance and pay, and greater attention is being paid to work output and more-clearly-stated performance requirements. Employees also have said they believe they have a meaningful role in developing performance plans; they are getting more feedback from their supervisors; and supervisors are more willing to make distinctions among levels of performance.[46] These accomplishments are far from insignificant. If human resources managers are fully committed to meeting the challenge, there is no reason to believe that similar results cannot be achieved in many public agencies.

■

NOTES

1. Georgia State Merit System, *The Merit System Performance Appraisal Instrument: A Manual for Supervisors* (Atlanta, GA, November 1981), p. 1.
2. George T. Milkovich and Alexandra K. Wigdor (eds.), *Pay for Performance: Evaluating Performance Appraisal and Merit Pay* (Washington, DC: National Academy Press, 1991), p. 45.
3. Lawrence R. O'Leary and Myron Scafe, "The Performance Appraisal: From Albatross to Motivational Tool," *The Police Chief*, February 1989, pp. 46–47.
4. Ibid., p. 51.
5. John M. Greiner, H. P. Hatry, M. P. Koss, A. P. Millar, and J. P. Woodward, *Productivity and Motivation: A Review of State and Local Government Initiatives* (Washington, DC: The Urban Institute Press, 1981), p. 227.
6. U.S. General Accounting Office, *Report to the Congress by the Comptroller of the United States: Federal Employee Performance Rating Systems Need Fundamental Changes* (Washington, DC, March 1978).
7. See Milkovich and Wigdor (eds.), *Pay for Performance*, pp. 48–67.
8. U.S. General Accounting Office, *Civil Service Reform: Development of 1978 Civil Service Reform Proposals* (Washington, DC, 1988), p. 12.
9. Ibid., p. 15.
10. See *Merit System Performance Appraisal Instrument*, pp. 1–4.
11. Milkovich and Wigdor (eds.), *Pay for Performance*, p. 46.
12. Ibid., p. 47.
13. Charles J. Fox, "Employee Performance Appraisal: The Keystone Made of Clay," in Carolyn Ban and Norma N. Riccucci (eds.), *Public Personnel Management: Current Concerns—Future Challenges* (New York: Longman, 1991), p. 60.
14. George W. Downs and Patrick D. Larkey, *The Search for Government Efficiency: From Hubris to Helplessness* (New York: Random House, 1986), pp. 190–200.
15. Larry M. Lane and James F. Wolf, *The Human Resource Crisis in the Public Sector: Rebuilding the Capacity to Govern* (New York: Quorum Books, 1990), pp. 107–114.

16. U.S. Merit Systems Protection Board, Office of Policy and Evaluation, *Working for America: A Federal Employee Survey* (Washington, DC, June 1990), p. 11.

17. Greiner et al., pp. 205–225.

18. Alan K. Campbell, "Remarks," in U.S. General Accounting Office, *Civil Service Reform*, p. 10.

19. U.S. General Accounting Office, *Report to the Director, Office of Personnel Management: New Performance Appraisals Beneficial But Refinements Needed* (Washington, DC, September 15, 1983).

20. U.S. General Accounting Office, *Managing Human Resources: Greater OPM Leadership Needed to Address Critical Challenges* (Washington, DC, January 1989), pp. 67–68.

21. Ibid., p. 71.

22. Ibid., p. 141.

23. John Nalbandian, "Performance Appraisal: If Only People Were Not Involved," in Frank J. Thompson (ed.), *Classics of Public Personnel Policy*, 2nd ed. (Pacific Grove, CA: Brooks/Cole, 1991), pp. 191–193.

24. U.S. General Accounting Office, *Blue Collar Workers: Appraisal Systems Are in Place, But Basic Refinements Are Needed* (Washington, DC, June 1987), p. 10.

25. Ibid., p. 11

26. Ibid., p. 12.

27. Ibid., p. 13.

28. Ibid., p. 13–14.

29. U.S. General Accounting Office, *Performance Management: How Well Is the Government Dealing with Poor Performers?* (Washington, DC, October 1990), p. 14.

30. Ibid., pp. 31–32.

31. Ibid., p. 37.

32. Ibid., p. 23.

33. Ibid., p. 41.

34. U.S. General Accounting Office, *Report to the Congress: An Assessment of the SES Performance Appraisal Systems* (Washington, DC, May 16, 1984).

35. Ibid.

36. U.S. Merit Systems Protection Board, *Federal Personnel Management Since Civil Service Reform: A Survey of Federal Personnel Officials* (Washington, DC, November 1989), p. 11.

37. Ibid.

38. U.S. Merit Systems Protection Board, *Working for America*, p. 23.

39. Ibid., p. 26.

40. Ibid., p. 25.

41. Peter Allan and Stephen Rosenberg, "Getting a Managerial Performance Appraisal Plan Under Way: New York City's Experience," *Public Administration Review*, vol. 40, no. 3 (July–August 1980).

42. Milkovich and Wigdor, Pay for Performance, p. 3.

43. Ibid., p. 144.
44. Ibid., p. 164.
45. Downs and Larkey, *Search for Government Efficiency*, p. 4.
46. Robert M. Glen, "Performance Appraisal: An Unnerving Yet Useful Process," *Public Personnel Management*, vol. 19 (Spring 1990), pp. 4–7.

Job Evaluation and Classification   6

Job evaluation and pay plans are major aspects of public personnel administration, especially in merit systems, where they are regarded as means of achieving the goals of equal pay for equal work and assuring that levels of compensation are logically related to job characteristics and skills requirements. Since job evaluation and pay have become technical specialties within public personnel, a detailed treatment of them is well beyond the scope of this text. In this chapter, therefore, we will focus on the managerial implications of job evaluation and classification policies in the public sector, and in Chapter 7 we will consider issues related to pay.

Job evaluation is the process of comparing individual positions and ranking them in value for pay purposes. Whatever the method used, it results in the assignment of each position to a pay level or grade. Job evaluation is based on job analysis, which is essential not only for setting pay differences but also for providing the detailed information needed for recruitment, selection, training, performance evaluation, and other aspects of personnel administration.

POSITION CLASSIFICATION

The usual method of job evaluation in the public services of the United States is position classification. In this approach, all positions that

are considered equal in duties, responsibilities, and qualification requirements are grouped in the same class, and the same salary range
or pay grade applies to all positions in that class. Position classification is based on an evaluation of the job as a whole according to classification standards, or the criteria used to assign positions to classes.

Classification Standards

In the federal service, classification standards, as set by the Classification Act of 1949, must take the following factors into consideration:

1. The nature and variety of work performed in carrying out the
   responsibilities of a position.
2. The amount and kind of supervision provided to the person
   occupying the position.
3. The nature of the available guidelines for performing the
   work.
4. The originality or independent decision making required.
5. The importance and scope of decisions, commitments, and
   conclusions that must be reached by the person occupying the
   position.
6. The number and kinds of other positions over which the person occupying the position exercises supervisory authority.
7. The qualifications required to successfully carry out the position's responsibilities.[1]

For federal positions, these factors are considered using one of
three classification methods, which vary according to the type of position. These are the narrative style, the factor evaluation system
(FES), and discretionary ways of classifying positions. Most standards set prior to 1975 are in a narrative format under which the
classification analyst "grades" the position by determining the
appropriate level for each factor. About half of the federal work
force, including all supervisors, is covered by narrative standards.
The factor evaluation system, adopted by the U.S. Civil Service Commission in 1975, uses nine factors. Factor points are assigned to each
position, and the total number of points determines the position's
grade. Roughly 30 percent of federal positions are covered by some
version of the FES. The other 20 percent of federal positions are not
covered by specific grading criteria. In these discretionary cases, the
classifier has to establish a grade for the position using either an FES
or narrative-style standard for an occupational series with similar
work requirements.[2]

Classification standards provide the basis for an internal alignment of classes. A city budget director position, for example, would be assigned to a much higher class than an entry-level typist position, and a senior clerk's duties would likely result in a higher classification than that of a beginning clerk. A primary goal of classification standards is to assure that positions involving similar levels of responsibility, difficulty, and qualification are in the same class ("equal grade for equal work"). Determining what class an existing or proposed position belongs in is usually the responsibility of classification analysts working in a jurisdiction's personnel agency. In large governments, the central personnel agency sets general standards and audits their implementation by department-level analysts.

Pay Grades

Hundreds and even thousands of positions may be placed in the same class (e.g., typist or carpenter), or the class may consist of only one position (e.g., budget director, fire chief, or county coroner). To each class of positions, a pay grade is assigned on the basis of the duties, responsibilities, and qualifications that are considered necessary for the grade level. Under the federal statute as well as state and local laws, pay ranges are established for workers according to their job assignments; according to the National Academy of Public Administration (NAPA), "This philosophy adheres to the principle of equal pay for substantially equal work." Thus pay is tied to how the work to be performed has been evaluated; it is not linked directly to the qualities or performance of the person holding the job.[3]

The number of pay grades varies from jurisdiction to jurisdiction. Some state and local governments have dozens of pay grades designed to reflect what are considered to be significant differences in job duties and qualifications, and the federal government currently has 15 grades in its General Schedule for white-collar employees. Under the Federal Employees Pay Comparability Act of 1990 (see Chapter 7), the GS–16 to GS–18 supergrades have been replaced with a single pay band, and members of the Senior Executive Service are under another plan.

PROBLEMS AND ISSUES IN POSITION CLASSIFICATION

The historic contribution of position classification was to bring relative order out of a chaotic situation of misleading job titles, grossly inequitable pay for the same kind and level of work, and recruitment and selection procedures uninformed by a detailed understanding of job content. The adoption of position classification and accompanying compensation plans, beginning in the early 1900s, constituted an important stage in the development of merit systems. It effectively curbed the widespread legislative practice of juggling pay rates for individual workers in order to reward political supporters. The position classification approach also gained wide support as an administrative reform that reflects the values of scientific management in its emphasis on job analysis and efficiency. It conveyed the image of "businesslike" administration.

Position classification systems should have two broad objectives, according to a 1991 report by the National Academy of Public Administration. They should support efforts to treat public employees fairly and equitably, and they should be designed to promote effective and efficient agency performance. The first objective is firmly imbedded in the goals and values of Civil Service Reform I, while the second is a product of the contemporary focus on human resources management. In line with the second objective, NAPA points out that the principal goal in modernizing classification systems is to bring them "more into the mainstream of essential processes in an organization's management structure." These should be as important as an agency's budget, information, or accounting systems; in fact, they should have the ability to interface with these and other administrative systems to enhance the management process.[4]

Assuring Fairness and Equity

Traditional position classification systems are currently under attack from critics who consider them incapable of achieving either of NAPA's two objectives. With regard to fairness and equity, the accuracy and objectivity of job analyses and classification actions has always been suspect.

Position classification, like all other forms of job evaluation, is inevitably a subjective process, even with methods that are considered quantitative. Some jobs are relatively easy to classify (e.g., messenger or janitor), but in many lines of work, conclusive differentiations as to levels of difficulty and responsibility are hard to make. This is particularly the case in clerical, fiscal, social service, medical, scientific, and administrative classes.[5] Classification analysts, therefore, must be far more than clerks plugging numbers into formulas; they are often required to exercise considerable discretion and judgment.

Classification audits conducted by central personnel agencies such as the OPM almost always reveal that a certain percentage of the decisions made by classifiers are in error, due to factual inaccuracies or misinterpretation of the classification standards.[6] Given the subjective nature of the process, classification errors of this type must be expected.

A more significant challenge to the fairness of the classification process and the equity of its outcomes comes from the perception that because it is discretionary in nature, it is open to personal and organizational bias and distortion. Managers with a stake in a classification action often try to influence the analyst's decision. Many instances of overgrading are attributable to pressures from managers who for one reason or another want higher salaries for their subordinates. Some critics have gone so far as to characterize classification analysts as organizational politicians who actively "bargain" with line managers and approve classifications they know are too high.[7]

Grade Creep

Another reason for doubts about the objectivity of position classification in government is the phenomenon of *grade creep*, a term that refers to a gradual rise in the average grade of all employees in a jurisdiction or agency. Periodically, legislative oversight committees or executive budget offices "discover" that average grades have risen, along with personnel budgets. In short order, there are calls for adjustments and downgrades, and legislators and taxpayers complain about overpaid and underworked bureaucrats and increases in salary costs. Some of this grade creep is the result of overgrading in order to raise someone's pay, so the agency can match outside offers, compensate for inflation, or give an employee special treatment. The result is an erosion of the principles of fairness and equity, and doubts are cast on the integrity of the personnel system.

Inflated job descriptions do occur, classifications are sometimes manipulated, and some public employees do receive salaries that are out of line with their job responsibilities and qualifications. If this goes on long enough and often enough, significantly higher average job grades can result. However, the reasons for grade creep are usually far more complicated than simple greed or favoritism. Much of it is associated with the changing nature of the public work force. Because government is employing increasing numbers of professional, administrative, and technical employees to carry out new, often complex programs, there is less reason to expect the largest share of public employees to be in the lowest grades.

Another major reason for grade creep is the connection between classification and pay plans. A great deal of overgrading happens because jobs are assigned to relatively narrow classes with pay grades that cannot be changed without legislation. Since legislative bodies and chief executives are notoriously reluctant to raise pay scales, pressure builds to place positions in higher grades in order to prevent turnover in jobs held by valued employees or to reward superior performance. From the viewpoint of organizational performance, grade creep may actually be a functional adaptation. Over time, however, the classification plan will collapse from the distortions of numerous reclassifications and the inequities created when positions are upgraded only for certain employees.

Negotiated Agreements with Employee Organizations

Another possible source of inconsistencies and distortions in classification plans is the agreements negotiated between management and employee organizations or unions. In most jurisdictions, the setting of job evaluation standards and the classification of individual positions are management prerogatives that are not negotiable; unions have traditionally concentrated on improving pay and benefits. This does not mean that the unions have always been content to leave job evaluation entirely up to management, however. In some cases, they have been able to make classification actions subject to negotiation and binding arbitration.

Most public managers are strongly opposed to the practice of making classification decisions through collective bargaining. They believe that without the authority to unilaterally determine the job evaluation plan and the classifications of individual positions, management will be undermined. To classification analysts, bargaining in these areas is an anathema, because they consider the process of evaluating and ranking jobs a strictly technical question, not to be decided through negotiations or compromise. For the most part, this point of view has held sway on all levels of government, but there are exceptions. One of these is the U.S. Postal Service, in which job evaluation is subject to negotiation under terms of the Postal Reorganization Act of 1970.

A particular problem faced by public employers who bargain collectively with unions representing several bargaining units is how to maintain a unified job evaluation and pay plan. When there are several units, no single union is likely to win representation in all of them, so the employer must bargain with a number of different unions. The union representing each unit will do all it can to improve pay and benefits for its members, but improvements negotiated for one unit may create inequities for employees doing the same kind and level of work in other units. As a result of unit-by-unit bargaining, therefore, separate job evaluation and pay plans eventually are created for each unit. The grading and pay are equitable *within* each unit, but not *between* units.[8]

Achieving Organizational Effectiveness and Efficiency

With varying degrees of success, public-sector classification systems have concentrated on the first objective of current position classification systems: achieving fairness and equity. In so doing, however, they have tended to neglect the organizational performance concerns of managers. Job evaluation processes and position classification structures have long been a point of contention between proponents of a management-centered approach and those who favor limiting management's discretion, especially in matters of pay.

Over the past 50 years, public administrators have rather consistently complained that the existing classification structures and processes were imposing barriers to overall effectiveness and efficiency. In its review of studies and articles published between 1941 and 1991, NAPA found the following problems were identified most often:

1. Classification standards were too complex, hard to understand, rigid, out of date, or inaccurate.
2. Central personnel agencies such as the OPM did not provide needed leadership and interdepartmental coordination and were notoriously reluctant to try new approaches or innovations.
3. Public managers saw the process as burdensome and unintelligible and perceived little reward in making an effort to classify positions accurately. Supervisors habitually pressured analysts to overgrade positions and did not use the system as a human resources management tool.
4. The rank-in-position approach was too rigid and inflexible and did not accommodate specific agency needs. Classification standards often did not consider employees' abilities or differences in level of performance.
5. Classification systems were typically at least several years out of date (many systems have not been revised for decades), making it difficult to recruit for new occupations or to meet staffing requirements in technical fields.
6. Grade definitions were often confusing and vague, allowing little pay differentiation between supervisors and subordinates, and tended to create "rigid job hierarchies that cannot change with organizational structure."[9]

NAPA's evaluation of the federal classification system revealed that these problems still exist, especially in the opinions of federal administrative officers and managers. The questionnaire survey, focus groups, and interviews used in the study revealed three serious problems: (1) the system is burdensome and inflexible, (2) classification standards are out of date, and (3) the OPM's leadership and coordination efforts are inadequate. Users of the classification system (administrative officers and line managers) were more critical than the system's managers (personnel directors and classifiers). The users observed that the system does not produce fair and equitable results, recruiting for new and emerging occupations is difficult, and there is a rigid job hierarchy that resists change.[10]

Overall, the federal personnel directors, classifiers, administrative officials, and managers surveyed favored several important changes in the existing system. These include: (1) skill-based pay differentials, (2) wider salary ranges within pay grades, (3) significant delegation of classification authority to line managers, and (4) fewer grade levels, or broadbanding (see the next section). These kinds of innovations are in place in agencies excluded from Title 5 of the United States Code in which classification policies covering most federal organizations are established.[11] Relatively high levels of satisfaction with innovative or alternative classification systems were found to be linked to the ability of these agencies to pay competitive salaries more in keeping with those offered in the private sector than is possible for agencies covered by Title 5.[12]

Similar changes were included in three OPM-sponsored demonstration projects implemented to test alternative approaches to aspects of personnel administration. In addition to making pay more competitive, the agencies conducting these projects cited at least three other problems in human resources management as reasons why the federal classification system should be changed. First, overly complex classification structures with too many narrowly defined occupations and grades were undermining management's efforts to recruit highly qualified personnel, to assign work effectively, and to sustain high levels of performance on the organizational level. Second, the classification of positions was taking far too long; often, months were needed to complete the process and fill a position. Third, the inflexibilities of the classification structure were forcing outstanding performers out of their primary areas of expertise and into higher-grade supervisory jobs in which they could make higher salaries.[13]

EFFORTS TO REFORM CLASSIFICATION SYSTEMS

The call for flexibility and responsiveness to specific agency needs in position classification has focused attention on the development of alternative approaches. Various ways to reform these systems in the public sector have been proposed, including the following:

1. Moving to governmentwide rank-based classification systems.
2. Allowing fragmentation, under which agencies are allowed to adopt systems tailored to their particular needs.
3. Implementing a comprehensive system that allows considerable agency-level discretion under general policies administered by central personnel agencies.

Rank-Based Classification

In many countries, personnel systems are structured around the concept of rank in the person; the pay and status of civil servants are determined by their background, educational qualifications, abilities, and experience, not simply by the jobs they hold. In the United States, in contrast, the concept of rank in position has dominated the public service on all levels of government. Rank-based systems generally have been used only in the foreign service, military services, and parts of quasi-military agencies such as the Department of Veterans Affairs (VA) and law enforcement or investigative agencies such as the FBI, CIA, and local police departments. Arguments in favor of such rank-based systems stress their flexibility and adaptability and their suitability to decentralized personnel management structures.

The U.S. Merit Systems Protection Board has favorably evaluated the modified rank-in-the-person system used by the VA, noting that Title 38 of the statute under the which this federal department operates establishes "a methodology in which the qualifications of each *person* are evaluated against agency-established qualification standards, and a grade (rank) is assigned to the person based on his or her individual qualifications regardless of the position held."[14] Another difference from the Title 5 model is the use of standards boards, or groups of VA employees in the same or related occupations, to recommend the grade to which a person should be assigned. The VA's approach is not a pure rank-in-the-person system, because an employee's ability to qualify for a higher-grade position is often determined by that employee's present position. For example, the three highest grades for registered nurses and the two highest grades for physicians are assigned exclusively on the basis of the position currently held.[15]

From its study of the VA's personnel system, the MSPB concluded that the rank-based system offers "potential alternatives to current Title 5 procedures within at least some agencies or occupations." Noting that VA managers who responded to the study generally said they believe the method used to set grades is "easier" and "more equitable," the MSPB recommended that reforms of the Title 5 system should consider the use of standards boards or peer panels as a part of the grade- and pay-setting process. Such employee groups, it said, increase flexibility and are more likely to reflect "an understanding of the actual work environment." The MSPB also applauded the VA's extensive delegation of personnel authority to local managers as providing a model that the rest of the federal service should consider.[16]

In recent years, there has been much support for the application of the rank-in-the-person concept to high-level professional and executive employees. The Senior Executive Service is a limited example in the federal government, and several states have established versions of the SES under which top managers are assigned ranks and pay grades. Nevertheless, the possibilities of either adopting the rank principle or loosening the restraints of position classification for middle- and lower-level jobs appear small. A primary objection is that this change would lead to a revisitation of the chaos and pay inequities that prevailed before the implementation of position classification plans. Public employees and unions are very much concerned with preserving the hard-earned victory of establishing the norm of equal pay for equal work. Also, rank-based classification schemes have generally been rejected as antidemocratic, largely because access to the higher classes and pay grades often is restricted to socioeconomic elites. Career lines traditionally do not cross class lines, and lateral entry into any class is virtually impossible.

Fragmentation of Classification Systems

The fragmentation option is favored by those who believe that a single classification system or concept cannot respond effectively to the needs and problems of human resources management in all agencies. In the federal service, the need to adapt classification systems to agency circumstances has been met with numerous complete and partial agency exclusions from Title 5, demonstration projects, and modifications of traditional classification practices. As the NAPA study published in 1991 notes:

> Each excluded agency, in accordance with its own priorities, needs and culture, established or is in the process of establishing its own posi-

tion classification system. These programs run the gamut from continued use of the GS grades and OPM position classification standards to not classifying positions at all, but rather adopting a rank-in-person classification system.[17]

Another NAPA report on the status of the federal civil service, published in 1986, noted "increasing support for proposals that would have the effect of 'splintering' the civil service into several separate pay schedules and formulas."[18] Much of this pressure to break up the pay schedule stems from efforts to make pay more competitive for certain occupations and to allow agency management greater flexibility in personnel matters. While such changes may be necessary, Charles Levine and Rosslyn Kleeman, authors of the report, foresee adverse consequences of adopting a series of incremental adjustments rather than comprehensive reform. While certain occupations and politically powerful agencies might thereby escape the limitations of the General Schedule, others would not. As Levine and Kleeman put it:

> Under such a process, the civil service system seems likely to break into two parts, "the haves" and the "have-nots," gradually fraying first the edges and then the core of the present system....The outcome, therefore, is likely to be a mixture of some up and a few down; i.e., a dual system that is fully competitive in some places and not competitive for top quality employees in others.[19]

Continued fragmentation could lead to a system so complex that it cannot be managed accountably, and pay disparities between occupations and agencies might completely undermine efforts to maintain fairness and equity. Extensive fragmentation, in these authors' judgment, could threaten the very idea of *a* federal civil service and, in effect, replace it with *several* services.[20]

Comprehensive Reform

In order to avoid the problems associated with rank-based classification and fragmentation, NAPA recently proposed a comprehensive reform of the federal classification system. These changes stress flexibility, simplicity, and a human resources management orientation, while keeping most federal agencies within the same system.

In overview, NAPA's approach requires the OPM to take the lead in consolidating some 459 occupational job series into seven groups called *occupational families*. These families would range from Office Services, or general office administration jobs, to Sciences, or "scientific occupations that have a positive education requirement."

Each occupational family would be broken down into three classification levels representing career paths: developmental, full performance, and senior/expert level. Of the seven families contemplated, at least five would have the same pay schedule. The Health and Law Enforcement families would probably have their own personnel systems because of fundamental, long-standing differences in such matters as pay administration and retirement systems.

Other features of NAPA's proposed comprehensive reform include the following basic changes in the federal classification system:

1. Each agency would have the discretion to build on the governmentwide occupational family standard by adding an agency-specific statement that further defines "the work at each competency level in terms of the activities and structure of the agency."
2. Each unit of the agency could add a mission statement, a work statement, and work-specific qualification requirements applying to each competency level.
3. The formulation of "performance plan and performance indicators that are directly related to the work statement" would be required. These would be used to determine both "pay progression through the grade band and level of competency for promotion purposes."
4. The definition of each work level within the occupational family would serve as the foundation for a career development planning guide. This would allow employees to see the relationships between levels of work and the competencies they need to progress within the occupational family.[21]

Other Reform Techniques

In addition to the three main types of reform discussed above, several more specific methods have been proposed for improving position classification systems in the public sector. These include techniques of broadbanding, the delegation of classification authority to line managers, and the position management approach.

Broadbanding Classes

Broadbanding addresses the need to make position classification systems more flexible and responsive to managerial and organizational concerns. Public managers widely support the elimination of numerous narrow classes of positions and the substitution of a relatively small number of occupational categories and pay grades.

American classification plans have traditionally used narrow classes containing a restricted range of duties that require specialized qualifications. Narrow classes have resulted from the emphasis on recruitment and selection to fill particular positions, with the expectation that those hired will be able to perform the duties of these positions without extensive on-the-job training. This greatly limits management's ability to adjust job tasks and rates of pay without having to seek position reclassifications from the personnel agency.

Broad classes, in contrast, incorporate a wide range of tasks and responsibilities that a qualified worker with a general background can be trained to perform. Such broadband classification structures and related pay scales make it much easier for managers to design and interrelate positions around work processes. They also facilitate recruitment on the basis of occupations and career planning, make moving people from job to job in the organization much less complicated, and support efforts to administer pay in ways intended to reward performance meaningfully and recognize differences in skills and abilities.

Delegation of Classification Authority

Broadbanding is usually associated with the extensive delegation of classification authority to line managers. Under these arrangements, managers apply general, understandable classification standards or criteria in placing specific positions in classes. The role of classification analysts working in personnel departments is to help formulate these general standards and to assist management in their application, rather than to make case-by-case classification decisions. Formal appeals processes and periodic audits are used to assure conformance with systemwide merit policies and to make sure that managers are not violating the norms of fairness and equity.

In addition to empowering managers and allowing them to use the classification process as a human resources management tool, decentralization may lower the overall cost of administering the classification plan by simplifying and speeding up the process. It may also relieve central personnel departments of large inventories of routine classification actions which must be handled before personnel specialists can respond to the organization's human resources development and management needs.

Position Management

From the perspective of human resources management, classification systems should promote the organization's capacity to design jobs in ways that take advantage of the available human resources.

The traditional concept of classification analysts is that they "photograph" the position as it is, and it is not their responsibility to recommend changes in administrative organization or the structuring of individual jobs. But this point of view has changed somewhat in recent years, and, in some jurisdictions, analysts have been asked to engage in position management, a function that has not been precisely defined. John Cole describes it as "a wide spectrum of management concerns about efficiency and effectiveness—from the organization of work and allocation of numbers of positions to full utilization of people."[22]

Classification analysts can make major contributions to agencies' efforts to meet the human resources management challenges they confront. As NAPA observes, however, position management is well beyond the scope of any classification system: "The realm of position management also includes employee training, career development, work force forecasting, performance appraisal, pay criteria, equal employment compliance, and budgeting for necessary funds to sustain the work force. A classification system is only one of the actors in this scheme of things."[23] But NAPA's perspective on position management does not minimize the potential contributions of position classification to agency performance. Rather it emphasizes the role of position classification in an overall effort to improve the capacity of organizations to manage work, not isolated positions.

■

NOTES

1. National Academy of Public Administration, *Modernizing Federal Classification: An Opportunity for Excellence* (Washington, DC: July 1991), p. B–4.
2. Ibid., p. B–11.
3. Ibid., p. B–10.
4. Ibid., p. 14.
5. Harold Suskin (ed.), *Job Evaluation and Pay Administration in the Public Sector* (Washington, DC: International Personnel Management Association, 1977), p. 99.
6. U.S. Office of Personnel Management, *A Federal Position Classification System for the 1980s: Report of the Classification Task Force* (Washington, DC, 1981).
7. Jay Shafritz, *Position Classification: A Behavioral Analysis for the Public Service* (New York: Frederick A. Praeger, 1973).

8. Anthony F. Ingrassia and Charles Feigenbaum, "The Union Impact on Job Evaluation and Pay Administration," in Suskin (ed.), *Job Evaluation and Pay Administration*, p. 548.

9. NAPA, *Modernizing Federal Classification*, pp. 17–18.

10. Ibid., p. 23.

11. Public Law 89–554, September 6, 1966, 80 Stat. 452.

12. NAPA, *Modernizing Federal Classification*, p. 33.

13. Ibid., pp. 33–34.

14. U.S. Merit Systems Protection Board, *The Title 38 Personnel System in the Department of Veterans Affairs: An Alternative Approach* (Washington, DC, April 1991), p. 17.

15. Ibid., p. 18.

16. Ibid., pp. 45–48.

17. NAPA, *Modernizing Federal Classification*, p. D–3.

18. Charles H. Levine and Rosslyn S. Kleeman, *The Quiet Crisis of the Civil Service: The Federal Personnel System at the Crossroads* (Washington, DC: National Academy of Public Administration, December 1986), p. 30.

19. Ibid., p. 31.

20. Ibid., pp. 30–31.

21. NAPA, *Modernizing Federal Classification*, p. xxv.

22. John D. R. Cole, "Position Management and Classification," *Civil Service Journal*, vol. 17, no. 1 (July–September 1976), p. 9.

23. NAPA, *Modernizing Federal Classification*, p. 42.

Pay in the Public Service

7

Virtually everybody is in some way interested in public employees' wages, salaries, and benefits. Taxpayers are prone to be outraged at what they consider excessive pay and overly generous benefits in the civil service, especially in light of what they consider to be inefficiency, ineffectiveness, and unresponsiveness. The media are alert to scandals involving "overpaid" and "underworked" public servants. As for public employees, they are likely to consider themselves underpaid and exploited, as well as unappreciated. They have seen their purchasing power slowly eroding while the pay of many workers in the private sector kept pace with inflation.

Legislators and elected executives with limited options for controlling budgets typically focus on personnel costs, and pay policies become pawns as politicians and interest groups maneuver for public support and votes. Since public-sector pay raises and other compensation reforms have virtually no effective political constituency outside of the workers themselves, the tendency is to put them off until "better times." Proposals for legislatively mandated improvements in pension plans and other long-term financial commitments cause experts in public finance and others to worry about finding the resources needed to meet these future obligations.

When employee unions demand "more," management counters

that due to fiscal stress, no increases or improvements in pay or benefits are possible, and cutbacks may be necessary. Public employees vote in local, state, and national elections and join organizations that support candidates for elective office. They lobby legislative bodies for better pensions and higher pay and threaten dire consequences if legislators turn a deaf ear.

Public administrators are confronted by problems in recruitment, retention, and motivation caused at least in part by their inability to offer pay and benefits that are competitive with those in the private sector. Pressures to fragment pay policies in order to deal with special problems on a case-by-case basis are resisted by administrators who are intent on preserving consistency and ensuring equity throughout the system. In many jurisdictions, management has little capacity to relate pay directly to performance. In others, there is considerable debate over how effective pay-for-performance systems have actually been, despite the enthusiasm for them among managers and politicians.

Women and minority groups see ample reason to conclude that they have been and continue to be victims of inequitable pay policies and practices. Proposals for reform are countered with the argument that they would inflate public budgets and the costs associated with pay administration. There are ongoing political, technical, and legal battles over these issues.

In contrast to the technical topics of job evaluation and classification, compensation for public employees sparks great public interest and controversy. Everybody has what he or she believes is an informed opinion. However, planning and administering compensation plans are highly technical functions that require the skills of trained specialists in fields such as economics and accounting. The discussion in this chapter is limited to broad policy issues, managerial concerns, and efforts to improve the effectiveness of pay practices in the public sector.

PAY POLICIES IN GOVERNMENT

The terms *compensation* and *pay* are often used interchangeably. Compensation, however, includes benefits such as medical insurance, contributions to pension funds, sick leave, and paid vacation time, as well as a salary or hourly wage. The monetary value of all of these benefits must be added to pay in order to determine an employee's total compensation. Comparisons based on paychecks are likely to be unreliable, because the dollar value of the employer's contributions to benefits is not considered.

While certain features of a benefit package may be translated in dollar terms for comparative purposes (e.g., employer contributions to group health insurance plans), others such as relative job security and training opportunities are more difficult to quantify. The Reagan administration argued that "attractive" features of federal employment such as job security, job mobility, and portability of benefits were worth 6 percent in total compensation. The General Accounting Office, Congressional Budget Office, and employee organizations disagreed, pointing out that in some regards federal fringe benefits were inferior to those of the private sector.[1]

The Politics of Prevailing Rates

In the United States today, the prevailing norm is that government should offer pay comparable to that offered by the private sector. This is a change from earlier times, when it was generally assumed that public servants, particularly white-collar workers, should expect to make financial sacrifices. The traditional argument in support of lower pay was that public employees enjoy far greater job security and better benefits than are offered in the private sector. For blue-collar workers, however, payment of the prevailing wage in specific labor markets does have a long history, going back as far as 1862 in the federal service. In that year, Congress passed a law directing the Navy Department to relate pay rates in the shipyards "as nearly as is consistent with the public interest, to prevailing private industry rates in the immediate vicinity" of the Navy yards.[2] Many state and local governments have also adopted the prevailing-rate standard for setting blue-collar pay.

In applying the principle of prevailing or comparable rates, public employers use information generated by the interplay of the forces of supply and demand in a labor market. Prevailing-rate surveys are done to establish pay rates for benchmark jobs, or jobs that are comparable across organizations and employment sectors. These jobs are then placed into a salary grade structure based on average competitive rates of pay. After reviewing this structure and adjusting jobs as necessary, management places other jobs in it on the basis of what is seen as their value relative to the benchmark jobs. This approach, according to John McMillan and Cynthia Biondi, "generally allows the market forces to dictate the relative value of jobs."[3]

In theory, public employees can use a prevailing-rate or market-pricing evaluation approach to construct pay scales that allow them to acquire and retain needed human resources without paying more than they need to. Although the methods used to conduct and interpret prevailing-rate surveys are complex, the purpose is straightforward: to identify and pay the going market price for a particular combination of skills, knowledge, and abilities (SKAs). But because prevailing rates are not sensitive to social-psychological and political distortions of the "ideal" or theoretical market, they may perpetuate long-standing inequities and patterns of economic discrimination in society. For example, one of the issues of pay administration discussed in Chapter 13 is comparable worth, or pay equity for women. In 1991 women still earned only 70 cents for every dollar earned by men, and this was down from 72 cents in 1990.[4]

Another relevant problem is the degree to which the criteria used to structure prevailing-rate surveys are influenced by the efforts of those who hold the stakes to skew the outcomes. The answers to a number of basic questions can affect the survey results. For example, should the survey be restricted to a metropolitan area, state, or region, or should it cover the nation? Professors at Georgia state universities might have a stronger case for pay raises if surveys by the Board of Regents were national as opposed to regional in scope. Should other governments and charitable organizations be included in the survey? Nurses in public hospitals have historically suffered economically because these institutions have routinely surveyed one another, thereby keeping nurses' pay at "Florence Nightingale" levels for years. Should benefits and "intangibles" be factored into the compensation equation? If so, relatively generous pension plans (a form of deferred compensation) may be used to justify keeping wages down. What criteria should be used to establish comparability between organizations? Is working in a small police department the same as working for a large metropolitan department? How should positions with no functional equivalents in the private sector be handled?

Public managers, executives, legislators, employee organizations, and taxpayers' associations are among the groups actively seeking to have these crucial decisions made in their favor. Thus the politics of prevailing rates is quite intense, and it is very relevant to the seemingly objective "numbers" produced by surveys of prevailing rates.

Achieving Pay Comparability in the Political Climate

The political climate inevitably has an impact on how information about prevailing rates is used (or not used) by legislative bodies and chief executives. Over the past 20 years, this reality has translated into a general reluctance to spend the money necessary to achieve comparability, especially at the higher levels of the civil service.[5]

States and localities may be forced to choose between achieving comparability and funding a variety of important programs with strong political constituencies. When authorizing changes in base pay, legislators tend to be more generous—sometimes much more so—with those in the lower ranks. Lower-paid workers are generally more numerous and more able to exert strong political pressure than managerial and executive personnel, who usually do not have much clout in the electoral process. Since pay at the top levels of the non-elected bureaucracy is relatively high anyway, legislators and the voting public are more likely to be responsive to the plight of the underdog. Moreover, the compensation of nonmanagerial personnel in many state and local governments is set through collective bargaining, and managers do not have aggressive unions to represent their interests.

In effect, a ceiling on federal executive-branch pay has historically been set by congressional salaries, since legislators have been opposed to paying civil servants more than they make themselves. In general, legislators' pay increases slowly because political firestorms are ignited by large adjustments; the federal government is no exception to this rule. This cap on federal pay, in combination with the yearly presidential refusals to recommend systemwide increases that would achieve comparability, has led to a steadily growing gap between federal and private-sector pay.[6]

Salary Compression

In addition to a steady erosion of comparability throughout the public sector over recent years, governments on all levels are experiencing serious problems of salary compression. As a result of caps on top salaries, grade creep, and across-the-board inflation adjustments to existing pay scales, the range of salaries is compressed. The net effect is to flatten the organization's pay structure, gradually closing the gap between the highest- and lowest-paying positions. Over time, therefore, salary compression frustrates efforts to establish meaningful differences in pay on the basis of job responsibilities and qualifications. This makes it difficult to recruit and retain highly qualified administrative and technical personnel, and obvious inequities in the salary structure undermine efforts to connect pay with performance.[7]

RECENT DEVELOPMENTS IN THE FEDERAL SERVICE

The controversies and difficulties in setting wages and salaries are illustrated by the experience in the federal government over the past

30 years or so. The Federal Employees Pay Comparability Act of 1990 is the latest in a long series of reforms in federal policies and practices used to set pay rates for General Schedule or white-collar workers. The wages of blue-collar (trade and craft) employees are determined by the Federal Wage System.

White-Collar Pay

The comparability principle was first established by Congress for white-collar workers in the Federal Salary Reform Act of 1962. This legislation provided that "federal salary rates shall be comparable with private enterprise salary rates for the same levels of work."[8] White-collar pay for federal workers was so far behind in 1967, however, that Congress enacted the Postal Revenue and Federal Salary Act to authorize the president, without congressional approval, to bring federal pay up to private rates "as nearly as practicable" in two big pay adjustments.

The Federal Pay Comparability Act of 1970

The salary-fixing authority for General Schedule and Foreign Service employees was delegated by Congress to the president in the Federal Pay Comparability Act of 1970. The president designates an agent to assist; presently, this consists jointly of the director of the OPM, the director of the Office of Management and Budget (OMB), and the secretary of labor. The 1970 legislation also established the Federal Employees Pay Council, consisting of five members from three employee organizations representing substantial numbers of GS employees, and the Advisory Committee on Federal Pay, with three members from outside the government who are noted for their impartiality and expertise in labor relations and pay policy. The president appoints members of these groups on recommendation from the director of the Federal Mediation and Conciliation Service and "other interested parties."

Under terms of the 1970 legislation, the Bureau of Labor Statistics (BLS) was to conduct a national survey of professional, administrative, and technical pay in the private sector (the PATC survey). The president's agent was to instruct the BLS concerning which jobs to include in the survey and the establishments to be surveyed, and the OPM and the BLS were to jointly maintain job descriptions for each of the various work levels in the occupations surveyed. Each work level was to be defined in a manner that allowed it to be compared with grade levels in the General Schedule. BLS data collectors were to visit the establishments included in the survey, identify the jobs that matched the BLS–OPM job descriptions, and collect the salary information. Since the act stated that comparability was to be with private-sector jobs, jobs in state and local governments were not to be included in the survey.

After reviewing the survey's findings, the agent was to prepare a report for the president with recommendations as to the size and form of pay adjustments needed to maintain comparability. The views and recommendations of the Federal Employees Pay Council and other unions that were not represented on the council were to be included in the report. The Advisory Committee on Federal Pay was to review the agent's report and submit a second, independent report to the president. The president then was to adjust federal pay rates, with changes to be effective on or after October 1 of the applicable year. However, if the president believed it inappropriate to make the adjustments suggested by the agent because of "national emergency or economic conditions affecting the general welfare," an alternative plan could be sent to Congress. This plan would go into effect within 30 days of transmittal unless either house of Congress passed a resolution of disapproval.

Because presidents routinely exercised their power to submit alternative plans providing for substantially less than full comparability, the gap in pay between white-collar workers in the federal service and in the private sector grew steadily, reaching crisis proportions by the late 1980s. In addition to the general erosion of comparability, federal competitiveness in certain geographic areas was crippled by a reliance on national averages to determine comparability, though private-sector pay rates actually varied across localities or labor markets. The 1988 BLS survey in San Francisco, for example, showed that a private-sector secretary was paid 60 percent more than one doing the same kind of work in Scranton, Pennsylvania, but federal pay for secretaries was the same in both cities. In some places the federal government paid more than the private sector, but the private sector paid more than the federal government in about 90 percent of the cases. In many metropolitan statistical areas (MSAs), the private sector enjoyed competitive pay advantages running well over 20 percent.[9]

Prior to passage of the Federal Employees Pay Comparability Act of 1990, the only way the federal government could vary GS pay by locality for certain occupations was by offering what were termed *special rates*. The OPM had to approve agency requests for special rates based on recruitment or retention problems "caused by higher private sector pay or other reasons." The agencies making these requests had to certify that they had the funds to pay the higher rates within their existing budgets.[10] By 1990, about 13 percent of the GS work force (190,000 employees) was on special rates, and severe problems in a number of agencies such as the FBI were adding emphasis to the need for a general reform of federal white-collar pay practices.[11]

The Federal Employees Pay Comparability Act of 1990

The Federal Employees Pay Comparability Act passed by Congress and signed by President Bush in late 1990 represented a compromise between those who favored comprehensive reform and action to reach comparability quickly and those who preferred incremental adjustments and close attention to budgetary consequences. Under terms of this legislation, the president retains across-the-board authority to alter pay recommendations, and the executive branch is given greater discretion in matters of pay administration. A nine-member Federal Salary Council, consisting of three neutral experts and six representatives of employee organizations, advises the president on matters of locality pay or prevailing rates in specific locations.

Four guiding principles for setting federal pay rates for white-collar workers under the General Schedule are stated in the 1990 legislation:

1. There should be equal pay for substantially equal work within each local pay area.
2. Within local pay areas, pay distinctions should be maintained on the basis of work *and* performance distinctions.
3. Federal pay rates should be comparable with all *nonfederal* (as opposed to only private-sector) rates for the same levels of work.
4. Any existing pay disparities between federal and nonfederal employees should be eliminated.

The act's main provisions, designed to allow greater flexibility than was possible under earlier legislation, incorporate the following changes in the GS pay system:

1. Setting up criteria and procedures under which pay disparities may be reduced by locality-based comparability adjustments to the GS base-pay schedule.
2. Instituting a special pay authority in order to allow agencies to fill critical positions.
3. Authorizing the establishment of special occupational pay systems.
4. Approving the delegation of a wide variety of case-by-case nonbase-pay decisions to the agency management level.

The legislation also sets up a new pay structure for the Bureau of Engraving and Printing and the U.S. Mint, and Title IV creates special pay structures and policies for federal law enforcement personnel.

Another significant change is the replacement of the old PATC survey with a new BLS survey that includes "nonfederal" jobs in state, local, and nonprofit agencies. A principal criticism of the methods used by the OPM and the BLS for determining white-collar comparability rates with the old surveys was their failure to include jobs in these sectors of the work force. The 1990 Comparability Act responds to these concerns by specifying that the president shall direct the pay agent to prepare a report in which the rates of pay under the General Schedule are compared with the "rates of pay generally paid to non-Federal workers for the same levels of work within each pay locality." These rates are to be determined on the basis of annual surveys conducted by the Bureau of Labor Statistics.

The exclusion of state and local governments in the PATC surveys is a good example of the politics of prevailing rates. When Congress passed the Federal Salary Reform Act of 1962, it excluded comparisons with jobs in state and local governments because it was convinced that salary data from this segment of the work force (then about six million workers) would be outweighed by data from the private sector.[12] But state and local employment has more than doubled since 1962, making this argument no longer valid. Certain kinds of occupations not included in the PATC survey (e.g., nurses, police officers, fire fighters, and social workers) include many of the jobs at the state and local levels of government. Since pay is often lower in small state and local governments, unions representing federal employees have always objected to including them in prevailing-rate surveys. The management point of view, of course, is that they should be included.

In the case of nonprofit workers in health services, education, and social services, the exclusion from the PATC surveys was by administrative determination, but the legislative history of the 1962 act suggests that this was not the intent of Congress.[13] Like state and local government employment, the nonprofit sector now is also very large, and it contains many jobs (e.g., health-care occupations) that constitute a major area of federal white-collar employment. Because not-for-profit organizations, especially the smaller ones, tend to offer relatively low pay, federal employees and their unions historically opposed including them in the survey; management and other groups concerned about the size of federal payrolls argued for their inclusion.

The 1990 legislation may produce survey results that actually narrow the gap between federal and nonfederal pay in certain localities; in others, the gap may disappear entirely or be replaced with a federal pay advantage. In other words, the redefined BLS survey may serve to moderate pay increases in some localities while it justifies real-dollar declines in places where GS workers are doing relatively well. Technically, surveying nonfederal jobs, as opposed to private-sector jobs only, should allow federal employers to fine-tune pay to the supply-demand forces operating in specific labor markets. Politically, the new language is a compromise under which increased federal payrolls in some areas will be underwritten in part by workers who have historically profited from a single, nationwide, GS pay scale.

Blue-Collar Pay

Prior to 1968, there was no comprehensive policy for setting the pay of trade and craft employees in the federal government. In some local areas, different federal agencies paid different rates for the same occupations. This situation was corrected with the implementation in 1968 by the U.S. Civil Service Commission of a Coordinated Federal Wage System (CFWS), which provided for a "common set of policies and operating procedures" covering "grade structures, occupational standards, survey coverage, labor organization participation, and other matters."[14] When Congress enacted the principal features of the CFWS into law in 1972, it added provisions that resulted in wages for government blue-collar workers that are widely considered to be too high.

The Federal Wage System

Under the Federal Wage System (FWS) established by the 1972 law, the OPM sets uniform national job-grading standards and criteria to be followed by agencies in defining wage areas, designing wage surveys, and setting up wage schedules. Advising the OPM is an 11-member Federal Prevailing Rate Advisory Committee consisting of five members representing the agencies, five representing the unions, and a full-time chairperson appointed by the director of the OPM.

While federal agencies do not formally negotiate blue-collar wages, the FWS does allow for considerable union influence in all phases of the process. Local wage surveys are done by "lead agencies," that is, those with large numbers of blue-collar jobs in the area (frequently the lead agency has been the Department of Defense). Each lead agency has an agency wage committee made up of two management members, two union members, and a chairperson appointed by the agency. This committee advises the lead agency on designing local surveys, interpreting survey findings, and establishing local wage schedules. The unions as well as management are represented on local wage survey committees, which oversee the conduct of the local surveys.

Certain features of the legislation establishing the FWS are considered responsible for the excessive rates of blue-collar pay. One is the Monroney Amendment, which requires that if there is an insufficient number of comparable positions in the local area, the lead agency must obtain wage data from outside the area and consider the outside as well as the local data in constructing wage schedules. The use of out-of-area data has often led to higher rates for federal workers than those paid for the same work by private employers in the area.

Another provision of the law prescribes five steps for each grade in an FWS regular nonsupervisory schedule. The first step provides 96 percent of the prevailing rate for a grade; the second step, 100 percent; and the third, fourth, and fifth steps, 104 percent, 108 percent, and 112 percent, respectively. Because most blue-collar workers progress to the top of their grade in a relatively short time, this ensures that most of them will make more than their private-sector counterparts.

The statutory requirement for payment of night-shift differentials that are substantially higher than those paid by private employers is another reason for high blue-collar rates, as is the exclusion of state and local governments in FWS wage surveys, even though they employ many blue-collar workers in the local areas.

Pay reform initiatives by the Carter and Reagan administrations addressed the bias of the FWS toward high pay for blue-collar workers. Among other things they sought to eliminate the Monroney Amendment, modify the night differential rates, and adjust the five-step wage schedules. But these efforts failed, and the 1990 Federal Employees Pay Comparability Act does not include changes in the FWS.

Current Pay Policies in the Federal Service

The president currently has no authority to limit wage-rate adjustments under the FWS, but Congress has imposed appropriations limitations under which blue-collar wage adjustments have been restricted to those granted to white-collar employees under the General Schedule. Speaking for the GAO before the Subcommittee on

Compensation and Benefits of the U.S. House, Richard Fogel stated in 1990 that as a result of these limitations, "large pay gaps with the private sector now exist in many wage areas." The GAO has recommended that the president should have the authority to take actions to assure that pay adjustment determinations for all pay systems, including any decisions to limit pay, are consistently applied. It has also supported efforts to change the method used to make general adjustments to the FWS five-step pay-grade structure.[15]

Federal white-collar pay policies have become more management-centered and flexible with the 1990 reforms. In large measure, the focus has shifted from equity and consistency throughout the federal service to competitiveness and managerial concerns such as recruitment and pay for performance. Structurally, the GS is now overlaid by a locality-pay system that represents a major step toward fragmentation of the federal service into several white-collar pay systems based on location, occupation, and specific agency problems and needs. The degree to which these reforms are actually implemented in the short term will depend heavily on the president's willingness and ability to budget the funds needed to achieve comparability. Over the long term, they provide the basis for a transformation of federal pay administration.

PAY PRACTICES AND POLICIES IN STATE AND LOCAL GOVERNMENTS

Although practices vary widely, some states and localities have long histories of progressive pay policies. Their governing bodies have reviewed pay rates annually or biennially and authorized adjustments considered necessary to make the rates more competitive. In a few states, such as California and Michigan, the legislature has delegated to the executive branch the authority to make adjustments in pay scales. Executive pay has been higher in some state and local governments than in the federal service, but, on average, it has been less.

For many state, city, county, and school district jurisdictions, the biggest change has been to collective bargaining with unionized workers (see Chapter 8). Pay and benefits are negotiable on the state and local levels, unlike in the federal government, and pay for some occupations (e.g., police officers, fire fighters, teachers, and nurses) has improved substantially since the 1960s. Jurisdictions feeling threatened by the possibility of employee unionization and collective bargaining have often moved unilaterally to upgrade pay as well as other aspects of compensation.

Contrary to popular belief, however, there is no evidence to suggest that collective bargaining has allowed state and local workers to "loot the treasury."[16] In fact, after the relatively brief catch-up period of the 1960s, state and local pay raises for most occupations have at best kept pace with inflation. In the present environment of fiscal stress, many employee organizations are now forced to concentrate on avoiding wage concessions or cuts in benefits.[17]

Current pay trends in state and local government parallel developments in the federal service; in both, traditional systems of classification and pay are being criticized as inflexible and not responsive to management's needs. John Matzer, Jr., describes recent developments at the state and local levels as follows:

> Employers are focusing on pay for performance, incentive pay, knowledge-based pay, and multiple pay systems. They are reviewing pay administration to identify ways to eliminate salary grades, reduce the number of salary ranges, and broaden job descriptions. They are also giving line managers greater authority to make pay decisions and to streamline the pay process.[18]

Two areas of particular importance in such developments are the concepts of pay for performance and comparable worth. Although comparable worth has had little effect on federal pay administration, 20 states and almost 1,000 localities have implemented some form of pay equity adjustment designed to address gender-based pay differentials.[19] Pay-for-performance systems of some kind were in place in over 20 states by 1988 and in the process of development in others.[20] Local governments across the country have been actively experimenting with pay for performance since the early 1980s; in the largest experiment prior to 1989, Denver put all of its 8,000 employees on a pay-for-performance basis.[21] Comparable worth and pay for performance are the principal topics discussed in Chapter 13.

■

NOTES

1. U.S. General Accounting Office, *Proposal to Lower the Federal Compensation Comparability Standard Has Not Been Substantiated: Report by the Comptroller General of the United States* (Washington, DC, January 26, 1982).
2. Raymond Jacobsen, "Efforts to Resolve Problems in Federal Compensation," in Harold Suskin (ed.), *Job Evaluation and Pay Administration in the Public Sector* (Washington, DC: International Personnel Management Association, 1977), p. 470.

3. John D. McMillan and Cynthia G. Biondi, "Job Evaluation: Generate the Numbers," in John Matzer, Jr., *Pay and Benefits: New Ideas for Local Government* (Washington, DC: International City Management Association, 1988), pp.47–48.

4. Associated Press news report, December 17, 1992; data from U.S. Bureau of Labor Statistics and interviews by *Working Woman* magazine.

5. Elder Witt, "Are Our Governments Paying What It Takes to Keep the Best and the Brightest?" *Governing*, December 1988, pp. 30–39.

6. U. S. General Accounting Office, *Federal Pay: Comparisons with the Private Sector by Job and Locality* (Washington, DC, May 1990), pp. 4–5.

7. U. S. General Accounting Office, *Recruitment and Retention: Inadequate Federal Pay Cited as Primary Problem by Agency Officials* (Washington, DC, September 1990).

8. Public Law 87–973, 87th Congress, 1962.

9. U. S. General Accounting Office, *Federal Pay*, pp. 5–17.

10. U. S. General Accounting Office, *Federal Pay: Special Rates, Effect on Recruitment and Retention for Selected Clerical Occupations* (Washington, DC, September 1990), p. 1.

11. Tom Shoop, "Wage Wars," *Government Executive*, June 1990, pp. 40–42.

12. *Staff Report of the President's Panel on Federal Compensation* (Washington, DC: U. S. Government Printing Office, 1976), p. 89.

13. Ibid., pp. 77–78.

14. Ibid., p. 107.

15. Richard L. Fogel, "H.R. 4716, 'Federal Pay Reform Act of 1990,'" testimony before the Subcommittee on Compensation and Employee Benefits, U.S. House of Representatives (Washington, DC, May 21, 1990), pp. 11–12.

16. Jeffrey S. Zax, "Wages, Non-Wage Compensation, and Municipal Unions," *Industrial Relations*, vol. 27 (Fall 1988), pp. 301–317.

17. Daniel J. B. Mitchell, "Concession Bargaining in the Public Sector: A Lesser Force," *Public Personnel Management*, vol. 15, no. 1 (Spring 1986), pp. 23–40.

18. John Matzer, Jr., "Introduction," in Matzer (ed.), *Pay and Benefits*, p. x.

19. Alice H. Cook, "Pay Equity: Theory and Implementation," in Carolyn Ban and Norma M. Riccucci (eds.), *Public Personnel Management: Current Concerns—Future Challenges* (New York: Longman, 1991), pp. 102–104.

20. U. S. General Accounting Office, *Pay for Performance: State and International Public Sector Pay-for-Performance Systems* (Washington, DC, October 1990).

21. Elder Witt, "Sugarplums & Lumps of Coal," *Governing*, December 1989, pp. 28–33.

Collective Bargaining in the Public Sector

8

Collective bargaining may be defined as a two-party or bilateral decision-making process in which authorized representatives of management and labor: (1) meet and in good faith negotiate wages, hours, and working conditions, (2) produce a mutually binding written contract of specified duration, and (3) agree to share responsibility for administering the provisions of that contract.

In the public sector, the history of collective bargaining is brief compared to its development in the private sector. As Ida Klaus noted in 1959, although many governmental units permitted their employees to organize and gave employee organizations some role in determining their conditions of employment, no government on any level had adopted a "thoroughgoing and systematic code of labor relations at all comparable in fundamental policy, basic guarantees and rights, and procedures for their enforcement, with those of prevailing labor-relations laws in the private sector."[1] The social and political turbulence of the 1960s, however, provided a fertile field for the unionization of government workers. This history is summarized in Chapter 2.

THE UNIONIZATION OF PUBLIC EMPLOYEES

Millions of public employees joined labor unions in the 1960s, many of them prepared to be militant in their efforts to win from management the recognition and advantages that had been realized by their counterparts in the private sector. White-collar workers eagerly joined unions affiliated with the consolidated American Federation of Labor and Congress of Industrial Organizations (the AFL–CIO). Public employee associations, once satisfied to consult with management and lobby legislative bodies for improvements in pay and benefits, were transformed almost overnight into labor organizations that made contractual demands and brought them to the bargaining table. Organized workers frequently engaged in strikes, slowdowns, and political action of various kinds in their efforts to extract pay raises, improved benefits, better working conditions, or the right to participate in policy-making. The "rules of the workplace," previously under the more-or-less benevolent unilateral control of the public employer, became issues to be resolved through bilateral negotiations between management and labor in many states and thousands of cities and counties. Even the federal service established a restricted form of collective bargaining in 1962 under President John F. Kennedy's Executive Order 10988.

Across the country, the public sector was invaded by labor-management practices and concepts already established in the private sector. Often this development was met with extreme discomfort by public administrators, who saw it as a threat to their authority and to the merit principle. Because little or no expertise in labor relations had been needed, most personnel systems were unprepared to help management negotiate or administer a traditional labor relations program. Many of the employee organizations suffered from a similar lack of experience and skill; numerous strikes and other disruptions were the direct result of incompetence and ignorance of the traditions and values underpinning the collective bargaining process.

On the management side, the needs for labor relations training programs in government and for governments to pool their efforts were soon recognized, and state leagues of municipalities and other existing organizations of public employers became active in these efforts. New organizations such as the Labor Management Relations Service of the United States Conference of Mayors were established in order to provide information, training, consulting, and other labor relations services. Labor organizations such as the AFL–CIO also expanded their consulting and training programs to include the public sector.

The unions' efforts to organize public employees and to secure legislation permitting or requiring collective bargaining were beaten back in some states, but by the early 1970s their numerous and sometimes startling successes during the preceding decade had fundamentally transformed public personnel administration. Labor-management relations and collective bargaining were firmly established in public personnel policy, and they became administrative responsibilities as well as areas of technical expertise.

The tidal wave of unionization and collective bargaining that engulfed the public sector in the 1960s and early 1970s was dramatically slowed by the 1973 recession, the deepest economic decline since the Great Depression of the 1930s. In the subsequent decade of widespread fiscal stress, the period of phenomenal growth and continuous successes by the public employee unions ended abruptly. Although most unions did not suffer great losses in membership, their ranks did not continue to expand at anything resembling the previous rate, and they generally were unable to win large salary increases and other concessions at the bargaining table.

The unions faced not only better-prepared management organizations and negotiators but also growing public hostility and stiffening resistance to tax increases. Public opinion had turned against them, and it became increasingly difficult to get collective bargaining legislation passed on the state and local levels. Organized labor then sought a federal law requiring *all* states and local governments to establish collective bargaining programs. This strategy failed when the Supreme Court ruled in *National League of Cities* v. *Usery* (1976)[2] that Congress did not have the authority under the commerce clause of the Constitution to extend provisions of the Fair Labor Standards Act (FLRA) of 1938 to state and local governments. This decision was widely interpreted to mean that the Court would strike down any federal attempts to mandate collective bargaining. The Court's stance, in combination with the lack of political support, ended any realistic expectation that Congress would act to advance the unions' interests.

By the end of the 1970s, many jurisdictions had experienced a "taxpayers' revolt," and initiatives such as passage of California's Proposition 13 were placing severe limits on government revenues and expenditures. In the 1980s, another recession and decreasing federal aid to states and localities combined to worsen the position of the unions and their members. The unions' public image was further undermined by the 1981 strike of the Professional Air Traffic Controllers Organization (PATCO) and the hard-line response of President Reagan, under which the strikers were fired and permanently barred from federal employment and the union was decertified. This dramatic event encouraged public employers around the country to be tough in their dealings with unions. Public employee organizations and their leaders were placed in the position of having to fight hard simply to preserve existing jobs and prevent drastic cuts in pay and benefits. By the end of the 1980s, union negotiators, instead of demanding real pay increases and improved benefits, were concentrating on offsetting inflation, opposing layoffs, resisting contracting-out or privatization, and mobilizing opposition to budgetary cuts in programs.

Despite the unions' difficulties, there is no indication that the existence of collective bargaining in the public sector is now threatened. In fact, for many governments, the practice has become routine and accepted as a way of handling much of the personnel function. During any given year, large numbers of public employees are involved in negotiations leading to contracts. In 1990, for example, there were collective bargaining negotiations in state and local governments that involved 884,000 of the 2.5 million workers covered by major agreements, or about 35 percent.[3]

Thus, even though the era of explosive union growth and spectacular advances at the bargaining table in the public sector ended some time ago, collective bargaining is far from dead. The unions achieved some legislative successes during the 1980s, such as the comprehensive collective bargaining statutes passed in the large industrial states of Illinois and Ohio. Historically, the effect of such legislation has been to promote strong growth in bargaining—especially when the employer is required to bargain in good faith with recognized unions.[4] Over half the states now require local employers to bargain with at least some categories of workers, particularly in police and fire departments.[5]

Nevertheless, the public sector is already highly organized, there is relatively little growth in the public work force, and major fiscal constraints continue. At the most, therefore, unionization of the public sector is expected to grow only slowly during the foreseeable future.

TYPES OF PUBLIC EMPLOYEE ORGANIZATIONS

Several types of employee organizations are active in the public sector. Some function at just one level of government, others at two or more. Some are organized along craft lines (e.g., electricians) and others by occupation (e.g., social workers). Some are analogous to private-sector industrial unions and include many different kinds of workers. There are AFL–CIO affiliated unions such as the American Federation of State, County, and Municipal Employees (AFSCME), and some public employees are represented by the International

Brotherhood of Teamsters (IBT). There are also independent associations of state and local government employees, as well as professional associations such as the National Education Association (NEA) which bargain collectively. Most public employees covered by negotiated contracts are included in one of the following types of organizations:

1. *Mixed unions.* These organizations have members in both government and the private sector. Most members work for private businesses, but in recent years some mixed unions have substantially increased their membership in public agencies.
2. *All-public or mostly public unions.* All or most of the members of these organizations are in government. Some are affiliated with the larger labor movement; the others are independent. Postal workers' unions are in this category, but police and fire organizations are considered separately.
3. *Professional associations.* These organizations draw their membership from particular professional occupations, such as teachers and registered nurses. They are not affiliated with national labor organizations such as AFSCME.
4. *Independent associations of state and local government employees.* Members of these organizations do many different kinds of work, and the groups function on a statewide or local basis. Most of them were created between 1920 and 1950, well before collective bargaining in government began to spread.
5. *Police and fire fighter organizations.* This classification overlaps some of the others. Included are all organizations, large and small, that represent police and fire fighters, both of which have been very active in collective bargaining.

Many public employees covered by contracts are not members of the unions that negotiated them, because requirements that workers join the union (a union shop) or pay dues (an agency shop) are very rare in government. Public employee unions therefore are often in the position of having to represent many "free riders," or employees who benefit from collective bargaining agreements but do not pay dues or belong to the organizations that negotiate them.[6] The American Federation of Government Employees (AFGE), for example, represented close to 650,000 federal workers in 1991, but it had only 177,000 members.

The Mixed Unions

This category of employee organizations includes a wide variety of unions that as a group crosscut all levels of government in the United States. Those with the strongest representation in state and local government are the Teamsters (IBT), the Service Employees' International Union (SEIU), the Amalgamated Transit Union (ATU), the Communication Workers of America (CWA), and the Laborer's International Union (LIU). With the exception of the Teamsters, all are AFL–CIO affiliates. In the federal government, the largest organization in this category is the Metal Trades Council, which is made up of several national craft unions.

The SEIU has a total membership of about 950,000 in 300 locals, roughly half of which are in the public sector.[7] In recent years, the bulk of its membership gains have come from government. This union has many members in California state and local government; in 1984 it acquired as an affiliate the large California State Employees Association. Taken together, the Teamsters, ATU, CWA, and LIU represent a total of about 200,000 local, state, and federal workers.

All-Public or Mostly Public Unions

The largest organization of this type is the American Federation of State, County, and Municipal Employees, AFL–CIO. It currently has 1,200,000 members in 2,991 locals, most of them in state and local governments. It includes workers of all kinds except teachers. The AFSCME started in 1936 as a small union dedicated to advancing the cause of merit in the states and localities. When the late Jerry Wurf became its president in 1964, it changed its orientation, aggressively recruited new members, enthusiastically endorsed collective bargaining, and achieved many successes at the bargaining table. Its growth did not end with the 1960s; between 1975 and 1987 AFSCME's membership expanded by over 350,000.

Another large, predominantly public union is the American Federation of Teachers (AFT). An AFL–CIO affiliate, the AFT now has 750,000 members in 2,400 locals. Most AFT members work for elementary and secondary schools in very large cities; in New York City alone, for example, the AFT represents over 75,000 employees. Recently many members have been enrolled from college and university faculties; the AFT now represents more faculty and staff than the National Education Association (NEA). The success of the AFT's largest affiliate, the United Federation of Teachers (UFT), in winning the 1961 collective bargaining election in New York City gave a great national impetus to bargaining in the public schools. The election was the first to be held in a large metropolitan school district, and the UFT succeeded in negotiating a comprehensive contract that was unprecedented in comparison with existing AFT local and NEA affiliate agreements.

Other large, mostly public unions operate in the federal service. With the exception of the postal service employee unions, they all have members in many kinds of positions in a number of federal agencies. Still by far the largest in terms of members and other employees represented is the American Federation of Government Employees (AFGE), AFL–CIO. In 1991 it represented close to 650,000 federal employees in exclusive bargaining units, down 7 percent from 690,000 in 1981. However, the AFGE lost over 30 percent of its dues-paying members in the same decade, dropping from 255,000 to 177,000; it currently has 172,000 members in 1,300 locals. The National Federation of Federal Employees (NFFE) is an independent organization that represented about 146,000 workers in 1991. Like the AFGE, it had suffered major membership losses (about 20 percent) between 1981 and 1991; it now has about 60,000 members.

The National Treasury Employees Union (NTEU), another independent union, started in the Internal Revenue Service, expanded to the Treasury Department, and recently extended its jurisdiction to include workers in other federal agencies. In contrast to the AFGE and NFFE, the NTEU managed to grow in both members and employees represented. Between 1981 and 1991, its ranks grew from 53,000 to 65,000, and the number of workers it represented for purposes of collective bargaining increased from 107,000 to 152,000. Since then the membership has declined somewhat, to 140,000 workers in 23 chapters. Nevertheless, the NTEU's ability as a federal employee union to generally maintain its membership appears to be due to its aggressive and often successful efforts to challenge government personnel policies in court. Its large legal staff also has a reputation for highly effective representation of individual employees in grievance proceedings and court cases.

The Postal Reorganization Act of 1970 granted workers in the U.S. Postal Service collective bargaining rights that are far more extensive than those available to other federal employees. Most important is their right to negotiate compensation. Labor relations in the Postal Service are under the jurisdiction of the National Labor Relations Board, the regulatory body that oversees collective bargaining in the private sector. Close to 450,000 postal workers are covered by negotiated contracts.

The American Postal Workers Union (APWU) and the National Association of Letter Carriers (NALC), both AFL–CIO, have about 330,000 and 311,000 members, respectively. The APWU was created in 1971 as the result of a merger between the AFL–CIO Postal Clerks, the independent National Postal Union, and three smaller AFL–CIO postal unions. The NALC, one of the first affiliates of the AFL–CIO, was established in the late 19th century. The NALC and APWU are very strong unions, both at the bargaining table and in lobbying Congress.

Professional Associations

By far the largest professional association in the public sector is the National Education Association; its members number well over 1 million, and it has 12,000 affiliates. The NEA was established to advance the teaching profession and provide a variety of services to members; it did not see itself as a labor organization. Until the 1960s, the leadership steadfastly rejected the idea that teachers need to bargain collectively with their employers. However, due to pressures from the membership and the strong competition offered by the AFT after its 1961 successes in New York City, the NEA was forced to officially adopt collective bargaining in 1962. Since then it has participated in many collective bargaining elections; in fact it is as much involved in bargaining and strike actions as the AFT is. It has rejected a merger with the AFT, largely because of the AFT's affiliation with the AFL–CIO. The NEA's membership is drawn primarily from public schools in suburban and rural areas.

Of the 1,712,000 registered nurses employed in the United States in 1991,[8] about 10 percent were members of the American Nurses Association (ANA). The ANA was the first professional association to adopt collective bargaining. In 1946, it approved an Economic Security Program which, according to Jacquelyn Gideon, was "committed to the use of collective bargaining as one of the most effective means of assuring nurses' rights to participate in the implementation of standards of nursing employment and practice."[9] The ANA's membership is open only to registered nurses, and it represents public-sector nurses on all levels of government. There are currently 53 constituent state associations.

Independent Associations of State and Local Employees

State employee associations were created for a variety of reasons. In some cases, the purpose was to provide some type of unified general representation for government employees. In others, the motive was to provide support for a particular cause or employee benefit. For example, several of these associations were organized to promote or protect a merit system, while others were created to support better retirement systems and insurance benefits. Most state associations limit their membership to state workers, but the number that admit local employees has grown recently.

Most of the state associations are federated with the Assembly of Government Employees (AGE), which was established in 1952. The AGE strongly supports merit systems; like most of its member associations, it did not welcome collective bargaining with open arms. Unions such as AFSCME were regarded as threatening to completely replace civil service laws and regulations with negotiated agreements. After collective bargaining statutes had been passed in a number of important states, however, the AGE faced the choice of adapting to the new public policy or recommending that its members not compete with the unions in collective bargaining elections. It chose to accommodate and to compete; many of the state associations have now been engaging in bargaining for some time.

The local associations were formed for basically the same reasons as the state groups. Like their state counterparts, they did not originally support collective bargaining, but some now serve as bargaining agents. An increasing number of state and local associations are affiliating with the AFSCME and other AFL–CIO organizations in order to build their bargaining power and resources.

Police and Fire Fighter Organizations

Of the 832,000 government employees providing police protection in 1990, by far the largest share, 664,000, were in local jurisdictions. Federal civilian police officers numbered 79,000, and there were 89,000 state police officers.[10] Police officers are members of several different kinds of organizations. A few belong to AFSCME or one of the mixed unions that admit police (e.g., the Teamsters and the SEIU). There are also many local police associations that are not affiliated with any of the three national organizations of police personnel: the Fraternal Order of Police (FOP), the International Union of Police Associations (IUPA), and the National Association of Police Officers (NAPO).

The members of the FOP, which was established in 1915, are regularly appointed or full-time law enforcement personnel of all ranks who work for state, local, or federal governments. The FOP does not consider itself a union, but some of its lodges engage in collective bargaining and have taken militant stands. It now has 1,860 affiliates and 225,000 members. The IUPA and NAPO were formed after the dissolution of the International Conference of Police Associations in 1978, when the state and local police associations comprising the group split over the issue of affiliation with the AFL–CIO. One segment formed the IUPA and became a charter member of the AFL–CIO in 1979; those opposed to affiliation created the NAPO as an independent, police-only association.

The International Association of Fire Fighters (IAFF), to which the majority of the nation's professional fire fighters belong, currently has about 172,000 members in 1,943 locals. There were 327,000 fire protection personnel in the United States in 1990, many of them in volunteer fire departments.[11] Most IAFF members are employed by municipalities, but there are some in the states and the federal service. This union, established shortly after World War I, has the longest continuous experience with local labor-management relations of any of the public employee unions. It has vigorously pursued bargaining agreements in most cities of any size.

ELEMENTS OF A COLLECTIVE BARGAINING SYSTEM

Collective bargaining usually takes place within a highly formalized system of rules and procedures. In the private sector, the National Labor Relations Act (NLRA) and its amendments provide the basis for the procedures and policies set forth by the National Labor Relations Board (NLRB). Title VII of the Civil Service Reform Act of 1978 established a system of labor relations for the federal service in which the Federal Labor Relations Authority (FLRA) "is responsible for issuing policy decisions and adjudicating labor-management disputes."[12]

Collective bargaining systems at other levels of government are based on state and local statutes or ordinances, except in a few cases where they have been set up by executive orders or bargaining on a de facto basis has been approved by the courts. In these cases, public management has for some reason decided to bargain with union representatives, and the courts have ruled valid the agreements entered into. In Ohio, for example, the state supreme court ruled in 1975 that public employers did have the "discretionary power to negotiate and engage in collective bargaining with [their] employees."[13] Enabling legislation *obligating* employers to bargain collectively was not passed in Ohio until 1983, however. In some states, such as Virginia, the courts have decided that public employees may not bargain collectively if the enabling legislation does not exist.[14]

The Labor Relations Agency

The collective bargaining programs of state and local governments are usually administered by an agency created expressly for that purpose. New York State's Public Employment Relations Board, Ohio's State Employment Relations Board, and New York City's Office of Collective Bargaining are examples. When collective bargaining is provided for by a local ordinance, the administering agency typically is a board or commission. Members of state boards or commissions are appointed by the governor, in most cases with confirmation of the state senate. In the federal government the agency is the FLRA, which consists of three members appointed by the president with Senate confirmation.

Bargaining Agents and Units

Within the traditional framework of collective bargaining, management representatives negotiate with the exclusive bargaining agent, the organization or union elected by the workers in a particular bargaining unit as their representative. All eligible workers within the unit are covered by the contract (as we noted above), even if they do not belong to the union that has won the right to act as the exclusive agent. Although there are variations in procedure, the norm is for exclusive agents to be selected by a majority of those voting in a representation election. The labor relations agency sets the procedures for these elections, oversees the process, and certifies the winner. Once certified, the bargaining agent has the exclusive right to represent the unit until it is defeated in another election or it is decertified by the labor relations agency because it violated the law governing collective bargaining in its jurisdiction. The most well-known recent example is the decertification of PATCO by the FLRA after it called for and orchestrated the illegal strike by federal air traffic controllers.

The Determination of Bargaining Units

Since bargaining units are the building blocks of collective bargaining, their size, membership, and number can have far-reaching effects on the efficient operation of the governmental unit, the workings of employee organization, the stability of the bargaining relationship, and the scope of bargaining, as well as the outcome of the representation election.[15] The criteria and procedures used to establish bargaining units therefore are of vital importance to both management and labor. These broad policy issues are dealt with on a political level through legislation or executive orders.

Historically, one of the principal functions of administering agencies has been to decide how bargaining units are to be constituted when management and labor disagree in their interpretations of the existing criteria. In the United States, three different ways of determining bargaining units have been used in the public sector:

1. Case-by-case determinations by the labor relations agency.
2. Stipulation in the enabling legislation.
3. Specification by the administrative agency through its rule-making powers.[16]

The case-by-case approach is the most commonly used on the local level, as well as the method used in the federal service. In general terms, the labor relations agency tries to group employees in units so there is a "community of interest" within each one, based on position classifications, the kind of work or occupation involved, or geographical location. However, these considerations must be balanced against the needs for administrative efficiency and an orderly or rational structure of bargaining units.

For public management, the existence of large numbers of fragmented units means that many contracts must be negotiated yearly. Besides increasing the workload, a multiplicity of units improves the unions' chances to benefit from the whipsaw effect of using a favorable agreement in one unit (e.g., police) to press for the same or better terms in another (e.g., fire fighters). Although management generally prefers a few large units to a scattering of small ones, neither management nor the unions invariably support either larger or smaller units. Each side develops its strategy in light of the situation it faces. If management is confronted by a powerful union or unions, it may try to divide that power by seeking several small units. Similarly, unions may try to create larger units if they believe this would increase their bargaining strength.

The case-by-case approach increases the risk of fragmentation because the administrative agency must deal with requests to establish units as they occur, and it may not be able to wait until the units can be rationally consolidated. In order to avoid this problem, the legislatures of a number of states (e.g., Hawaii and Wisconsin) have specified the units for certain state workers in their legal authorizations. In Hawaii, the legislation requires over a dozen units, including those for nonsupervisory blue-collar positions, registered nurses, fire fighters, police officers, and professional and scientific employees. In Massachusetts, the legislature does not specify units, leaving this task to its Labor Relations Commission. This Commission rejected a case-by-case approach; instead it uses its rule-making powers to create a system of broad units based on occupations.

The legislative and rule-making approaches to setting up bargaining units can avoid fragmentation and quickly produce a comprehensive, workable unit structure. However, a legislature may not be able to develop a successful unit framework, especially if there is intense competition among unions and management and labor cannot agree in advance on the form the framework should take. As Stephen Hayford, William Durkee, and Charles Hickman point out, "In the absence of such firm policy guidance, the legislative body, which typically lacks expertise in such matters, would probably base its decision on factors (primarily political in nature) other than those normally relied on in unit determination."[17] The rule-making approach does not eliminate political considerations; instead it shifts the task of dealing with them to the administrative agency.

The Status of Supervisors

One bargaining-unit issue that is unique to the public sector is the status of supervisory personnel. In the private sector, with the exception of a few skilled craft unions, supervisors from the foreman level up are considered to be a part of management and so are excluded from bargaining units. This arrangement is firmly imbedded in a larger tradition of clearly differentiating between management and labor. The NLRA excludes supervisors from bargaining rights, and most employers have strongly insisted that supervisors must be regarded as part of the management team. For many public employers, however, the line between supervisors and nonsupervisors is blurred and controversial.

Three questions are involved in the issue of the status of supervisors. First, it may be hard to determine whether or not a particular position is actually supervisory in nature. Merit systems covering entire work forces have not stressed this distinction. The definition of a supervisory position set forth in the collective bargaining statute may be detailed, but there are frequent disagreements over whether the supervision exercised justifies excluding a particular position from a nonsupervisory bargaining unit. In reality, many public employees occupy positions in so-called supervisory classes that actually involve little or no supervisory activity. Since the size of a unit is important to a union's bargaining position, unions usually try to have ambiguous cases classified as nonsupervisory. Management, on the other hand, tries to reduce union strength by convincing the labor relations agency to define these kinds of jobs as supervisory, in order to exclude them from the bargaining unit.

Most collective bargaining statutes do not specify which individual positions are to be considered supervisory. This determination is left to the administrative agency that decides bargaining units, and some of these agencies closely examine the actual duties of positions with supervisory titles and exclude only those involving clearly supervisory duties and powers. Nonetheless, disagreements among management, the unions, and the administrative agency over which positions are supervisory are commonplace in the public sector.

The second question has to do with the desirability of having units that contain both supervisors and nonsupervisors. In government, the work force is predominantly white-collar rather than blue-collar, and there are numerous levels of supervision. From the beginning, employee associations contained both supervisory and nonsupervisory personnel. Supervisors often were primarily responsible for creating these associations, and it was not unusual for them to hold leadership positions in them. Most of the mixed, predominantly public, and all-public employee unions admit lower-level supervisors. Against this historical background, when collective bargaining programs were established, union leaders resisted legislation prohibiting "mixed" bargaining units. Nevertheless, most state statutes contain such a prohibition and use the definition of supervisors set forth by the National Labor Relations Act.

The reason for the private-sector precedent of not mixing supervisors and nonsupervisors is the possibility of a conflict of interest. In these terms, supervisors and other workers have opposed, not common, interests. Supervisors represent management's interests; the interests of workers are represented by the union. Since bargaining units are supposed to be composed of persons with a community of interest, having them both in the same unit does not make sense. Either the supervisors will permeate the unit with a management point of view, thereby undermining the collective bargaining rights of the workers, or they will "defect," weakening management's position.

Union leaders who favor mixed units argue that the conflict-of-interest argument does not hold for the public sector. One of their key points is that supervisors in government do not have the kind of authority and discretion typical of their counterparts in business and industrial settings. Another perspective is that in some occupations and services, supervisors and nonsupervisors share a community of interest that outweighs differences between management and labor. Representatives of nurses, teachers, and police and fire service employees have strongly advanced this point of view. In some local governments, almost all levels of supervision in certain departments have been included in the same bargaining unit as nonsupervisory employees; cases frequently cited are in police and fire departments. When this happens—and it occurs largely because the unions have been politically effective—there may be only a few executives left to define and represent management's interests.

The third question is whether or not supervisors should be allowed to form their own units and bargain collectively with an employer. In the private sector, under the Taft-Hartley amendment to the NLRA, organizations of supervisors do not have bargaining rights. For the most part, government has followed this model, but some states (e.g., New York, Hawaii, and New Jersey) do grant bargaining rights to all or some supervisory personnel.

The rationale for not allowing bargaining with units of supervisors is that they are a part of the management team and should represent management's interests in the administration of personnel policies. In other words, if supervisors bargained, it would be very difficult to define managerial roles and responsibilities clearly. Also, if supervisors had bargaining rights, they might see themselves as "labor" and, for example, sympathize with strikes by rank-and-file workers. When strikes or other job actions take place, management often relies on supervisors to perform essential work, and supervisors who have strong feelings of solidarity with organized labor may be unwilling to undermine the workers' position.

For largely practical reasons, many supervisors in both sectors disagree with the idea that consultations with top management are the best way to determine supervisory pay and benefits. It is fairly common for supervisors' compensation to be informally linked to the provisions of negotiated agreements, but agency managers are not required to do this. In that case, public-sector supervisors are in a very dependent position; it is not unusual for them to consider themselves disadvantaged in comparison to unionized workers who have bargaining rights and the organizational resources needed to pressure management. It is clear that many public employers have given inadequate attention to the pay and other needs of their supervisory personnel. While there may be compelling reasons for not authorizing supervisors' bargaining units, this does not lessen the need to develop alternative organizational mechanisms for representing their interests.

Employee Rights

Employee rights normally are stated in the legal authorization for collective bargaining. The most basic is the right to form, join, and participate in employee organizations for the purpose of conferring and bargaining collectively with management. This includes the workers' right to be represented by the majority union in grievances over the terms and conditions of employment. The right of workers *not* to join unions or associations may or may not be stated. If it is stated, management cannot agree to contracts that require workers in bargaining units to join the union or pay dues. This arrangement is what is known as an *open shop*.

With an open shop, exclusive bargaining agents are often faced with situations in which they are negotiating contracts for units that have more nonmembers than members—that is, more free riders. A large percentage of free riders weakens a union's financial position, and its bargaining power may be affected because it cannot depend on strong, unified support from all those in the unit. For obvious reasons, management prefers to negotiate in an open-shop environment; the unions much prefer statutory language that does not specify the right of employees to refuse to join a union that has been selected as an exclusive bargaining agent.

In the public sector, most states and the federal government require open shops. Where this is not the case (e.g., in Pennsylvania and Hawaii), unions have succeeded in negotiating union or agency shops for some units.

Union shops are common in the private sectors of states that have not enacted right-to-work laws, which prohibit making union membership a qualification for employment. With a union shop, workers who do not join the majority union within a specified time period after being hired lose their jobs. With an agency shop, membership is not mandatory, but the equivalent of the union dues must be paid in return for services provided by the exclusive bargaining agent. The agent is required to represent the interests of all persons in the bargaining unit, whether or not they are members of the majority union.

The Scope of Bargaining and Management Rights

A key to the relative balance of power between management and the unions is the range of personnel policies and practices that are defined as negotiable. In general, unions prefer a wide range; management usually seeks to narrow the scope of bargaining. In the private sector, the NLRA broadly defines the scope of bargaining as including wages, hours, and working conditions. The NLRB has identified three types of collective bargaining issues: (1) those that are nonnegotiable, (2) those that must be negotiated, and (3) those that may be negotiated if management agrees to do so.

Overriding laws and court rulings may effectively remove certain issues from the bargaining table; for example, if the enabling state legislation for public employees requires an open shop, union and agency shops are not negotiable. On the national level, the closed shop (requiring union membership before employment) is illegal. With regard to mandatory issues, it is up to the NLRB and often the courts to decide what the language of the NLRA means in specific circumstances. Employee relations boards and commissions in the public sector are empowered to interpret legislative intent, subject to judicial review. Although they are not bound by NLRB precedents, these agencies have in practice generally followed the NLRB's threefold classification of issues.

Legislative Provisions in the Public Sector

Throughout government, the scope of bargaining is likely to be narrower than it is in the private sector. Provisions of civil service laws, state educational codes, special legislation covering the pay of blue-collar workers, and other statutes—federal, state, and local—make many issues nonnegotiable. Typically, the legal authorization covering public employees limits the range of negotiations by providing that subjects already covered by existing laws (particularly civil service statutes) may not be negotiated. Federal law restricts the scope of bargaining to *conditions of employment*, a term it defines as "personnel policies, practices, and matter, whether established by rule, regulation, or otherwise, affecting working conditions, except that such term does not include policies, practices, and matters...[that] are specifically provided for by Federal statute." Since the pay and benefits of federal workers are set by law, they are not negotiable.

In addition to limits set by other legislation, a "management rights" clause often is included in legislative authorizations. It is designed to specify managerial powers that may not be bargained away or shared with labor organizations. Traditionally, enumerated rights give management control over agency missions, administrative structures, and operating technologies. Other rights include directing the work of employees and the authority to hire, evaluate, promote, assign, or transfer employees in light of agency requirements. Typical of such clauses is the language of the Civil Service Reform Act on management rights:

> ...nothing in this chapter shall affect the authority of any management official of any agency (1) to determine the mission, budget, organization, number of employees, and internal security practices of the agency; and (2) in accordance with applicable laws (A) to hire, assign, direct, layoff, and retain employees in the agency, or to suspend, remove, reduce in grade or pay, or take other disciplinary action against such employees; (B) to assign work, to make determinations with respect to contracting out, and to determine the personnel by which agency operations shall be conducted.

Management rights clauses are replicated in agreements reached with unions, but determining what they mean in specific cases is often a responsibility of the public employment board or commission. These interpretations are important because they set the scope of bargaining. Does the right to determine the organization and methods of work mean that management may unilaterally decide the classification level of individual positions? On this question, the Federal Labor Relations Authority has interpreted the word *organization* to include individual positions and duties; thus federal agencies are not required to negotiate over job content.[18]

Court and Agency Rulings

Rulings of labor relations agencies and courts concerning which issues are mandatory or permissive in the public sector vary from state to state. Student-teacher ratios are negotiable in some states but not in others. There are also variations in an area of great importance to the unions: contracting-out, or privatization (see Chapter 3). Timothy Chandler and Peter Feuille found in a study of municipal unions and contracting-out that most of the unionized cities in their sample were not contractually barred from contracting-out sanitation services, for example. In about 25 percent of the cities, contracting-out was specified as a management right; in 20 percent management was required to consult with the union before contracting-out; and in a few cases, negotiated contracts prohibited the practice.[19] On the same issue, the FLRA and federal courts have effectively blocked union efforts to participate in agency decisions, and the federal unions are now supporting legislation that would allow them some voice in which functions are subject to contracting-out and would give employees and their union representatives agency-level appeal rights.[20]

Based on their analysis of numerous court decisions on management rights, Walter J. and Gladys Gershenfeld concluded that the courts:

> . . . have tended to be more concerned with preserving those rights that it believes management must possess to carry out its public duties and responsibilities under enabling statutes than with providing a safety valve for employees. The courts appear to be likely to rule borderline issues as nonmandatory, but they do provide some flexibility for employee organizations by making the impact of management actions on wages, hours, and working conditions negotiable.[21]

In other words, what is known as *impact bargaining* expands the arena of mandatory negotiations to include the effects of management decisions on those in the bargaining unit.

In personnel matters, impact bargaining means that management keeps its power to make program decisions, such as whether or not to carry out a reduction in force or to implement a pay-for-performance system. However, since these kinds of actions almost certainly have an impact on working conditions, management is obliged to negotiate with the union over procedural issues and ways of dealing with the consequences for employees. In such negotiations, the union may want management to agree to give laid-off workers first consideration when positions become available. In the federal service, the unions may negotiate aspects of pay-for-performance systems that have an impact on working conditions, with the major exceptions of position classifications and other matters specifically provided for by federal statute. Management is not compelled to grant union demands regarding impact issues, but it cannot simply say they are nonnegotiable.

Unfair Labor Practices

In their dealings with each other, management and labor are constrained by rules defining the term *unfair labor practices*. These rules are designed to prevent "union busting" by management, to make sure that unions do not engage in coercive behavior, and to ensure that both parties negotiate in good faith. Such practices by the employer commonly are defined to include the following:

1. Interfering, restraining, or coercing employees who are trying to exercise their collective bargaining rights. An example is threatening to fire or transfer workers who participate in union activities.
2. Dominating, obstructing, or assisting in the formation, existence, or administration of any employee organization. It is an unfair labor practice for employers to try to create "company unions" or to put "their people" into union leadership positions.
3. Encouraging or discouraging membership in any employee organization through discriminatory personnel practices. Discriminating against union members in hiring, promoting, or offering training opportunities to employees is an unfair labor practice.
4. Discouraging or discriminating against employees because they have joined a union or filed a grievance under the collective bargaining agreement. An example is assigning unpleasant work to an employee who has filed a grievance.

5. Refusing to negotiate with the union in good faith. Lying, distorting information, deliberately provoking conflict, and other measures intended to undermine negotiations are unfair labor practices.

Unfair practices by employee organizations involve the following kinds of behaviors.

1. Interfering with, restraining, or coercing employees in the exercise of their bargaining rights. For example, a union may try to coerce workers to vote for it as the exclusive bargaining agent.
2. Obstructing an employer's efforts to select its labor relations team, including negotiators and representatives in the grievance process. Unions have been known to use political pressure and threats to undermine management's capacity to function effectively.
3. Refusing to negotiate in good faith with the employer. A good-faith effort by both sides to negotiate and resolve differences is the foundation of the collective bargaining relationship.

Charges of unfair labor practices are filed with the labor relations agency authorized to investigate them. If the agency finds that the charges are justified, it orders the violator to stop the practice and to take whatever remedial actions are necessary. In the case of dismissals for union activity, management usually is ordered to reinstate fired employees with back pay. These kinds of orders may be appealed to the courts for a final decision.

Effective labor relations depend in large measure on each side's fully understanding the rules of the game. From time to time, labor relations agencies such as the NLRB and the FLRA issue rulings that both management and labor are expected to understand and to follow as guidelines. During the early stages of the expansion of collective bargaining in the public sector, it was not unusual for the actions of inexperienced managers or union members to be met with charges of unfair labor practices. A derogatory statement about a union and its leadership made in the presence of union members is often enough to bring a complaint against management. Unless management negotiators are aware of which overt acts the labor relations agency will consider as offering evidence of a lack of good-faith bargaining (such as routinely putting off meetings with the union bargaining team or simply refusing to meet with it), they run a great risk of being found guilty of an unfair labor practice. The penalties can be substantial. In this as well as other regards, collective bargaining adds a new dimension to public personnel administration.

CONTRACT NEGOTIATION

Most negotiated agreements in the public sector cover one or two years, which means that both sides are almost constantly preparing to negotiate the next contract while they are administering the provisions of the one in force. In addition to the bilateral bargaining that takes place across the table, both sides are conducting a process of multilateral bargaining with constituencies and authorities that must be recognized and accommodated in any negotiated contract.[22]

In the corporate or business environment, it is fairly easy to identify the membership of the management team responsible for making preparations, conducting negotiations, and committing the organization to contractual obligations. In government, however, it is often difficult to say who is in charge. When collective bargaining began to spread in government, an important issue for management was clearly defining who should have the responsibility for labor relations and the authority to enter into contractual relationships with unions. In an address delivered in 1966, Douglas Love observed that:

> . . . one of the most difficult problems is to find management and, having found it, to clothe it with the authority it needs to play the part. In a public service setting, managerial authority tends to be divided between a legislature and an executive, between politicians and bureaucrats, between independent commissions and operating departments. Because badly dispersed, it tends to lack substance and definition and almost, at times, to disappear in a forest of checks and balances.[23]

In addition to the intentional dispersal and sharing of power within the formal institutions of government, external interest groups seek influence in the collective bargaining process. Many potentially conflicting roles and points of view make up the management side of the collective bargaining relationship. While elected executives may recommend or request budgetary appropriations, it is up to the legislative body to make them. Even when legislators delegate to agency executives the authority to set pay scales, they do not give up their control over fiscal and budgetary matters; in fact, they may refuse to make needed funds available. Moreover, where tax increases would be required to finance negotiated pay scales, organized interests of many kinds are likely to be very active in the debate. Personnel departments, the courts, and other levels of government may be drawn in by contractual provisions concerning issues such as position classifications, appeals processes, and seniority systems.

On the union side, important players include national or state labor organizations, factions within the union itself, and community and special-interest groups with a stake in the outcome of negotiations.

The Labor Relations Function in Government

The fragmentation of authority and power in public employers led to much confusion and lack of coordination on the management side during the early years of collective bargaining. It was not unusual for city councils to reject or attempt to change contracts negotiated in good faith by a management team. Lack of coordination among personnel departments, budget offices, and line managers frequently produced contracts that were inadequately costed-out and at cross purposes with efforts to improve productivity. Recognizing this weakness, unions often bypassed management negotiators and, in effect, tried to negotiate with legislators. At the same time, management might be covertly trying to mobilize legislators, courts, and taxpayer groups in a effort to achieve a dominant position.

An effect of the movement to unionization and collective bargaining since the 1960s has been the centralization of management structure in the public sector.[24] In jurisdictions where collective bargaining is well established, professional managers have been expected to take the lead in labor relations, with the result that there has been a significant decline in legislative influence over personnel matters. The administrative pattern has been for executives to establish a direct line of authority over the unit having responsibility for labor relations.

In state and local governments, the labor relations function often is assigned to the director of personnel or to a separate office of labor relations. In either case, specialists in labor relations are responsible for the program. Many small jurisdictions use part-time consultants to represent management at the bargaining table. In the federal government, all bargaining takes place on the agency level, and the OPM serves as a management adviser on labor relations. In most cases, the federal agency's labor relations program is handled by a specialized unit of its personnel office or department. A few agencies have a completely separate office of labor relations, a model that is typical of the private sector.

When one office is responsible for labor relations and another for

personnel, experience has shown the need for close coordination between the two. Managers negotiating agreements must be thorough-
ly familiar with personnel laws and regulations and should be aware
of any personnel problems or issues that relate to the agency's dealings with organized employees. Likewise, the personnel department
must be in a position to understand and respond to the implications
of proposed contractual agreements. When the functions are combined in one office but are handled by different staffs, similar coordination is needed. Whatever the structure of responsibilities, those
responsible for labor relations should be in constant contact with line
managers in order to assure that management's needs and perspec-
tives are represented in the negotiating process.

Strikes and Impasse Resolution

At one time, strikes by public employee organizations were probably
the single most feared aspect of collective bargaining, at least from
management's point of view. Strikes by private-sector workers are
legal, and unions see that right as absolutely essential in order to
maintain an economic balance of power between management and
labor. In contrast, strikes by public employees are illegal in most
states and the federal government. Two primary reasons are offered
for denying the right to strike: (1) many public services are essential
and the public has no comparable alternatives, and (2) strikes by
public employees are essentially political weapons that give unions
an unfair advantage.

Statutory penalties include dismissal of striking workers, crimi-
nal prosecution of union leaders, fines against union treasuries, and
decertification of unions calling strikes. Nonetheless, many strikes or
work stoppages have taken place in government, most of them
against local employers and school districts. Although they generally
have been relatively short, some have become protracted media
spectaculars. In many instances, legal penalties cannot be enforced,
and settlements provide for amnesty. In cases where legal penalties
have been imposed, such as the PATCO strike that resulted in the firing of over 10,000 air traffic controllers, it may take years for the
agency (in this case, the Federal Aviation Administration) to return
to normal operation.[25]

The experience of public management with strikes, while unpleasant, has taught it that agencies can survive them if they are prepared. One measure of confidence on the employer's side is
legislation in ten states that permits strikes by nonessential workers.
Most of these laws were passed in the late 1970s, after the period of

explosive growth in unionism; more recently, the number and duration of work stoppages has declined. The overall maturation of the
relationship between management and labor has been a contributing
factor, along with fiscal stress and public opposition to strikes. In the
current environment, both sides have many incentives to avoid
strikes and job actions such as slowdowns and "sickouts," or actions
in which workers call in sick as a form of protest or to exert pressure
on management.

Legally authorized collective bargaining programs almost always set up procedures for resolving bargaining deadlocks or impasses. In contrast to the private sector, in which labor and
management have relative flexibility in deciding how to resolve impasses, in the public sector these rights and privileges are greatly
limited.[26] By 1985, over 40 states had passed some kind of law dealing with impasses. The administering agencies are responsible for
seeing to it that these laws are followed and arranging for the services of mediators, fact finders, and/or, in some cases, arbitrators to
help break impasses. Traditionally, each side shares equally in the
costs associated with such third-party interventions.

The Impasse Resolution Process

Mediation is usually the first step in impasse resolution. Mediators focus on getting the negotiation process back on track and facili-
tating communication between the parties. If mediation fails, the
next step may be fact-finding. Often "the facts" (e.g., a jurisdiction's
ability to pay) are in dispute. Fact-finding is a semijudicial process in
which both sides present their version of the facts with documenta-
tion such as cost-of-living data and information on prevailing rates
of pay. Expert witnesses are likely to be called in to support each
side. The fact finder or a fact-finding panel studies the evidence and
issues a report containing a recommended settlement. If these are
not accepted by one or both of the parties, in some states the parties
may agree to go to binding arbitration, under which an agreement is
imposed.[27] In others, a limited strike is a legal option. In about 20
states, the law requires police and fire fighters to submit to binding
arbitration if they cannot resolve an impasse at the bargaining table.

The 1983 Ohio legislation on impasse resolution provides a useful example of how these various elements may be combined in a
legally mandated process. The state legislature stipulated the detailed procedures to be followed in cases where collective bargaining
results in an impasse. As Ron Portaro notes:

> The term impasse takes on an expanded meaning under the new
> law. Impasse has been commonly known as the point in the negotiating

process where the parties cease to make progress. Ohio law accepts this view, but also states that impasse results if a labor agreement is not reached forty-five days before the expiration of the current collective bargaining agreement.[28]

The Ohio legislation requires the following schedule of procedures, which may range from 61 days before expiration to the expiration date:

1. *Sixty-one days before the expiration of the existing contract,* one of the parties must notify the other and the State Employment Relations Board (SERB) that it intends to negotiate another contract. Negotiations may start earlier.
2. *Sixty days before expiration,* negotiations must begin. In the 15 days between this time and 45 days before expiration, the sides may "submit issues in dispute to the board and each other for consideration under any mutually agreed-upon dispute settlement procedure."[29] The agreed-upon procedure then takes precedence over the legislated process.
3. If requested to do so, *50 days before expiration* SERB will respond to requests to investigate disputes relating to charges that one side or the other is not bargaining in good faith.
4. If the parties have not reached an agreement *45 days before expiration,* SERB will appoint a mediator to facilitate negotiations. If the mediator reports that the sides have reached an impasse, SERB will immediately appoint a fact-finding panel.
5. If an agreement has not been reached by *30 days before expiration,* SERB must appoint a fact-finding panel. Depending on the situation, SERB may order continued mediation and/or negotiations.
6. The findings and recommendations of the fact-finding panel must be sent to the employer, employee organization, and SERB *16 days before expiration.*
7. The employer and SERB must be notified of an intent to strike by workers who have that right *10 days before expiration.*
8. *Nine days before expiration,* the employer's legislative body and the union's membership vote on the panel's recommendations. Rejection by either side requires a 60 percent vote. If neither party rejects the recommendations, "they shall be deemed agreed upon as the final resolution of the dispute, and a collective bargaining contract shall be executed."[30]
9. If one or both sides rejects the recommendations, SERB makes the fact-finding panel's findings and recommendations public. Negotiations and mediation efforts may continue.

10. If the employees concerned do not have the right to strike (most of these are law enforcement personnel and fire fighters), SERB orders a final-offer settlement procedure to begin *three days before expiration.* A "conciliator" must hold a hearing within *30 days. Five days before the hearing,* each side submits its final offers on all issues in dispute and a justification for each offer. Under Ohio law, conciliators are empowered to impose a final resolution by accepting the offers of management or labor on an issue-by-issue basis. Conciliators' awards are subject to review by the state court of common pleas.

11. *On the expiration date,* employees with the right to strike may do so if they have given the required ten-day notice. SERB can initiate mediation efforts at its discretion.

In both fact finding and arbitration, management is required to carefully prepare its case. Personnel departments usually have much of the responsibility for collecting, organizing, and displaying information that supports the employer's position. Although most public-sector labor leaders prefer the strike option, fact finding and arbitration do compensate somewhat by requiring employers to present a rational justification of the positions they have taken at the bargaining table.

Approval of Agreements

Public management is seldom in the position of being able to finalize a contractual agreement with a union. In many municipalities, agreements must be approved by the local governing body, such as the county board of supervisors or city council, and, in most school districts, approval by the school board is required before a contract may go into effect. In some state governments, the legislature must ratify the agreement; in most, this is not the case. Agreements take effect in the federal service when agency heads approve them. With the exception of public authorities having their own sources of revenue, the legislative body must vote funds to finance contracts and so may exercise a veto power.

Ideally, both agency leadership and the union membership have been kept fully informed about the status of negotiations, have in some manner consulted with their negotiators, and will not be surprised by the content of a proposed contract. When management presents an agreement to those legally empowered to give final approval, it should be prepared to fully explain the terms and likely consequences for such matters as budgets and tax rates. On the union side, contracts may be submitted to the membership for a ratification vote, but procedures vary. In the federal service, such votes are not required. Union leaders are responsible for explaining a contract's terms to the members of the bargaining unit and recommending its approval or rejection if a ratification vote is required.

CONTRACT ADMINISTRATION

Although negotiations attract the most public attention, effective day-to-day administration of agreements is the foundation of a successful labor relations program. Once a contract has been signed and ratified, the labor relations program enters the contract administration phase, another bilateral process in which management and labor share responsibility for implementation of the provisions of the agreement. The emphasis is on building a cooperative relationship in which disputes over how to interpret certain provisions can be handled fairly and effectively.

In a recent study of the federal labor relations program, which it called "A Program in Need of Reform," the GAO concluded that a cooperative or joint problem-solving orientation often is sadly lacking:

> Several cases on which FLRA decisions were made in 1990 illustrate the minor issues that the parties referred to FLRA rather than agreeing among themselves: the use of a radio at a worksite, consumption of surplus coffee during breaks, cancellation of a 1984 annual picnic, removal of a water cooler, change in office seating arrangements, removal of two office partitions and a typewriter, and a requirement that civilian guards salute the military.[31]

This GAO report notes that in the private sector, labor-management cooperative programs "reflect the growing view that an 'us versus them' approach is outdated and unworkable."[32] Representatives of management and unions in the federal service strongly disagree on the extent to which there is cooperation throughout the system. Nevertheless, they do cite two successful cooperative efforts: the Internal Revenue Service's Joint Quality Improvement Process and the PACER SHARE productivity improvement program at the Sacramento Air Logistics Center. The first involves the National Treasury Employees Union and agency management in attempts to improve effectiveness throughout the IRS. PACER SHARE is a five-year demonstration project in which the agency and employees affiliated with the American Federation of Government Employees share cost savings generated by productivity improvements. Both programs are credited with enhancing productivity and greatly reducing union-management litigation.[33]

On the state and local levels, joint labor-management committees (LMCs) are increasingly popular. While they are not a substitute for bargaining, LMCs provide a mechanism for cooperative efforts to solve a wide variety of problems such as workplace safety, quality control, and communication. Joint LMCs are created by contract to deal with a single issue such as health care. There is joint representation of both labor and management on the committee, but the final decision is reserved for management. Cities such as Phoenix and San Diego have negotiated agreements establishing LMCs, as have the states of Ohio and Massachusetts.[34]

The Roles of Supervisors and Stewards

Because supervisors have the most direct contact with rank-and-file workers, they are considered key figures in the administration of a public personnel program. Perhaps the single most positive impact of collective bargaining on personnel administration has been its focus on the administration of these contracts by supervisors. Supervisors are expected to understand a contract's provisions and to be able to prevent disputes and resolve conflicts before they result in formal grievances that undermine cooperation. While some grievances are unavoidable, many are provoked by supervisory ignorance and a confrontational approach.

For supervisors unused to working under a negotiated contract, the role of union stewards may come as somewhat of an unpleasant shock. Stewards, elected by the union membership, and supervisors are counterparts in the process of contract administration. These union officers are often more diligent than management or personnel offices in detecting supervisory deficiencies, particularly as they relate to contractual requirements.

Since stewards are situated in the workplace alongside supervisors, they have access to intimate knowledge of work activities and problems affecting both management and the workers. Some may be overzealous or so antagonistic toward management that supervisors have some cause for considering them troublemakers, but a capable, conscientious steward is in fact a troubleshooter who can be a valuable problem solver for both the union and management. Studies of the steward's function have revealed that in large measure it has been a positive factor in improving supervisory skill and assuring equitable treatment of employees in personnel policies and practices.[35] For supervisors and stewards alike, adequate training in labor relations is crucial to a smoothly functioning collective bargaining relationship.

Grievance Resolution

An important aspect of contract administration is the process through which disputes over how a contract is interpreted and how it is administered are resolved. Typically, authorizing legislation requires all contracts to contain a mechanism for resolving grievances. The standard mechanism is a negotiated grievance procedure that is designed to have "finality." In this procedure, disputes that cannot be resolved by the parties are submitted to a third-party "neutral" or arbitrator who makes a final and binding decision. Such finality is essential to avoid interminable conflicts and ambiguities over how to interpret one part or another of the contract. While one of the parties inevitably is disappointed by the arbitrator's decision, at least it provides a clean end to the dispute and makes it easier to avoid future misunderstandings.

The definition of a grievance set forth in legislation determines what issues employees will be able to present as grievances under a negotiated process, as opposed to the system established under civil service laws and regulations. For example, the language of the CSRA is very broad; a grievance is defined as "any complaint about employment, or the interpretation and application of the negotiated agreement or any law, rule, or regulation affecting employees' working conditions." Unless the parties agree to exclude them, this means that the negotiated grievance procedure can be used to deal with matters already covered by the statutory appeals process.[36] Not surprisingly, many managers object to broad definitions of grievances because they believe this exposes most management decisions on personnel matters to potential reversal by arbitrators.[37]

THE IMPACT OF COLLECTIVE BARGAINING ON PUBLIC PERSONNEL ADMINISTRATION

Probably the greatest concerns about collective bargaining in the public sector have been its effects on the merit principle and on managerial effectiveness. Despite dire predictions that it would "negotiate-away merit" or undermine the ability of public management to manage human resources, collective bargaining appears to have done neither.

In some ways, collective bargaining may have actually strengthened both merit and management. Unions historically have been opposed to patronage systems, and where they have established collective bargaining relationships with public employers, they have negotiated contracts that Richard Elling considers "may be stronger bulwarks against spoils practices than the trappings of civil service." In fact, extensive collective bargaining and extensive merit system coverage often coexist. In states such as California, New York, Michigan, and Vermont, collective bargaining is available to the high percentage of state employees who are in the classified service. In other states, such as Texas and Arizona, both civil service coverage and collective bargaining are limited or nonexistent for state employees.[38]

With regard to management's capacity to manage human resources effectively, at best there is evidence to support the proposition that collective bargaining has encouraged at least some agencies to use human as well as material resources more efficiently and to develop better supervisory skills.[39] At worst, it seems that provisions of negotiated contracts are no more serious impediments than traditional civil service rules and procedures are.[40]

In most jurisdictions with dual personnel systems (both merit systems and collective bargaining), an accommodation of sorts has been reached between the two. Collective bargaining has partly replaced the unilateral civil service system in such areas as compensation and grievances, but the prediction that civil service boards and departments would be limited to recruitment and examination functions has not been realized.[41] They generally retain broad policy authority over promotions, transfers, reductions in force, performance standards and evaluation, position classifications, and other aspects of the in-service personnel program. But the procedures used to implement civil service laws and policies are likely to be governed by contract provisions in all or many of these areas, so the powers of civil service agencies have in fact been meaningfully diminished.

Joel Douglas sees a pressing need to eliminate the confusion and conflict typical of dual personnel systems:

> ...where collective bargaining laws have been implemented, civil service merit systems have become tired institutions, are in a period of decline, and may be at the twilight of their existence.... for state employees, LRS [labor relations systems], more than CSMS [civil service merit systems], have become the primary forces in human resource policy formulation and implementation. Living with dual personnel systems is an option widely followed yet not recommended. The task ahead is the enactment of statutory revocation provisions for state civil

service merit systems that conflict with labor relations systems and the preservation of merit principles within the context of collective bargaining.[42]

In a number of states such as Hawaii and Illinois, the authorizing legislation for state employees requires that negotiated contracts take precedence over civil service rules where conflicts exist. Some states have arrangements whereby contractual agreements on certain subjects (e.g., wages, hours, discipline, and layoffs) have precedence. In others, contracts prevail only on a few specific topics, such as union security provisions. In most local governments, contracts do not automatically supersede civil service, and negotiated terms that conflict with existing law may take effect only if the governing body changes the law.

The most profound impact of collective bargaining in the public sector has been a transformation of the relationship between employer and employee. Traditional civil service merit systems are based on the proposition that the "rules of the workplace" set the terms of the relationship between the employer and the *individual worker*. Under collective bargaining, management is required to negotiate those rules with another *organization*, the labor union or employee association. Beyond bilateral negotiations, these two organizations co-implement and coadminister the rules as they apply to members of bargaining units. This means that employees may not individually negotiate terms of employment, and for management to deal with them on this level is an unfair labor practice. It means that management must extensively share power over and responsibility for the personnel program with the leadership of an organization created to serve the interests of the worker.

To the degree that the merit systems that emerged from Civil Service Reform I were predicated on unilateral control, collective bargaining has radically altered public personnel administration. But like the human resources management approach, it is only one of many forces for change in concepts, policies, and practices.

■

NOTES

1. Cited in B. V. Schneider, "Public Sector Labor Legislation: An Evolutionary Analysis," in Benjamin Aaron, Joseph R. Grodin, and James L. Stern (eds.), *Public Sector Collective Bargaining* (Washington, DC: Bureau of Na-

tional Affairs, 1979), pp. 191–192.
2. *National League of Cities* v. *Usery,* 426 U.S. (1976).
3. William M. Davis and others, "Collective Bargaining in 1990: Health Care Cost a Common Issue," *Monthly Labor Review,* vol. 113, no. 1 (January 1990), p. 3.
4. Jeffrey S. Zax and Casey Ichniowski, "Bargaining Laws and Unionization in the Local Public Sector," *Industrial and Labor Relations Review,* vol. 43, no. 4 (April 1990), pp. 447–462.
5. Ibid., p. 449.
6. Marick F. Masters and Robert Atkin, "Bargaining Representation and Union Membership in the Federal Sector: A Free Rider's Paradise," *Public Personnel Management,* vol. 18, no. 3 (Fall 1989), pp. 311–323.
7. Data on current union membership and numbers of locals and affiliates in this section are from "Labor Union Directory," *World Almanac and Book of Facts 1993* (New York: Pharos Books, 1992), pp. 159–160.
8. U.S. Bureau of the Census, *Statistical Abstract of the United States: 1992,* 112th edition, (Washington, DC, 1992), Table 629.
9. See Jacquelyn Gideon, "The American Nurses Association: A Professional Model for Collective Bargaining," *Journal of Health and Human Resources Administration,* vol. 2, no. 1 (August 1979).
10. U.S. Bureau of the Census, *Statistical Abstract of the United States: 1992,* Table 482. Also see Table 1.1 in Chapter 1 of this text.
11. Ibid.
12. U. S. General Accounting Office, *Federal Labor Relations: A System in Need of Reform* (Washington, DC, July 30, 1991), p. 13.
13. Ron M. Portaro, "Public-Sector Impasse Legislation: Is It Working?" *Employee Relations Law Journal,* vol. 12, no. 1 (Summer 1986), p. 112.
14. Joel A. D'Alba, "The Nature of the Duty to Bargain in Good Faith," in Public Employment Relations Services, *Portrait of a Process: Collective Negotiations in Public Employment* (Fort Washington, PA: Labor Relations Press, 1979), p. 156.
15. Stephen L. Hayford, William A. Durkee, and Charles W. Hickman, "Bargaining Unit Determination Procedures in the Public Sector: A Comparative Evaluation," *The Employee Relations Law Journal,* vol. 5, no. 1 (Summer 1979), p. 85.
16. Ibid., p. 86.
17. Ibid., p. 95.
18. Paul A. Krumsiek, "Contract Negotiation and the Classification Specialist," *Public Personnel Management,* vol. 11, no. 1 (Spring 1982), p. 32.
19. Timothy Chandler and Peter Feuille, "Municipal Unions and Privatization," *Public Administration Review,* vol. 51, no. 1 (January–February 1991), p. 18.
20. Katherine C. Naff, "Labor-Management Relations and Privatization: A Federal Perspective," *Public Administration Review,* vol. 51, no. 1 (January–February 1991), p. 28.
21. Walter J. Gershenfeld and Gladys Gershenfeld, "The Scope of Collective

Bargaining," in Jack Rabin, Thomas Vocino, W. Bartley Hildreth, and Gerald J. Miller (eds.), *Handbook of Public Personnel Administration and Labor Relations* (New York: Marcel Dekker, 1983), p. 349.

22. Irving O. Dawson, "Trends and Developments in Public Sector Unions," in Steven W. Hays and Richard C. Kearney (eds.), *Public Personnel Administration: Problems and Prospects*, 2nd ed. (Englewood Cliffs, NJ: Prentice-Hall, 1990), pp. 153–157.

23. Douglas Love, "Proposals for Collective Bargaining in the Public Service of Canada: A Further Commentary," in Gerald C. Somers (ed.), *Collective Bargaining in the Public Service: Proceedings of the 1966 Annual Spring Meeting, Industrial Relations Association*, Milwaukee, Wisconsin, May 6–7, 1966, p. 28.

24. Richard C. Kearney, "Monetary Impact of Collective Bargaining," in Rabin, Vocino, Hildreth, and Miller (eds.), *Handbook of Public Personnel Administration*, p. 381.

25. U.S. General Accounting Office, *FAA Staffing: The Air Traffic Control Workforce Opposes Rehiring Fired Controller* (Washington, DC, October 1986).

26. Portaro, "Public Sector Impasse Legislation," p. 111.

27. See Gregory G. Dell'Omo, "Capturing Arbitrator Decision Policies under a Public Sector Interest Arbitration Statute," *Review of Public Personnel Administration*, vol. 10, no. 2 (Spring 1990), pp. 19–38.

28. Portaro, "Public Sector Impasse Legislation," p. 113.

29. Ibid., p. 114.

30. Ibid., p. 115.

31. U.S. General Accounting Office, *Federal Labor Relations: A Program in Need of Reform* (Washington, DC, July 1991), pp. 20–21.

32. Ibid., p. 63.

33. Ibid., p. 64.

34. Dawson, "Trends and Developments in Public Sector Unions," pp. 158–159.

35. George T. Sulzner, *The Impact of Labor-Management Relations upon Selected Federal Personnel Policies and Practices*, (Washington, DC, U.S. Office of Personnel Management, 1979), p. 36.

36. U. S. General Accounting Office, *Federal Labor Relations*, pp. 58–59.

37. Steven A. Rynecki, Douglas A. Cairns, and Donald J. Cairns, *Police Collective Bargaining Agreements: A National Management Survey* (Washington, DC: National League of Cities and Police Executive Research Forum, 1978), p. 16.

38. Richard C. Elling, "Civil Service, Collective Bargaining and Personnel-Related Impediments to Effective State Management: A Comparative Assessment," *Review of Public Personnel Administration*, vol. 6, no. 3 (Summer 1986), p. 83.

39. Hervey Juris and Peter Feuille, "Police Union Impact on the Chief's Ability to Manage," in David Lewin, Peter Feuille, and Thomas A. Kochan, *Public Sector Labor Relations: Analysis and Readings* (Glen Ridge, NJ:

Thomas Horton and Daughters, 1977), pp. 434–448.

40. Elling, "Civil Service, Collective Bargaining, and Performance-Related Impediments," pp. 87–89.

41. Jerry Wurf, "City Hall Labor Policies," in Frank J. Thompson (ed.), *Classics of Public Personnel Policy*, 2nd ed. (Pacific Grove, CA: Brooks/Cole, 1991), pp. 328–334; Harry H. Wellington and Ralph K. Winter, Jr., *The Unions and the Cities* (Washington, DC: The Brookings Institution, 1971).

42. Joel M. Douglas, "State Civil Service and Collective Bargaining: Systems in Conflict," *Public Administration Review*, vol. 52, no. 1 (January–February 1992), p. 169.

Equal Employment Opportunity and Affirmative Action

9

Political, social, and economic forces in the United States over the past 30 years have produced heavy pressure on public employers to remove long-standing barriers to the hiring and career progression of minorities and women. Those who make and administer public personnel policies are expected to pursue the goal of a representative public work force; that is, the public service should mirror the demography of the society it serves. Since the early 1960s, public policy in this area has been structured around the idea that equal employment opportunity is the foundation of a representative public service. Laws requiring equal employment opportunity have had a major impact on personnel practices and, to a meaningful extent, on the composition of the American public service.

As we noted in Chapter 2, the federal mandate to employers to provide equal employment opportunity (EEO) means that they may not discriminate in hiring and other personnel actions on the basis of race, sex, age, disability, religion, or national or ethnic origin. EEO is required by the Equal Employment Opportunity Act of 1972, which amends Title VII of the Civil Rights Act of 1964; the Age Discrimination in Employment Act of 1967, as amended in 1978; and the Vocational Rehabilitation Act of 1973 and the Americans with Disabilities Act of 1990. Many states and localities have also passed EEO legislation. For all practical purposes, EEO is now well-established in law and public policy, and the *idea* that hiring and other employment actions should be based solely on a person's qualifications, ability, and job performance is widely shared in American society. However, the primary instrument for achieving EEO—affirmative action—is far more controversial.

Karen Ann Olsen defines affirmative action as "a good faith effort by an employer to achieve equal employment opportunity by developing and implementing results-oriented procedures."[1] The Equal Employment Opportunity Commission (EEOC), in its *Affirmative Action Guidelines* issued in 1979, states that affirmative action consists of personnel policies and procedures designed "to overcome the effects of past or present practices, policies, or other barriers to equal employment opportunity."[2] Thus affirmative action can be defined as a remedial concept that requires the employer "to analyze and then correct its own recruitment, hiring, promotional, and other employment practices that appear to have a disparate effect on the employment of persons protected by the federal statutes"[3] and by state or local laws as well.

The principle behind affirmative action is that a "court order to 'cease and desist' from some discriminatory practice may not be sufficient to undo the harm already done, or even to prevent additional harm as the result of a pattern of events set in motion by the prior illegal activity."[4] As a concept, affirmative action predates the Civil Rights Act of 1964 and applies to many questions besides the rights of minorities and women. For example, the National Labor Relations Act of 1935 not only provided for cease-and-desist orders against employers that engage in illegal antiunion activities but also for affirmative remedial actions by employers, such as the reinstatement of unlawfully fired workers with back pay and the posting of notices that the employer would stop such illegal practices. In other words, affirmative action means not only stopping or eliminating discriminatory practices but also taking steps to repair the damage they have already caused.[5]

AFFIRMATIVE ACTION PLANS

Public agencies set up affirmative action plans or programs most often in response to political pressures or legislative mandates. The courts also may order the implementation of affirmative action plans designed to eliminate discriminatory personnel practices and to achieve a representative work force in the shortest possible time. More likely is the issuance of executive orders such as President

Nixon's 1969 Executive Order 11748, under which affirmative action by federal agencies is required to achieve EEO in recruitment, hiring, and other personnel practices. In today's legal environment, public employers often establish affirmative action plans in order to protect against possible charges of discrimination and avoid litigation.

The Civil Rights Act of 1964 did not require affirmative action plans, but the EEOC stated in its 1974 *Guidebook for Employers*: "The certainty of increased legal action, and consistent record of court-required affirmative action to remedy discrimination found under Title VII, emphasize the advantage to you, as an employer, of instituting an effective affirmative action program voluntarily and speedily."[6] And in 1979 it recommended that "each person subject to Title VII should take voluntary action to correct the effects of past discrimination and to prevent present and future discrimination without awaiting litigation."[7]

Since public as well as private employers are potentially vulnerable because they lack representative numbers of minorities and women in some or all job categories, many have voluntary affirmative action plans that include remedial procedures designed to accelerate the hiring and promotion of employees in these demographic groups. In *Johnson v. Transportation Agency, Santa Clara County, California* (1987)[8] the Supreme Court ruled against a male transportation worker who had claimed "reverse discrimination" because he had been passed over for promotion in favor of a qualified female candidate. While the Court ruled that voluntary affirmative action plans of this kind do not violate Title VII, it did not rule on their constitutionality under the equal protection clause.

Affirmative action goals that favor women and minorities remain politically controversial. Despite the Supreme Court's decision in *United Steelworkers of America* v. *Weber* (1979) (see Chapter 2), both Presidents Reagan and Bush went on record as strongly opposed to any form of preferential treatment for women and minorities, on grounds that it is illegal and unconstitutional.[9]

Components of an Affirmative Action Plan: The Virginia Beach Example

The EEOC, OPM, and other federal agencies responsible for enforcing EEO requirements have published extensive guidance for public as well as private employers. We will use the example of the *1989–1990 Affirmative Action Plan* of the City of Virginia Beach, Virginia, to illustrate how this guidance translates into the major components of an affirmative action plan.

Statement of Policy

First, affirmative action plans should include a written EEO policy, clearly state an affirmative action commitment, and specify a top official as responsible for carrying out the program. Virginia Beach's plan offers a good example in its EEO policy statement:

> It shall be the policy of the City of Virginia Beach to maintain and promote equal employment opportunity for all employees and applicants for employment, without regard to race, color, national origin, sex, age, religion, handicap, or other non-job related factors. This policy affects all aspects of employment practices including, but not limited to, the following: recruitment, testing, selection, compensation, promotion, transfer, demotion, layoff, termination, training or any other personnel action.[10]

The EEO policy statement then establishes the requirement of "continued affirmative action throughout the City to ensure that any discriminatory practices that impede equal employment opportunity with the City are identified and eliminated." It assigns overall administrative responsibility for the plan to the city manager and the director of personnel. In addition, Virginia Beach has created the position of EEO/affirmative action coordinator, with responsibility for day-to-day management of all phases of the plan. And an EEO Advisory Committee made up of city employees representing various categories of workers is set up to monitor implementation of the plan, make recommendations, and serve "as a forum for employees to raise questions concerning the Plan and its implications, and to discuss general concerns."[11]

The City of Virginia Beach sets forth the following positive goals and objectives for its affirmative action plan:

1. To ensure equal opportunity in all personnel policies and procedures through the identification and elimination of policy and procedural areas that unlawfully discriminate on the basis of race, religion, color, national origin, sex, age or disability.
2. To identify areas of needed concentration, to assess underutilization of protected classes at all levels of employment, and to work toward appropriate utilization of these classes throughout the workforce.
3. To develop, coordinate, and/or present employee training programs which are designed to assist supervisors and employees in learning how to comply and work effectively with equal employment and affirmative action provisions.
4. To encourage movement of qualified women and men into non-traditional jobs and management positions.

5. To design and implement an on-going internal assessment process which will allow for the monitoring and reporting of hiring and promotional procedures.
6. To provide a vehicle for the publication and dissemination, both internally and externally, of the City's goals and objectives regarding equal employment opportunity and affirmative action.[12]

Communications Provisions

It is important for the EEO policy and affirmative action plan to be fully publicized, both internally and externally. Virginia Beach provides for communication of the plan to department heads and supervisors, all other employees, job applicants, and the general public. Highlights of the city's communication strategy include the following methods.[13]

Supervisors and department heads. Copies of the plan are distributed in conjunction with meetings to explain it attended by the city manager, director of personnel, and EEO/AA coordinator. There are provisions for training sessions to communicate legal requirements and for sensitivity and awareness training for these personnel to "explore attitudinal and employment barriers which may affect their hiring practices." Executive and administrative personnel are held accountable for having individual affirmative action goals as well as other performance evaluation goals.

All employees. Orientation and supervisory skills training includes information on EEO requirements. EEO and sexual harassment policies and discrimination complaint procedures are posted on the city's bulletin board, and EEO articles are included in city publications. The EEO/AA coordinator is available to meet with employees to inform them of the plan.

Applicants and the general public. All recruitment sources are notified in writing annually of the city's EEO policies and affirmative action plan. Minority media are used for recruitment efforts, and minority, female, and disabled employees are pictured in promotional materials. All city contracts, purchase orders, and leases must have an EEO clause and provide for revocation in cases of noncompliance. In order to inform the general public, the city's affirmative action plan is summarized in a brochure which is distributed to community leaders and citizens.

Utilization Survey and Action Plan

The next major component is a utilization survey to determine the existence and extent of underutilization of women and minorities in departments and major occupational classifications. Underutilization exists when the percentage of minorities and women in an occupational category is lower than that found in the relevant labor market. In Virginia Beach, this survey was conducted as follows:

> An internal analysis of the City's workforce was completed by race, sex, and EEO job categories. Additionally, an external analysis was conducted using the appropriate relevant labor market areas. The combined analysis provides a basis for determining how our City is utilizing the available labor markets to fill its jobs and obtain and maintain proportional representation....Utilization of minorities and females at the departmental level will be analyzed by the EEO/AA Coordinator on a quarterly basis and reports shall be provided to the City Manager....[14]

Based on the results of the utilization study, the next major component is the "action plan," which sets forth specific steps to be taken in order to eliminate discriminatory practices and correct underutilization. Timetables or target dates for implementation are specified, and one or more units of the organization are assigned responsibility for accomplishing each EEO goal. Virginia Beach's action steps are divided into five broad categories: (1) recruitment, (2) selection and placement, (3) compensation, (4) training and development, and (5) miscellaneous. Table 9.1 provides examples drawn from each category.

Monitoring and Evaluation

The affirmative action plan should provide for ongoing monitoring or auditing of progress toward achieving EEO goals and objectives. Not only does a sincere commitment to EEO require careful program evaluation, but auditing is critical because of the possibility of legal sanctions against the employer if the EEO program is not implemented properly. Accordingly, a record-keeping system should be developed to keep track of sex and race and ethnicity representation as regards applicant flow, hiring, wages and benefits, promotion, transfer, demotion, layoff and recall, disciplinary action and discharge, and training and career development programs.[15] These data are used to track progress toward EEO goals and to identify problem areas that must be addressed.

The Virginia Beach plan requires the EEO/AA coordinator to conduct a quarterly analysis of the utilization of minorities and women on the departmental level. These reports are provided to the city manager and the director of personnel and to department heads

Table 9.1   City of Virginia Beach Action Steps 1989–1990 Affirmative Action Plan

Recruitment	Responsibilities	Target Date
Identify potential recruitment sources for protected class members	Testing and selection EEO/AA coordinator	Continuing
Design recruitment literature/ videos with photographs of protected-class members	Testing and selection	June 1989
Selection and Placement	**Responsibilities**	**Target Date**
Revise selection procedures for management and midmanagement to improve entry and upward mobility opportunities	Testing and selection	1989
Identify protected-group employees and community persons available to participate in selection committees	Testing and selection EEO/AA coordinator Department heads	Continuing
Compensation	**Responsibilities**	**Target Date**
Review new and existing positions to ensure proper classification and eliminate any possibility of discrimination	Compensation	Continuing
Training and Development	**Responsibilities**	**Target Date**
Include EEO training in general supervisory training programs	EEO/AA coordinator Training and development	Continuing
Provide appropriate training opportunities for employees on all levels	Training and development	Continuing
Miscellaneous	**Responsibilities**	**Target Date**
Include in the monthly personnel report statistics on minority and disabled workers	Compensation	April 1989
Establish EEO/AA goals for all executive/administrative personnel	Department heads	Continuing
Send all bids, as appropriate, to minority contractors and require EEO clause in all contracts	Purchasing City attorney	Continuing
Provide appropriate workshops to enhance personal and career development	Training and development Employee relations	Continuing

to assist departments in monitoring hiring and promotional practices within their own departments and functional areas. In Virginia Beach, top management monitors implementation of the plan on all levels of the organization.

The city manager is responsible for periodically reporting the plan's progress to the city council and assuring the development of effective monitoring mechanisms. Deputy and assistant city managers are held accountable for seeing to it that the provisions and intentions of the plan are carried out in their assigned departments. They review and evaluate departmental employment practices and statistics, develop progress reports, and make recommendations to the director of personnel and the EEO/AA coordinator.

Department heads have primary responsibility for implementation and evaluation, including making sure that supervisors understand the plan and have the information and resources needed to implement it effectively. Department heads must include support of the plan as part of the annual performance evaluation of all supervisory personnel. They also must attend training sessions and develop budgets that provide the funds needed to carry out provisions of the plan.

The director of personnel, who has overall responsibility for administration of the plan, is charged with monitoring progress and recommending changes and improvements to the city manager. In support of the director of personnel, the EEO/AA coordinator has several important duties, including:

1. Developing and implementing auditing and monitoring systems that permit continual measurement of the effectiveness of the Affirmative Action Plan.
2. Comparing the available data on the participation of minorities and women in the labor force with the city's work-force data on a quarterly basis to identify possible areas of underutilization. These findings are reported to the director of personnel.
3. Providing quarterly work-force analysis reports to management in order to monitor progress on a departmental basis.
4. Conducting regular audits on hiring and promotional patterns and techniques to ensure that the provisions of the plan are being carried out and its goals and objectives are being met.

The EEO Advisory Committee participates in the monitoring process by submitting its own quarterly reports to the city manager on EEO progress and needs. It also contributes to monitoring efforts by reviewing and responding to reports developed by the EEO/AA coordinator and the director of personnel.

Evidence of Commitment

Affirmative action plans also should offer concrete evidence of the employer's commitment to advancing EEO. This final component usually takes the form of brief descriptions of specific policies, practices, and good-faith efforts. The City of Virginia Beach gives several examples in its plan.

Recruitment and selection. The city targets minority and disability-related organizations, minority media, and schools with high proportions of minorities and women in its recruitment efforts. It does everything possible to assure nondiscriminatory selection procedures, and it provides accommodations to help persons with disabilities take examinations.

Upward mobility and promotional procedures. Employees are encouraged to seek promotions and transfers to new or challenging jobs. In support of this policy, career ladders and "bridging positions" have been created to allow employees to change career paths. Career counseling is available, and there is a tuition reimbursement program to support employee-development goals. The personnel department also offers training courses in areas such as reading, mathematics, and computer use.

EEO discrimination complaint procedure. This procedure provides a means for internal resolution of complaints of sexual harassment or discrimination based on race, color, national origin, sex, age, religion, or disability. Under the appropriate circumstances, it may be used as an alternative to the general employee grievance procedure.

Disabled employee assistance. Virginia Beach provides funding to an independent living center for severely disabled adults. The center's staff has conducted sensitivity awareness programs regarding persons with disabilities for the city's department heads, and the EEO/AA coordinator helps the center find employment for its residents. The city has also worked with other local agencies to provide both unpaid work experience and placement of disabled persons in city jobs, where they are accommodated on an as-needed basis.

Internship programs. A Municipal Fellows Summer Program offers an opportunity for college students to work for the city in their field of study as paid summer interns. In 1988, eight of the nine interns were members of protected-class groups (i.e., minorities, women, or disabled persons).

GOALS, TIMETABLES, AND QUOTAS

Although affirmative action involves far more, the term is often treated as synonymous with the use of goals, timetables, and quotas for the hiring and promotion of minorities and women. In fact, however, the courts have consistently made it clear that voluntary affirmative action plans should not impose fixed quotas on any aspect of the personnel system, but involuntary plans, imposed by the federal courts, may include numerical hiring and promotion ratios. If remedial goals and timetables are carefully tailored to address specific EEO problems and "avoid trammelling the legitimate interests of nonminority or male employees," they are legally acceptable components of voluntary affirmative action plans.[16]

Goals and timetables were first used by an EEO enforcement agency in 1968, when the Office of Federal Contract Compliance Programs of the Department of Labor (DOL) required contractors to develop "specific goals and timetables for the prompt achievement of full and equal opportunities." In 1971, the U.S. Civil Service Commission (CSC) issued a policy statement encouraging federal agencies to use goals and timetables in:

> ...problem areas where progress is recognized as necessary and where such goals and timetables will contribute to progress, i.e., in those organizations and localities and in those occupations and grade levels where minority employment is not what should reasonably be expected in view of the potential supply of qualified members of minority groups in the work force....[17]

Controversy quickly developed over the extent to which "goals" are actually "quotas" that must be met by a given date. Critics argued that quotas are illegal under Title VII of the Civil Rights Act. As this controversy intensified, the CSC, the EEOC, and the DOL's Office of Federal Contract Compliance Programs issued a joint memorandum in which they tried to distinguish between goals and quotas, as follows:

> A quota system, applied in the employment context, would impose a fixed number or percentage which must be attained or which cannot be exceeded; the crucial consideration would be whether the mandatory numbers of persons have been hired or promoted. Under such a quota

system, that number would be fixed to reflect the population in the area, or some other numerical base, regardless of the number of potential applicants who meet necessary qualifications. If the employer failed, he would be subject to sanctions....

A goal, on the other hand, is a numerical objective, fixed realistically in terms of the number of vacancies expected, and the number of qualified applicants available in the relevant job market. Thus, if through no fault of the employer, he has fewer vacancies than expected, he is not subject to sanction, because he is not expected to displace existing employees or to hire unneeded employees to meet his goal. Similarly, if he has demonstrated every good faith effort to include persons from the group which was the object of discrimination into the group being considered for selection, but has been unable to do so in sufficient numbers to meet his goal, he is not subject to sanction.[18]

The joint memorandum goes on to state that because goals do not require employers to hire or promote unqualified candidates in order to meet numerical objectives, "a goal recognizes that persons are to be judged on individual ability, and therefore is consistent with the principles of merit hiring." Quotas, in contrast, "may call for a preference of the unqualified over the qualified, or of the less qualified over the better qualified."

While the difference between goals and quotas is clear in theory, it may be blurred in practice. Political, economic, and legal pressures on employers to achieve formal goals may have the effect of converting them into informal quotas. When President Bush vetoed the 1990 Civil Rights Act, he claimed that several of its provisions would have forced employers to set informal quotas in order to avoid expensive litigation. Under heavy political pressure, he signed a similar bill in 1991 (see Chapter 2).

Where the courts have imposed numerical ratios or quotas, they have been confronted with extreme, obvious cases of deeply entrenched discrimination by employers unwilling to take effective voluntary action. The usual approach for the courts has been to order the establishment of two eligibility lists: one for white males and another for women and/or minorities. Candidates are then selected from these lists in the ratio ordered by the court for a specified period, or until a representative work force is achieved in the job categories covered by the judicial order.

Situations such as these almost always give rise to complaints of reverse discrimination because the creation of two lists means that a white male with a test score higher than that of a woman or minority may be passed over repeatedly and may never be appointed. However, as we noted in Chapter 4, the validity of selection and promotion tests is often dubious. The courts have never ordered employers to hire or promote unqualified candidates, but they have questioned the assumption that those with the highest *passing* scores are necessarily the most qualified.

In an effort to have judicially mandated quotas declared unconstitutional by the Supreme Court, the Reagan administration challenged a federal court order requiring "one-for-one" promotion of African Americans in the Alabama Department of Public Safety if qualified candidates could be found. In this case, the judge had determined that the employer was not in compliance with the terms of a consent decree. In *United States* v. *Phillip Paradise* (1987),[19] the Court upheld the judge's action, ruling that the one-for-one promotion plan served not only a governmental interest but also the interests of society.[20] The standard applied had been set forth previously in *Wendy Wygant* v. *Jackson Board of Education* (1986),[21] a case involving voluntarily negotiated layoff procedures. In that case, where it had been proven that the employer had discriminated, Justice Sandra Day O'Connor wrote in her opinion:

> ...a public employer, consistent with the Constitution, may undertake an affirmative action program which is designed to further a legitimate remedial purpose and which implements that purpose by means that do not impose disproportionate harm on the interests, or unnecessarily trammel the rights of innocent individuals directly and adversely affected by a plan's racial preference.

Court Scrutiny of Preferential Treatment

While the conservative Supreme Court that is the heritage of the Reagan-Bush appointments may narrow the conditions under which affirmative action remedies are deemed legal and constitutional—and decisions such as *Wards Cove* and *McLean* (see Chapter 2) suggest that it is predisposed to do so—it has reaffirmed its support for the principle of affirmative action and "race and sex conscious relief." Recent decisions, however, emphasize the Court's inclination to subject all forms of preferential treatment to "strict scrutiny."[22] The basic standard is that the preferential treatment must serve a "compelling state interest," namely dismantling patterns of illegal discrimination and guaranteeing constitutional rights. Other factors that the courts are likely to consider concern the questions raised in the following paragraphs.

Is the plan carefully tailored to the specific problem and designed to avoid unnecessary intrusions on the interests and legitimate expectations of nonminorities and males? In their efforts to remedy past discrimination, employers should proceed with care and moderation. Flexible, gradual, and case-by-case methods that "realistically" deal with hiring and promotion decisions are strongly preferred by the Court.

How and with what degree of severity are others affected? Although "innocent" persons may be required to "share the burden" of correcting past injustices, the type of employment decision involved may be crucial. The Court stated in *Wygant* that layoffs of nonminority workers with more seniority than minorities would impose greater injury than hiring goals because "[d]enial of a future employment opportunity is not as intrusive as loss of an existing job." Similarly, denial of a promotion "unsettled no legitimate... expectation on the part of the petitioner."

Does the plan require or imply quotas and set-asides? Voluntary plans should not impose fixed ratios or quotas, and positions should not be set aside for minorities or women. Plans should explicitly state that goals are not to be treated as quotas. Affirmative action concerns should be a part of the overall evaluation of qualified applicants.

Is the plan clearly a temporary deviation from traditional merit practices? Although they do not have to set a termination date, affirmative action plans should contain language showing that the employer has no intention of using them permanently. "An affirmative action plan which both limits its long term goal to the attainment (not maintenance) of proportional representation and considers gender or race as a 'plus' factor in close decisions among qualified candidates will be considered sufficiently temporary under *Johnson*."[23]

Does the plan make some workers ineligible for promotion? There can be no absolute denial of promotional opportunities. Although they may not be promoted to a particular position because of an affirmative action remedy, nonminority and male employees should be eligible for other promotions.

Can the employer show that minorities and women who are hired or promoted under affirmative action programs are qualified for the positions? The Court has established the principle that sex and race may be used as factors "in choosing among closely qualified applicants."[24]

SENIORITY ISSUES IN AFFIRMATIVE ACTION

In recent years, as reductions in force have become more common in the public sector, affirmative action plans calling for preference for minorities and women in the order of layoffs have become controversial. The Bush and Reagan administrations considered preferential layoff policies to be an illegal and unconstitutional form of reverse discrimination.

During periods of growth in the public service, affirmative action goals are more likely to be attainable without win-lose situations in which the gains of minorities and women come at the expense of nonminorities. Stagnation or decline in the size of the work force, however, is likely to promote conflict, because one group or the other must lose. This is particularly true in the case of layoffs, where the rule of "last hired, first fired" has long been followed in negotiated agreements.

In the civil service, length of service is usually the single most important factor in determining the order of layoffs. Since minorities and women are likely to have less seniority because of past discrimination, they are often the first to be let go under traditional seniority systems. Thus, reductions in force can seriously undermine ongoing affirmative action programs and wipe out previous accomplishments.

The Civil Rights Act provides in Section 703(h) of Title VII:

> Notwithstanding any other provision in this title, it shall not be an unlawful employment practice for an employer to apply... different terms, conditions, or privileges of employment pursuant to a bona fide seniority or merit system... provided that such differences are not the result of an intention to discriminate.

Exactly what Congress meant by a bona fide seniority system has been a hotly debated issue. The legislative history may be interpreted in at least two ways. Many unions maintain that Congress intended to "immunize neutral seniority systems from attack even if such systems tended to perpetuate the effects of past discriminatory practices."[25] Minority and women's organizations strongly disagree, arguing that "Congress could not have intended to permit the continuation of employment practices that institutionalized the effects of past discrimination."[26]

During the 1970s and 1980s, the Supreme Court issued a series of decisions that clarified some issues. In *Franks* v. *Bowman Transportation Co.* (1976),[27] it ruled that a seniority system that perpetuates discrimination suffered by an employee *after* passage of the Civil Rights Act of 1964 must be changed, and retroactive seniority must be granted. In this case, the plaintiffs were discriminated against until 1972.

The following year, in *Teamsters* v. *United States* (1977),[28] the

Court ruled that the "literal terms of Section 703(h) and its legislative history demonstrate that the act was not meant to be applied retroactively." Accordingly, a bona fide seniority system that perpetuates pre-1964 discrimination is legal, and retroactive pay and seniority rights may not be granted. In this decision, the Court addressed an issue not resolved in *Franks* v. *Bowman*: whether those who had *not* applied for jobs because of the discriminatory practices could also be granted relief. It ruled that such relief could be granted to this category of employees because they must have been deterred from applying, considering it futile to do so in light of the employer's discriminatory practices. Under Title VII, court-ordered relief must compensate those actually harmed by a discriminatory action. The case therefore was remanded to the district court to determine the "actual relief to be granted...whether the individual plaintiff either was or would have been an applicant, whether the applicant was qualified and therefore would have been hired but for the unlawful practices, and whether and when vacancies...had occurred."

Franks v. *Bowman* and *Teamsters* v. *United States* were private-sector cases, but the federal courts have used them as precedents in deciding public-sector conflicts between seniority systems and affirmative action. Earlier in the 1970s, federal appeals and district courts had issued rulings in public-sector cases that were supported by *Franks* and *Teamsters*.

In *Chance* v. *Board of Examiners* (1972), a federal appeals court reversed a district court's approval of a rule providing for quotas in layoffs in order to maintain existing minority-white ratios. In effect, this rule would have meant that white supervisors with more seniority "could be laid off before junior minority employees." The appeals court ruled that "to lay off in such a manner would amount to 'constitutionally forbidden reverse discrimination.'" However, it approved the granting of "constructive seniority" to individual employees "denied promotion because of a test since invalidated as discriminatory." Specifically, the court agreed to the employer's offer to grant such workers a fictional date of employment which would be the mean (average) appointment date of those who did pass the examination.

Along similar lines, the same appeals court ruled in *Acha* v. *Beame* (1972) that if employees can prove that "but for the employer's discriminatory hiring practices" they would have been employed early enough to have the seniority needed to protect them from layoff, then laying them off would violate Title VII. The court limited relief to those who could show that they were actually the victims of discrimination.

In June 1984, in *Memphis* v. *Stotts*,[29] the Supreme Court did rule on the legality of court orders setting aside the normal seniority rights of workers who were not minorities. In 1980, under terms of a district court–approved consent decree, the City of Memphis adopted a goal of increasing minority representation in the fire department to about the same proportion of African Americans as in the labor force of Shelby County, Tennessee. The court decree said nothing about layoff policy in relation to this goal, and in 1981 the city announced that it would make layoffs following the rule of last hired, first fired. The district court then issued an order, later affirmed by the appeals court, requiring the city to refrain from applying a seniority policy that would lower the percentage of black employees in the fire department. In compliance with the court order, some nonminority employees were laid off or reduced in rank, but all were reemployed a month later, and those who had been demoted were offered their old positions.

Voting six to three, with Justice Byron White writing for the majority, the Court ruled that the case was not moot, since the district court's order remained in force and would have to govern any future reductions in force. Furthermore, noted White, the fired employees had lost a month's pay and seniority that had not been restored. The Court ruled that the district court's order was an improper modification of the original consent decree because that decree had made no mention of layoffs. On the preference issue, White wrote that the congressional debates on Title VII made it clear that relief could only be given to those who themselves have been the victims of illegal discrimination. Further, there had been no finding that the African Americans protected from layoff had been victims of discrimination, nor had awards of retroactive seniority been made to any of them. White cited *Teamsters* v. *United States* as establishing the precedent that mere membership in a class (minorities) was insufficient to justify a *seniority* award; each individual had to prove that he or she had been injured by a discriminatory practice.

Stotts caused great excitement in the Reagan administration, some of whose members expressed the belief that the Court was on the way to a blanket ban on all forms of preference established under affirmative action plans. This, however, was not the case.

Although the Supreme Court overturned racial preference in a negotiated layoff procedure in *Wygant* (1986), it did not challenge the constitutionality of affirmative action or race/gender preference under appropriate conditions. In other 1986 decisions, most notably *Firefighters* v. *City of Cleveland*[30] and *Sheet Metal Workers* v. *EEOC*,[31] the Court upheld the legality of voluntary agreements giving relief to persons who were not directly victimized by discriminatory practices, and it reaffirmed the courts' authority to "order race-conscious remedies." In the latter case, it stated that the purpose of affirmative action is "to dismantle prior patterns of employment discrimination and to prevent discrimination in the future. Such relief is provided to the class as a whole rather than to individual members; no individual is entitled to relief, and beneficiaries need not show that they were themselves victims of discrimination."

AFFIRMATIVE ACTION: EFFECTS AND PROSPECTS

Although the lasting effects of affirmative action policies and programs are difficult to isolate, minorities and women did make substantial progress in the public sector during the 1970s.[32] This is not to say that the goal of a representative public service was achieved in many occupational categories and on the higher levels of the civil service. It is nevertheless fair to say that EEO became a serious policy objective in thousands of jurisdictions across the country, and this objective was supported by personnel reforms designed to eliminate unintentional as well as intentional forms of employment discrimination.

Starting with the Civil Rights Act of 1964, the federal government assumed a leading role in the effort to make EEO the foundation of both public- and private-sector employment, and it rather consistently supported affirmative action programs. During the 1980s, however, the Reagan administration orchestrated a determined effort to scale back the government's enforcement of EEO policy. Florence Perman, former director of the Federal Women's Program in the U.S. Department of Health and Human Services, reported in 1988 that in the preceding seven years, actions (or inactions) and policies of the EEOC, the Office of Federal Contract Compliance Programs, and the Employment Litigation Section of the Civil Rights Division of the Justice Department had brought "enforcement of national policy on EEO...to a standstill."[33]

The Reagan administration opposed race- and sex-conscious remedies as reverse discrimination. It asserted that those who are not directly discriminated against are not entitled to any relief and argued that affirmative action undermines the functioning of a free market economy. The Justice Department contested numerical goals and court-ordered remedies for classes, and the EEOC, endorsing the administration's contention that goals and timetables are quotas, abandoned them.[34] Perman concluded:

...it is clear that for federal enforcement of equal employment opportunity the rule of law was replaced in the 1980s by the rule of men for whom ideology was the criterion for action. When they could not persuade the Congress or the U.S. Supreme Court that affirmative action and goals and timetables were unconstitutional, they ignored their failure and let ideology drive their public policy actions.[35]

The degree to which the Reagan and Bush administrations' hostility to affirmative action actually eroded previous gains by minorities and women is uncertain. Many federal administrators continued to enforce standing EEO and affirmative action programs, despite pressure to do otherwise from the White House.[36] The inauguration of President Clinton in 1993 abruptly ended 12 years of presidential hostility toward affirmative action. He has promised to support it and other programs designed to promote diversity in the work force.

The 1990s as a whole will almost certainly be characterized by ongoing political and legal conflict over the meaning of EEO and methods of affirmative action. This struggle is taking place in the context of continuing social and demographic changes, as we noted in Chapter 1. Minorities and women are becoming the new majority in the labor force, and this reality will shape our definition of affirmative action in the 1990s and beyond.

■

NOTES

1. Karen Ann Olsen, *Equal Employment Opportunity and Affirmative Action: A Guide for Mayors and Public Officials Prepared by Labor Management Relations Service* (Washington, DC: United States Conference of Mayors, 1979), p. 17.
2. U.S. Equal Employment Opportunity Commission, "Affirmative Action Guidelines," Part XI, *Federal Register*, vol. 44, no. 14 (January 15, 1979), p. 4422.
3. Bonnie G. Cebulski, *Affirmative Action versus Seniority: Is Conflict Inevitable?* (Berkeley, CA: Institute of Industrial Relations, University of California, 1977), p. 3.
4. Thomas Sowell, "Affirmative Action Reconsidered," *Public Interest*, vol. 42 (Winter 1976), p. 48.
5. Ibid.
6. U.S. Equal Employment Opportunity Commission, *Affirmative Action and Equal Employment: A Guidebook for Employers*, Vol. 1 (Washington, DC, 1974), p. 13.

7. U.S. Equal Employment Opportunity Commission, "Affirmative Action Guidelines," *Federal Register*, vol. 44, no. 13 (January 19, 1979), p. 4426.
8. 55 U.S.C. W. 4379 (1987).
9. Steven M. Woodside and Jan Howell Marx, "Walking the Tightrope between Title VII and Equal Protection: Public Sector Voluntary Affirmative Action after *Johnson* and *Wygant*," *The Urban Lawyer*, vol. 20, no. 2 (Spring 1988), pp. 367–388.
10. City of Virginia Beach, *1989–1990 Affirmative Action Plan* (Virginia Beach, VA: Office of the City Manager, January 1989), p. 23.
11. Ibid., p. 10.
12. Ibid., p. 5.
13. Ibid., pp. 15–16.
14. Ibid., p. 3.
15. Olsen, *Equal Employment Opportunity and Affirmative Action.*
16. Woodside and Marx, "Walking the Tightrope," pp. 385–388.
17. Elliot Zashin, "Affirmative Action, Preferential Selection and Federal Employment," Public Personnel Management, vol. 7, no. 6 (November–December 1978), pp. 383–384.
18. Joint memorandum from the U.S. Civil Service Commission, the U.S. Equal Employment Opportunity Commission, and the Office of Federal Contract Compliance Programs of the Department of Labor, "Permissible Goals and Timetables in State and Local Government Employment Practices," March 23, 1973.
19. 107 S.Ct. 1053 (1987).
20. Krishna K. Tummala, "Affirmative Action: A Status Report," *International Journal of Public Administration*, vol. 14, no. 3 (1991), p. 395.
21. 54 LW 4485 (1986).
22. Tummala, "Affirmative Action," p. 396.
23. See Woodside and Marx, "Walking the Tightrope," pp. 388.
24. Ibid., p. 387.
25. Robert N. Roberts, "'Last Hired, Fired' and Public Employee Layoffs: The Equal Employment Opportunity Dilemma," *Review of Public Personnel Administration*, vol. 2, no. 1 (Fall 1981), p. 31.
26. Ibid.
27. 424 U.S. 747 (1976).
28. 431 U.S. 324 (1977).
29. 52 LW 4764 (1984).
30. 106 S.Ct. 3063 (1986).
31. 92 L. Ed. 2nd 344 (1986), pp. 386-387.
32. J. Edward Kellough, "Integration in the Public Workplace: Determinants of Minority and Female Employment in Federal Agencies," *Public Administration Review*, vol. 50, no. 5 (September–October 1990), pp. 557–566.
33. Florence Perman, "The Players and the Problems in the EEO Enforcement Process: A Status Report," *Public Administration Review*, vol. 46, no. 4 (July–August 1988), p. 832.
34. Tummala, "Affirmative Action," p. 387.

35. Perman, " The Players and the Problems," p. 832.
36. Gregory B. Lewis, "Progress toward Racial and Sexual Equality in Federal Civil Service?" *Public Administration Review*, vol. 48, no. 3 (May–June 1988), p. 705–706.

New Issues and Challenges in the 1990s

III

AIDS and the
Public Service

10

Personnel administration in the 1990s is deeply involved in the human problems of employees in the public service. Alcoholism, substance abuse and addiction, chronic physical and mental illness, and other tragedies afflicting public employees are no longer simply ignored or handled by dismissal at the first opportunity, nor are applicants with a history of such problems automatically excluded from consideration for employment. Instead, the emphasis is on prevention, treatment, or accommodation. Many public employers offer programs to educate workers about health risks, make counseling and other support services available, include drug and alcohol rehabilitation and psychological care in their insurance benefits, and accommodate workers with disabilities. They are concerned with the physical and social-psychological effects on workers of addiction, mental illness, and a wide range of physical disabilities, including chronic diseases such as cancer, diabetes, and most recently, AIDS, or acquired immunodeficiency syndrome.

The spread of AIDS has had sociocultural, political, and psychological effects on public employers. The issues raised are not unique to AIDS but apply to any life-threatening communicable disease. Fortunately, most of these diseases may be prevented with vaccines or successfully treated with modern drugs. AIDS does not fall into either category.

The first reports of an unusual type of immune system disease started to appear in the United States among gay men in June 1981. A little more than a decade later, at the Eighth International AIDS Conference held at Amsterdam in July 1992, *Time* magazine reported a somber mood, "reflecting a decade of frustration, failure and mounting tragedy." Billions of dollars had been spend on research and education and other attempts at prevention, but humanity did not seem to be any closer to conquering the disease. As *Time* put it, "There is no vaccine, no cure and not even an indisputably effective treatment."[1]

Thus AIDS now confronts public employers with a rapidly spreading disease that threatens to become one of the leading causes of disability and death among young and middle-aged workers, who historically have been relatively low-risk groups. Estimates of the number of Americans infected with the human immunodeficiency virus (HIV) that causes AIDS and the number of reported cases and deaths due to the disease must be differentiated carefully. The American Foundation for AIDS research (AmFAR), a health-related organization that solicits funds for research, education, and public policy purposes, estimated in January 1993 that over 1.5 million Americans were carrying the AIDS virus. According to the U.S. Centers for Disease Control (CDC), the cumulative number of AIDS cases between 1984, when AIDS first became a notifiable disease, and June 30, 1992, was 230,179, and there had been 152,153 deaths.[2] In 1991 alone, 43,671 cases were reported to the CDC, 45.6 percent of them people between the ages of 30 and 39 and 87 percent of them males.[3] The death rate from AIDS in 1991 was 11.3 per 100,000, one of the fastest growing causes of death in the United States.[4]

Public personnel is most directly concerned with the number of people in the work force with active AIDS or infected with HIV. In its issue of January 25, 1993, *U.S. News & World Report*, using data from the Agency for Health Care Policy and Research of the CDC, reported that the U.S. labor force included 20,800 workers with active AIDS and 44,800 who had been identified as carrying HIV. Two-thirds of large companies and 1 in 12 small businesses reported they had knowingly employed a worker with AIDS or HIV.[5]

AIDS therefore is not only a disaster for individual victims and their families and a social and economic threat to American society, it is also at least potentially a calamity for public as well as private employers. In this chapter, we will examine AIDS as a workplace problem, one that public employers must deal with now and in the foreseeable future.

EMPLOYERS' INFORMATIONAL AND EDUCATIONAL PROGRAMS

Among the many difficult problems AIDS presents to employers, not the least is widespread fear and ignorance. Despite a decade of efforts to educate the American public, a substantial proportion still does not have a firm grasp of the scientifically established facts related to the transmission of the HIV virus. The high level of ignorance in the United States is compounded by the relationship between AIDS and homosexuality and intravenous drug use that marked its initial appearance.

Many Americans still assume that if they are not homosexual males or intravenous drug users, the only way they can become infected is if they received a contaminated blood transfusion before 1985, when screening of donated blood became standard practice. But the number of heterosexually transmitted cases is increasing in the United States. In August 1992, *Time* reported that in AIDS clinics in large urban areas such as San Francisco and New York City, women made up 30–50 percent of all new patients, and about half of them had become infected through heterosexual contact. More women also were passing on the virus to their children in childbirth.[6]

At the other extreme are those who believe that AIDS can be transmitted through casual contact, such as sharing a glass of water, hugging, or shaking hands. There has been no credible evidence to support such fears. Despite the obvious need to educate employees about the causes and consequences of AIDS, by 1987 less than 40 percent of the nation's public employers had AIDS education programs in place.[7]

Public employees have the same beliefs and fears as the general population. Unless accurate, up-to-date information about AIDS is made available to all members of the organization, the workplace is likely to be rife with rumors, hostility toward AIDS victims, and irrational concerns about the risks involved. In addition to the risks of infection associated with ignorance and misperceptions, morale and productivity may be affected.

Programs designed to inform and educate can be carried out in many ways. In the federal service, the Guidelines for AIDS–HIV Information and Education issued by the Office of Personnel Management suggest the following means of providing information to employees about AIDS: agency news bulletins, personnel management directives, meetings with employees, expert speakers and counselors, question-and-answer sessions, films and audiotapes, employee newsletters, union publications, fact sheets, pamphlets, and brochures. Employee assistance programs (EAPs), which allow workers to talk with professional counselors confidentially, are described in the guidelines as an excellent source of information and advice. Employees who do not know much about the disease and associate it strictly with sex and drugs often are afraid and reluctant to openly admit their ignorance. Moreover, a worker who is HIV positive or who has a family member at risk for AIDS may hesitate to reveal it to supervisors or coworkers for fear of discrimination or loss of insurance coverage. EAPs can offer not only factual information but nonjudgmental support and counseling that is urgently needed by many employees and family members.

AIDS information and education programs should have strong training components. The OPM recommends that federal agencies establish training and education programs on the medical and personnel management dimensions of AIDS for all managers and supervisors. In the OPM's words:

> These programs can be used to educate managers and supervisors on the latest research on AIDS in the workplace, to provide advice on how to recognize and handle situations which may arise in their organizations, and to convey the importance of maintaining the confidentiality of any medical and other information about employees' health status.[8]

The Department of Defense (DOD) has developed a very structured HIV/AIDS education program that requires each of its uniformed services to establish policies to implement the program and ensure that commanders receive educational information about HIV.[9]

Agency educational programs should be based on established facts and communicated in a clear, unbiased manner. Employees' anxieties, feelings of shame, and tendencies to assign guilt must also be addressed. One example of such an effort is the following statement in the Policy on the HIV/AIDS Epidemic adopted in 1990 by the City of Los Angeles:

> Persons with HIV diseases are not to blame for their illnesses. AIDS education and awareness programs must emphasize that all persons with AIDS are innocent, and deserving of care and compassion. It is inaccurate and counterproductive to refer to some persons with HIV as "innocent victims," as if others are guilty of something.[10]

In the long term, effective education about HIV/AIDS in the nation's schools and information provided to the public by the mass media should establish a solid foundation for programs conducted by public employers. In the short term, however, public agencies must expect to shoulder major responsibilities in this area.

AIDS POLICIES IN THE PUBLIC SECTOR

A common argument against having a personnel policy on a given problem is that it may deny the organization and its managers the flexibility they need to deal with unforeseen situations. This approach makes sense when not enough is known about the problem to allow the development of a prescribed way of dealing with it, which may have applied to AIDS in the early 1980s but no longer is the case. A great deal is now known about the disease, the virus that causes it, and how it is transmitted from one person to another. Accordingly, formal policies for dealing with it in the workplace are appropriate and needed.

After a slow start during the 1980s (fewer than 20 percent of public employers had a formal policy by 1987), federal, state, and local governments are moving rapidly to establish basic policy guidelines to be followed by public employers. The City of Los Angeles was the first jurisdiction in the country to set forth a formal policy in an ordinance passed in 1985 that prohibited discrimination against persons suffering from AIDS.[11] Similar legislation was passed in a few other states and municipalities. On the national level, the federal courts have issued rulings that, together with the Americans with Disabilities Act of 1990, have established AIDS policies to be followed by employers throughout the country.

In adopting their own policies of nondiscrimination, public employers have had to deal with active discrimination against persons with AIDS in employment, housing, education, and public services. Should public employers hire people who are HIV positive or have active cases of AIDS? Should employees who are diagnosed after they are hired be separated from or treated differently than other workers? As they seek answers to such questions, public employers must rely on their understanding of the disease, human resources management concepts, and the direction of legislatures and the courts.

The Courts and AIDS: The Arline Case

In March 1987, the U.S. Supreme Court ruled that a person may not be discriminated against in employment *simply* because he or she has a contagious disease. In *School Board of Nassau County, Florida, et al.* v. *Arline*,[12] the Court stated that there had to be strong medical evidence of a substantial danger of transmission to others before any action could be taken against those having a contagious disease. The *Arline* decision strongly supports the proposition that AIDS is to be treated as a handicap or disability, and therefore that its victims are protected against discrimination by the Vocational Rehabilitation Act of 1973 (Section 504).

Gene Arline taught elementary school in Nassau County from 1966 until 1979. She had been hospitalized for tuberculosis in 1957, but for the next 20 years her condition was in remission. Then in 1977, and again in 1978, she suffered a relapse. At the end of the 1978–1979 school year, the school board discharged her, "not because she had done anything wrong," but because of the continued recurrence of tuberculosis. After exhausting the available administrative appeals, Arline sued in a U.S. district court, claiming that her condition made her a "handicapped individual," and she had been dismissed solely because of her handicap.

Section 504 of the Rehabilitation Act of 1973 contains the following language: "[N]o otherwise qualified handicapped individual ... shall, solely by reason of his handicap, be excluded from participation in, be denied the benefits of, or be subjected to discrimination under any program or activity receiving Federal financial assistance." The following year, Congress expanded the definition of the term *handicapped individual* by adding these words: "[A]ny person who (i) has a physical or mental impairment which substantially limits one or more of such individual's major life activities, (ii) has a record of such impairment, or (iii) is regarded as having such an impairment." Department of Health and Human Services (HHS) regulations define major life activities as "functions such as caring for one's self, performing manual tasks, walking, seeing, hearing, speaking, breathing, learning, and working."

The district court ruled against Arline because it did not regard her as a handicapped person under the act; even if she were, she was not considered qualified to teach in an elementary school because of the danger to her students. The U.S. Court of Appeals disagreed, holding that persons with contagious diseases are covered by Section 504. It remanded the case to the district court for further findings concerning the extent to which Arline's condition created risks to students that disqualified her from teaching. If the court deemed the risks substantial, it was to determine if some reasonable accommodation could be made for her employment as a teacher or in some other position.

On appeal, the Supreme Court affirmed, and Justice William Brennan stated in the majority opinion:

The fact that *some* persons who have contagious diseases may pose a serious health threat to others under certain circumstances does not justify excluding from the coverage of the Act all persons with actual or perceived contagious diseases. Such exclusion would mean that those accused of being contagious would never have the opportunity to have their condition evaluated in light of medical evidence and determination made as to whether they were "otherwise qualified." Rather they would be vulnerable to discrimination on the basis of mythology—precisely the type of injury the Congress sought to prevent.

Justice Brennan noted that the Supreme Court, like the Court of Appeals, did not have the facts needed to determine if Arline was "otherwise qualified" for her teaching position. The district court had not made any findings about the duration and severity of Arline's condition, had not examined the probability that she would communicate it to others, and had not determined if the school board had reasonably accommodated her. Therefore, the case was remanded to district court to "determine whether Arline [was] otherwise qualified for her position."

In its decision, the Court provided guidance in the form of a brief submitted by the American Medical Association, which recommended that:

... individualized inquiry should be conducted, based on: (1) the nature of the risk (how the disease is transmitted); (2) the duration of the risk (how long the carrier is infectious); (3) the severity of the risk (what is the potential harm to third parties); and (4) the probabilities the disease will be transmitted and cause varying degrees of harm.[13]

The next step, wrote Justice Brennan, was for the district court to determine if the employer could reasonably accommodate the employee in light of the medical findings.

The Supreme Court's reasoning in *Arline* has been applied to AIDS-related cases by the lower federal courts. Public employers seeking to discharge workers because they have AIDS, or to not hire them in the first place, should expect such actions to be subjected to close scrutiny under the provisions of Section 504 and the Court's guidelines. In *Arline*, the Court set a precedent that the contagiousness of AIDS and fear of contagion are not sufficient grounds for firing an employee. If employees with AIDS can still perform their jobs satisfactorily, there is no compelling reason for dismissal. Like any other disabled worker, employees with AIDS or HIV are entitled to reasonable accommodations by the employer.[14]

The Americans with Disabilities Act of 1990

Shortly after the *Arline* decision, the Congress included a provision in the Civil Rights Restoration Act of 1988 that amended the definition of the term *handicapped individual*. As a result, Section 504 now "protects all HIV–infected individuals, symptomatic or asymptomatic, who are not a direct threat to the health and safety of others . . . and who are able to perform the duties of the job."[15]

Then, in July 1990, Congress enacted more comprehensive legislation entitled the Americans with Disabilities Act, which prohibits discrimination against disabled persons in employment, public services and transportation, and public accommodations. Personnel functions covered by the act include job application and hiring procedures, promotions and dismissals, pay and other compensation, job training, and "other terms, conditions, and privileges of employment." It applies to all state and local governments as well as to the administrative agencies of the federal government. The legislative history of this act makes it clear that Congress has defined the term *disabled person* (like the term *handicapped individual*) to include those suffering from AIDS or infected with HIV.

MANDATORY TESTING FOR HIV

Public employers may be tempted to adopt policies requiring mandatory testing of employees and job applicants for HIV on the grounds that the workplace must be made safe, even if the risk of transmission is low. This was the reasoning of the Eastern Nebraska Community Office of Retardation (ENCOR), a unit of the Eastern Nebraska Human Service Agency, which provides a variety of social and medical services for the mentally retarded. When ENCOR management became alarmed by the possibility that HIV could be transmitted from staff members to retarded clients, a policy was adopted in 1988 that required HIV testing for persons holding or applying for several job titles. These positions included home teachers, residential assistants, vocational program managers, and registered and practical nurses, all of which involve extensive contact with clients. ENCOR employees in these positions responded by bringing a class action suit in federal district court, arguing that mandatory testing for HIV violates their Fourth Amendment right "to be secure in their persons, houses, papers, and effects, against unreasonable searches and seizures."

The reasoning used by the district court in reaching its decision in *Patricia Ann Glover et al.* v. *Eastern Nebraska Office of Retardation*[16] offers useful guidelines for public employers considering mandatory testing. The court concluded that the ENCOR policy was not reasonable and therefore violated the constitutional rights of the affected employees. It observed initially that ENCOR staff had received extensive training "to enable them to deal with violent and/or aggressive clients in a nonabusive manner." Although violent and aggressive behavior was not typical of ENCOR's clients, enough cases had occurred for the court to conclude from the evidence that the training was highly effective. This finding, in combination with extensive medical testimony, led the court to conclude that the risk of transmission from staff to clients was "near zero."

As to the primary rights of the employees bringing the suit, the court declared that "the mandatory testing required by the policy [was]...an involuntary intrusion into the body by the State for the purpose of withdrawing blood and constitutes a search and seizure for purposes of the Fourth Amendment." Having decided that the Fourth Amendment applied, the court then had to decide if this invasion of individuals' privacy was reasonable. In this case, under this set of circumstances, and in light of an almost "non-existent" risk of transmission, the court ruled that ENCOR's managers had gone too far. In its words, ENCOR had attempted to implement a sweeping policy that "ignored" and "violated" its employees' constitutional rights.

Public employers should consider mandatory HIV testing for job applicants and current employees only for positions where there is a meaningful risk of transmission. Otherwise, unless the employer is able to show that being HIV positive will make it impossible for the individual concerned to perform satisfactorily, no compelling reason exists for mandatory testing. In addition to the Fourth Amendment issue, actions taken against those testing positive would probably be judged discriminatory under existing law.

The most widely used test for HIV antibodies (enzyme-linked immunosorbent assay, or ELISA) often produces false positives. ELISA is an extremely conservative test developed to screen donated blood; according to some estimates, up to 80 percent of positive test results may be false. A second ELISA test is almost always recommended when a positive result is found, and a conclusive determination requires a different, more precise, procedure. In regard to the predictive value of the AIDS antibody tests, Robert Elliott and Thomas Wilson cite an article in the newsletter of the International Personnel Management Association that concluded, "there appears to be...little evidence in general to support the utility of screening for the virus for the purpose of detecting potential AIDS victims among applicants and employees."[17]

Overall, for the employer, the benefits of mandatory testing appear to be heavily outweighed by the costs. It may be appropriate under special circumstances, however. For example, if an employee is exposed to HIV through a needle-stick accident, efforts are made to identify the "source person." A statute may authorize testing of suspected source persons if they do not agree to it voluntarily.[18]

High-risk jobs may also warrant mandatory testing. In *American Federation of Government Employees* v. *The United States Department of State* (1987),[19] a district court refused to grant an injunction against testing of foreign service officers. Its reasoning was that while HIV-infected foreign service employees are considered handicapped under Section 504, they are not otherwise qualified for worldwide duty. In some countries, the court reasoned, medical facilities and sanitary conditions are so poor that there would be "sufficient prospect of serious harm" to weakened immune systems to justify testing before assigning people to these countries. Those testing positive could then be posted to countries where conditions are less risky.

Testing in the Department of Defense

The largest mandatory testing program is conducted by the Department of Defense. Uniformed personnel are often required to function under conditions that pose serious hazards for those infected with HIV. Combat and training situations also carry a substantial risk of transmission through wounds and injuries.

The DOD testing program consists of three components. First, all civilian applicants for military service are tested to prevent those infected with HIV from being appointed to or enlisting in the armed forces. Second, all active duty, reserve, and National Guard members undergo both initial HIV tests and retests in conjunction with periodic physical examinations. Third, testing of active-duty personnel is required of those who seek prenatal care or services for sexually transmitted diseases, or those who are enrolled in drug or alcohol programs. In 1990, the Army and Air Force planned to retest all personnel every two years; the Navy planned to retest all personnel in overseas and deployment units annually and other personnel in conjunction with their routine physical examinations.[20]

The DOD's comprehensive mandatory testing program for military personnel has four specific purposes:

1. To prevent assignment of HIV-infected service members to areas of endemic disease.
2. To make sure that those having the virus are not given live vaccine inoculations that might be hazardous to their health.
3. To help ensure the safety of the military's blood supply and to minimize the risk of transmission under battlefield conditions.
4. To respond to the requirements of some host countries that all entering soldiers be certified free from HIV.

Given the unusually high risks confronted by uniformed personnel and the potential for damage to military effectiveness, DOD's mandatory testing would appear to be a reasonable—indeed necessary—precaution. Moreover, excluding applicants who test positive protects them from a number of serious risks to their own health.

PROTECTING EMPLOYEES AND CLIENTS FROM HIV INFECTION

Although AIDS is not spread by casual contact, in some occupations there is a meaningful (although statistically low) risk of contracting HIV through contact with blood and body fluids. Doctors, dentists, nurses, laboratory workers, and others who routinely come into contact with these substances are in the greatest danger. Agency clients also need to be assured of protection from infection by health-care workers. Policies and guidelines designed to reduce the risk of contracting HIV for these two groups to the lowest level feasible are needed.

CDC Guidelines to Protect Employees

In the Health Omnibus Programs Extension Act of 1988, Congress directed the secretary of Health and Human Services to develop guidelines for reducing the risk of HIV transmission among health workers, public safety personnel, and emergency-response employees. The Centers for Disease Control has prepared and distributed these guidelines and has developed curriculum guides for use in training programs for those at risk of workplace exposure to HIV.[21] Rules requiring employers to follow the CDC's guidelines have been issued by the Occupational Safety and Health Administration (OSHA) of the Department of Labor.

Under the guidelines, employers classify work activities into one of three categories of potential exposure to HIV. Employees in the two highest categories of risk must be provided with certain protective gear. Employers must also prepare standard operating procedures (SOPs) for handling situations where there is the potential for exposure to HIV. Workers should be given training in these SOPs and on how to use protective equipment, and employers should monitor the workplace to ensure that required work procedures are followed and protective clothing and equipment are provided and properly used. Complete records must be maintained of all training activities and programs designed to prevent employees' exposure to HIV.

To the extent feasible, public employers are expected to implement administrative procedures that reduce the risk of exposure in the workplace. According to the CDC guidelines, for example, "jails and correctional facilities should have classification procedures that require the segregation of offenders who indicate through their actions or words that they intend to attack correctional-facility staff with the intent of transmitting HIV." Policies also should specify how to handle situations where an exposure to HIV may have taken place. If a source person has been identified, a blood sample should be drawn and tested immediately. If the test is positive, or the suspected source refuses to be tested, the worker who may have been exposed should be evaluated clinically for evidence of HIV infection as soon as possible after the exposure. These initial steps should be followed up with periodic retests. If the tests reveal that the exposed worker has contracted HIV, appropriate counseling and medical care should be made available.[22]

Protection of Agency Clients

The first strong evidence of HIV infection caused by a health-care worker was reported by the CDC in 1990. The agency's investigation revealed that a Florida dentist who died of AIDS, Dr. David Acer, apparently had infected a patient, Kimberly Bergalis (who died in 1991 after testifying to Congress on the hazard) and four other patients. Florida health officials advised all of Acer's 2,500 patients to be tested for HIV, and a teenaged girl became the sixth known victim in 1993. This case received national coverage by the media and unleashed a storm of controversy over three issues: Should periodic HIV testing be mandatory for doctors, dentists, nurses, and other health-care workers? Should those testing positive be required to reveal their condition to clients? And should those with HIV be limited in the kinds of services (e.g., invasive procedures such as surgery) they can provide, in order to minimize the possibility of transmission to patients and clients?

Needless to say, these questions are highly charged with the fears and uncertainties associated with AIDS. For the most part, the health-care professions have advocated a voluntary approach that relies heavily on the ethical obligation to protect patients. Even in the instance involving Dr. Acer, the means of transmission was unclear. Noting that proper sterilization procedures may not have been followed, *The New York Times* concluded that "equipment contaminated with HIV by use on other patients may have been more important in transmission than the dentist's HIV status." It was reported that the dentist "reused disposable equipment, did not always wear gloves and was seen using his own tools on himself."[23] The argument is that rather than trying to identify and segregate HIV-infected health-care providers, a more effective approach would be to see to it that all providers know and follow the rules on equipment use and sterilization.

In July 1991, the CDC issued new guidelines that stress careful adherence by health-care workers to standard infection-control measures. These guidelines recommend that those performing certain kinds of surgery should be tested voluntarily for HIV, and if they test positive, should get the informed consent of their patients before performing invasive procedures. Although these guidelines are not binding, they are influential because of the CDC's prestige. Mandatory testing was rejected by the CDC because the "chance of transmission from a doctor, dentist, nurse, or other health care worker to a patient is tiny."[24] In fact, the CDC data suggest that health-care workers are far more likely to be infected by patients.

Public opinion, informed and otherwise, is a major factor in this issue. One U.S. senator has proposed legislation that would impose long prison sentences on doctors who perform surgery without informing their patients that they are HIV positive. This kind of extreme response to public concerns demonstrates the need for public employers to do everything legally and technically possible to protect their clients from exposure to HIV.

PROBLEMS IN HUMAN RELATIONS AND SUPERVISION

If employees refuse to interact with coworkers who have AIDS or are known to be HIV positive, organizational productivity may suffer.

Although fear and hostility may not be rational in light of the medical evidence, these situations test the ability of managers and supervisors to educate and lead their subordinates.

Since much of the fear of AIDS is based on misinformation or prejudice, supervisors must know the medical facts and be able to communicate them. They also must be able to recognize and deal with interpersonal and group problems arising from AIDS-related situations. Once the source of these problems is identified, education and counseling are often effective remedies. Workers who are unable to overcome their fears or prejudices may have to be transferred or reassigned.

Supervisors' efforts to deal effectively and compassionately with workers' reactions to AIDS are more likely to be successful if their agencies have comprehensive policies in place. Nondiscrimination policies provide a firm basis for dealing with workers and others who demand that an AIDS victim be fired or physically isolated from coworkers or agency clients. Similarly, the existence of policies specifying procedures for identifying and handling situations that could involve the risk of exposure are of great value in establishing management's efforts to provide a safe work environment. The agency's expectations with regard to the behavior of supervisors must be clearly spelled out and visibly enforced. Public employers, in other words, must do whatever they can to create formal and informal organizational climates that discourage AIDS hysteria and give supervisors the tools they need to deal with the impact of AIDS in the workplace.

If employees do not respond to organizational and supervisory efforts to resolve a problem such as refusal to work with an HIV-infected coworker, the employer is justified in taking disciplinary measures. The OPM's Guidelines for AIDS/HIV Information and Education recommend "appropriate corrective or disciplinary action" if "an employee's unwarranted ... refusal to work with an HIV-infected employee is impeding or disrupting the organization's work."[25]

A related problem occurs when a health-care employee refuses to carry out assigned tasks on HIV-contaminated blood or body fluids. In one such instance, a laboratory worker in Indiana refused to perform tests on vials of blood to which AIDS warnings were affixed. The employer discharged the employee, and the Indiana Court of Appeals upheld this action. In this case, the employer convinced the Court that it had followed the CDC guidelines for protecting workers, and the employee had not demonstrated that the precautions taken by the organization were inadequate.

EMPLOYERS' INSURANCE COSTS AND FINANCIAL LIABILITIES

The cost of the AIDS epidemic to public employers goes beyond the issues already raised in this chapter. Informational and educational programs, mandatory testing, efforts to protect employees and clients from infection, human relations problems that result in lost productivity—all represent real costs to the employer. On an even larger scale, however, are the potential costs of providing insurance coverage for AIDS treatment for employees and dependents and meeting the liabilities that may result from lawsuits by employees who have been exposed to HIV in the workplace.

Medical and Disability Benefits

Medical and disability insurance costs to employers have skyrocketed over the past decade. In the absence of comprehensive national health care, employer insurance plans are essential, but they are increasingly difficult to finance as health-care costs continue to rise at rates far exceeding overall inflation. This situation has forced employers to take a serious look at what employee benefits they can afford to provide through their insurance programs.

In part, the continuing increases in health-care costs are a function of the availability of expensive new medical equipment and drugs. Many of the drugs currently used to inhibit HIV and to treat the opportunistic infections that characterize AIDS are very expensive, and the latter stages of the disease require intensive, around-the-clock care. Insurance carriers are raising premiums accordingly.

A problem for insurance companies, and for public employers paying premiums, is the prospect of millions of cases of AIDS over the next 20 years. For many conditions such as cancer and circulatory diseases, risk factors for specific populations have been established and there is relative confidence in projected claims costs. Estimates of the number of HIV-positive cases currently in the population vary widely, and this uncertainty means that premiums are likely to be based on worst-case projections of medical costs.

Typically, public employers negotiate contracts for group insurance plans for their workers with large private carriers. Alternatives include self-insurance and contracts with health maintenance organizations (HMOs). The goal is to offer the best possible health care and disability benefits for the available premium dollars. Employers may pay these premiums in full, or the cost may be shared with employees. In either case, group insurance plans are far less expensive than individually purchased insurance policies.

Under a group plan, of course, everybody receives the same coverage and benefits. Since the Rehabilitation Act of 1973 and the Americans with Disabilities Act of 1990 prohibit discrimination against handicapped or disabled persons with respect to all terms, conditions, and privileges of employment, victims of HIV/AIDS are entitled to the same sickness and disability benefits as are provided to other employees. Under law, they may not be excluded from these benefits.

Employers confronted with rapidly escalating insurance premiums thus do not have the option of lowering costs by refusing to cover certain employees for certain conditions such as AIDS. There is a possibility, therefore, that increasing numbers of public employers will be tempted to try to control costs by simply excluding *everybody* from coverage for these conditions. This is especially likely in self-insured organizations, which are not tightly regulated by state laws; moreover, the Supreme Court has let stand a lower-court decision that upheld an employer's right to decide what kind of health insurance coverage will be offered.[26] This option could be exercised by management unilaterally in some jurisdictions; in others, it would have to be negotiated with employee organizations or unions. Without insurance covering HIV/AIDS, employees would be forced to buy individual policies if they or their dependents become infected, or to try to qualify for two Social Security Administration programs: Supplemental Security Income (SSI) and Social Security Disability.

According to some observers, there are no legal restrictions on the employer's right to decide whether to provide AIDS-related coverage in a medical benefits package. Others are not so sure; Elliott and Wilson, for example, maintain that "all of the legal issues revolving around AIDS-related medical coverage are far from resolved, [and] it is apparent that, in the near future, the courts will necessarily give employers some guidance in this area."[27]

Liabilities of Public Employers

Employers may be held accountable if an employee contracts AIDS or suffers otherwise as the result of exposure to HIV in the workplace. The potential liability can be large in dollar terms if the employee sues and a court finds that the exposure was caused by the employer's negligence. Some public employers may be covered by statutes that make it possible for individuals to sue the government for damages. Others may find that the doctrine of sovereign immunity has been eroded to the point that it no longer protects them from civil suits and substantial damage awards.[28] To avoid the possibility of having to pay such costs, public employers must make every effort to see that employees are aware of how HIV is transmitted and take the proper precautions against contracting the virus in the workplace.

THE FUTURE OUTLOOK

When the first cases of AIDS were diagnosed in 1981, some medical experts predicted that the disease would be contained within a relatively short period. This optimistic scenario vanished as the number of AIDS cases increased rapidly and the difficulties associated with developing a vaccine for the HIV virus, a cure for the disease, or treatment for its complications became painfully obvious.[29] Because public employers cannot be isolated from the effects of AIDS on American society, personnel specialists must be prepared to help management respond to its effects in the workplace.

Public attitudes about AIDS initially reflected the belief that it is a disease of drug abusers and homosexuals. Policymakers were slow to respond with programs designed to educate the public about the risks to everybody, and prevention programs were halfhearted and underfunded. Most public employers made little or no effort to inform workers about the risk factors associated with AIDS. Today, with about 1.5 million Americans infected with HIV and overwhelming evidence that it crosses all social and geographic boundaries, it has become clear that the AIDS epidemic is a calamity that pervades American society—and the world.

Personnel policies in the 1990s will have to conform to the law and be based on available knowledge about how HIV is transmitted. More resources will have to be devoted to dealing with the organizational problems created by AIDS. Growing numbers of active cases of AIDS in the public work force will make the need for employee assistance, counseling, and other services more critical, and benefit plans, already under heavy financial pressure in many jurisdictions, will be subjected to further stress. Despite these difficulties, public employers, employee organizations, insurance carriers, and public policymakers will be expected to provide a decent and humane level of care for AIDS victims. Public personnel administration has an important role to play in meeting these challenges.

■

NOTES

1. Christine Gorman, "Invincible AIDS," *Time*, August 3, 1992, pp. 30–34.
2. "AIDS in the U.S.," *World Almanac and Book of Facts 1993* (New York: Pharos Books, 1992), p. 953.
3. U.S. Bureau of the Census, *Statistical Abstract of the United States: 1992*, 112th edition (Washington, DC, 1992), Table 192.
4. "AIDS in the U.S.," p. 954.
5. Amy Saltzman, "Ill—But Willing to Work," *U.S. News & World Report*, January 25, 1993, p. 72.
6. Gorman, "Invincible AIDS," p. 34.
7. John Matzer, Jr., "Introduction," in Matzer (ed.), *Personnel Practices for the '90s* (Washington, DC: International City Management Association, 1988), pp. xvi–xvii.
8. U.S. Office of Personnel Management, *Acquired Immune Deficiency Syndrome (AIDS) in the Workplace*, Federal Personnel Manual Letter 792-21 (Washington, DC, April 24, 1991), p. 3.
9. U.S. General Accounting Office, *Defense Health Care: Effects of AIDS in the Military* (Washington, DC, February 1990), p. 17.
10. City of Los Angeles, "Policy on the HIV/AIDS Epidemic," adopted by the Los Angeles City Council, October 16, 1990, p. 11.
11. See David I. Shulman, "AIDS Workplace Law and Policy: A Systematic Analysis," *St. Louis University Public Law Review*, vol. IX, no. 11 (1990), pp. 548–549.
12. No. 85–1277 (March 3, 1987).
13. See Robert H. Elliott and Thomas M. Wilson, "AIDS in the Workplace: Public Personnel Management and the Law," in Matzer (ed.), *Personnel Practices for the '90s*, p. 176.
14. Ibid., p. 179.
15. See Walter B. Connolly, Jr. and Alison B. Marshall, "An Employer's Legal Guide to AIDS in the Workplace," *St. Louis University Public Law Review*, vol. ix, no. 11 (1990), p. 567.
16. U.S. District Court, D. Nebraska, March 29, 1988, 686 Federal Supplement, p. 246.
17. Elliott and Wilson, "AIDS in the Workplace," p. 178.
18. See City of Los Angeles, "Policy on the HIV/AIDS Epidemic," pp. 16–18.
19. 662 Federal Supplement 50 (D.C. 1987).
20. U.S. General Accounting Office, *Defense Health Care*, pp. 12–13.
21. U.S. Department of Health and Human Services, Centers for Disease Control, National Institute for Occupational Safety and Health, *Guidelines for Prevention of Transmission of Human Immunodeficiency Virus and Hepatitis B Virus to Health Care and Public-Safety Workers* (Washington, DC, February 1989); and *Curriculum Guide for Public-Safety and Emergency Response Workers* (Washington, DC, February 1989).
22. U.S. Department of Health and Human Services, *Guidelines for Prevention of Transmission of Human Immunodeficiency Virus*, pp. 8–11.

23. David E. Rogers and Bruce G. Gellin, "AIDS and Doctors: The Real Dangers," *The New York Times*, July 16, 1991.
24. Ibid.
25. U.S. Office of Personnel Management, *Acquired Immune Deficiency Syndrome*, p. 5.
26. Saltzman, "Ill—But Willing to Work," pp. 74–75.
27. Elliott and Wilson, *AIDS in the Workplace*, p. 181.
28. Kenneth O. Eikenberry, "Governmental Tort Litigation and the Balance of Power," *Public Administration Review*, vol. 45 (November 1985), pp. 742–745.
29. See Gorman, "Invincible AIDS, " p. 31, and Susan Brink, "Triple Teaming the Deadly AIDS Virus," *U.S. News & World Report*, March 1, 1993, p. 60.

Drug and Alcohol Abuse

11

When the authors of the Pendleton Act (the Civil Service Act of 1883) included the statement that "no person habitually using intoxicating beverages to excess shall be appointed to, or retained in, any office, appointment, or employment to which the provisions of this act are applicable," they were recognizing a fact of American life. Americans have a long history of using and abusing alcohol and other intoxicating substances, and public employers have not been insulated from the effects of this problem. Postmaster General Amos Kendall's 13 rules of conduct for federal employees set forth in 1829 included one warning that "[g]ambling, drunkenness, and irregular and immoral habits will subject any clerk to instant removal."

The failed federal experiment with Prohibition (1919–1933) and today's faltering "war on drugs" reveal how difficult it has been to attempt to control, much less eliminate, the widespread use of illegal drugs and alcohol in American society. Like other social problems, alcoholism and drug abuse are not left at the entrance when public employees come to work. They confront public employers with real threats to productivity, workplace safety, and the well-being of coworkers, clients, and the public.[1] According to Robert Coulson and Mitchell Goldberg:

> American workers consume an *enormous* amount of alcohol and drugs. It has been estimated that twenty million sample marijuana, and

millions more are heavy drinkers. The consumption of such substances *saturates* our society. On the job, it creates many kinds of problems for management, including increased absenteeism and reduced productivity.[2] (emphasis added)

In recent years, public attention and the concern of policymakers have focused on illegal drugs such as cocaine, marijuana, and heroin. However, by far the largest percentages of respondents in the National Household Surveys of Drug Abuse by the U.S. National Institute on Drug Abuse report they have used or are using alcohol. In 1991, almost 89 percent of the respondents 26 years of age and older said they had used alcohol, and over 50 percent said they were current users. The percentage saying they were current users of illegal drugs that same year was minute in comparison: Marijuana was reportedly being used by less than 4 percent of respondents age 26 and older, cocaine by less than 1 percent, and heroin use reported was so small that it was not even included.[3] Labor authority Tim Bornstein says, "My experience as a labor arbitrator...confirmed by conversations with labor and management representatives, health care professionals, and a review of statistical data—has been that alcohol abuse is the most serious, widespread, and intractable problem in the workplace."[4]

Excessive drinking is a problem found on all levels of American society and in all occupational categories. It does not distinguish between executives, middle managers, or clerical workers. The damaging effects of alcohol abuse on the individual's health and the well-being of his or her family have been well documented. The organizational effects are also substantial: high rates of absenteeism, above-average use of sick leave, and more injuries on the job.[5] The costs to the organization and the taxpayer include those due to lost productivity and poor work quality, as well as outlays for sick leave, hospitalization, addiction treatment, and death benefits.

There are important social, political, and organizational reasons for the current emphasis on illegal drugs, in particular their connection with organized crime, violence, and social disorganization. Dealing with alcohol abuse, however, should also be a high priority for public as well as private employers.

THE MANDATORY DRUG-TESTING CONTROVERSY

Public personnel administrators are deeply involved in the controversial issue of mandatory testing of employees for drug or alcohol use. Some public employers, most notably police departments, national security agencies, and the armed forces, have been routinely testing job applicants for many years. As a part of the Reagan-Bush war on drugs, considerable pressure was exerted on public employers to provide a "drug-free workplace" by testing all applicants for civil service positions and requiring numerous workers to submit to periodic testing as a condition of employment. In addition to the obvious question of whether or not this approach represents an effective strategy for controlling substance abuse, attempts to enforce it have raised serious constitutional issues.

A number of state legislatures and local governments have passed laws dealing with substance abuse that include mandatory testing provisions. Efforts on the federal level were initiated in 1986 with the Reagan administration's Executive Order 12564, under which federal agencies were required to set up sweeping drug-testing programs. Public employee organizations and others have challenged the constitutionality of mandatory drug testing, especially where there is no concrete reason to suspect that an employee is using illegal drugs. One measure of the intensity of the issue is the number of federal court decisions on drug testing between 1987 and 1990: Out of a total of 136, 69 dealt with the public sector.[6]

Key Supreme Court Decisions

Prior to March 21, 1989, there had been much uncertainty about how the Supreme Court would rule on drug and alcohol tests in the workplace, since lower court decisions had failed to establish a consistent pattern and were at times contradictory. On that day, the Court handed down two important decisions related to mandatory testing of employees.

The Railway Labor Executives Case

The Court's ruling in *Samuel K. Skinner, Secretary of Transportation, et al. v. Railway Labor Executives' Association, et al.*[7] reaffirmed the long-standing tradition of balancing public against individual interests in Fourth Amendment cases. This case dealt with regulations of the Federal Railroad Administration (FRA) that permit railroads to require workers involved in train accidents to submit to blood and urine tests. The FRA had decided that government intervention was necessary because the railroad industry's efforts to curb workers' use of alcohol and drugs were not yielding satisfactory results. In the process of reviewing the industry's accident investigation reports, the agency had identified a long list of serious incidents in which alcohol or drug use was a contributing factor.

The Railway Labor Executives' Association and certain of its member organizations challenged these regulations in federal district court, requesting that their application be enjoined on statutory and constitutional grounds. The labor organizations based their case largely on the Fourth Amendment provision that "the right of the people to be secure in their persons, houses, papers, and effects, against unreasonable searches and seizures, shall not be violated." The district court ruled that the railroad employees do "have a valid interest in the integrity of their own bodies" that deserves protection under the Fourth Amendment. However, their interest is outweighed by the "public and governmental interest in the...protection of...railway safety, safety for employees, and safety for the general public." Accordingly, it upheld the FRA regulations.[8]

The Ninth Circuit Court of Appeals overruled the district court. It maintained that, although the railroads are privately owned, government subsidies and regulation of their operations justify their being considered instruments or agents of the government for purposes of the Fourth Amendment. The court's reasoning was that "individualized suspicion" is essential to a finding that toxicological testing of a particular railroad employee is required. In other words, there would have to be "reasonable suspicion" that the performance of a worker involved in an accident had been impaired by alcohol or drugs.[9] But the Supreme Court, hearing the case on appeal, upheld the FRA regulations. In essence, it agreed with the district court's reasoning that an overriding public interest in safety made testing of railroad employees constitutionally acceptable.[10]

The Von Raab Case

The other Supreme Court case decided on March 21, 1989, was *National Treasury Employees Union et al.* v. *Von Raab, Commissioner, United States Customs Service.*[11] The issue was U.S. Customs Service rules requiring drug testing of employees seeking transfers or promotions to certain positions, those included in drug interdiction programs, requiring authorization to carry firearms, or involving the handling of classified materials. For these kinds of jobs, the last stage in the screening process was a requirement that the applicant pass a closely supervised urine test for illegal drugs.

The NTEU challenged the Custom Service drug-testing program in federal district court, arguing that it violates employees' Fourth Amendment rights. The district court agreed, finding the program to be an "overly intrusive policy of searches and seizures without probable cause or reasonable suspicion, in violation of legitimate expectations of privacy." It enjoined the testing program, but the circuit court of appeals vacated the injunction.

The appeals court stated that drug testing is indeed a search within the meaning of the Fourth Amendment, but it held that the Custom Service program is "reasonable" because of its rational connection to the agency's law enforcement mission and its need to maintain public confidence in its integrity.

The Supreme Court, in terms consistent with its reasoning in *Railway Labor Executives*, upheld most of the Custom Service testing program. It did exclude applicants for positions handling classified materials because of the agency's lack of precision in defining that term and the related criteria to be used in determining when drug testing should be used.

Public employers contemplating drug-testing programs will find the Court's reasoning in *NTEU* v. *Von Raab* instructive. Referring to its decision in *Railway Labor Executives*, the Court cited its statement that "where a Fourth Amendment intrusion serves special governmental needs,... it is necessary to balance the individual's privacy expectations against the government's interests to determine whether it is impractical to require a warrant or some level of individualized suspicion in the particular context." In the opinion of the majority, the Supreme Court concluded that the Customs Service's effectiveness would be compromised if it were "required to seek search warrants in connection with routine, yet sensitive, employment decisions." Further, under certain conditions, the government's need to know about and to prevent substance abuse by employees "is sufficiently compelling to justify the intrusion on privacy entailed by conducting such searches without... individualized suspicion."

Balancing Public and Individual Interests

The Supreme Court's rulings in *Railway Labor Executives* and *NTEU* v. *Von Raab* made it clear that it was not predisposed to agree with those who argue that *all* mandatory blood and urine tests are unconstitutional under the Fourth Amendment. Employers should understand that such tests are "searches," and they must be "reasonable." There are, however, no universally accepted standards for judging the extent of the government's needs and the degree to which the intrusiveness of its actions are reasonable in relation to the privacy rights of citizens. Rather, the effort to balance public and individual interests requires a case-by-case approach, and this leaves ample room for judicial disagreement and public controversy.

This situation is illustrated by Justice Antonin Scalia's dissenting opinion in *NTEU* v. *Von Raab*. Scalia said he had joined the Court's decision in *Railway Labor Executives* because the frequency of drug and alcohol use by railroad workers, as well as the connection between "such use and great harm," had been demonstrated. The Customs Service, however, had not demonstrated frequency of use or a potential for great harm. In fact, Von Raab, the Customs Service commissioner, had stated that "Customs is largely drug-free," and that "the extent of illegal drug use by Customs employees was not the reason for establishing the program." He also said that he expected to receive "reports of very few positive findings through drug screening." His prediction turned out to be accurate: "out of 3600 employees tested, no more than 5 tested positive for drugs." With regard to actual or potential damage to the service, the government had not given the Court a single incident where drug use was connected to bribe-taking, bad aim, ineffective or biased law enforcement, or the compromising of classified materials.

In light of these facts, Scalia concluded that the Customs Service testing program was really a symbolic effort to show that the federal government was serious about its war on drugs. The commissioner had made no secret of the program's symbolic content, saying that "implementation of the drug screening program set an important example in our country's struggle with the most serious threat to our national health and security." Under these circumstances, Scalia argued that taking urine samples with a member of the same sex listening for "normal sounds" was "particularly destructive of privacy and offensive to personal dignity." In short, for Scalia, the government's justification for testing in this case was very weak and the invasion of privacy was very great.[12]

Scalia's dissent notwithstanding, and despite protests by employee organizations and other groups, a majority of the Supreme Court appeared to be inclined to give employers the benefit of the doubt on issues related to the balancing of public and individual interests. However, its own rulings established that public employers must demonstrate a rational connection between the public interest and drug-testing programs that do not involve individualized suspicion, and they must be able to show that such programs are not unreasonable violations of privacy under existing conditions. Considerable room exists for interpretation by the lower courts, and according to Frank Thompson, Norma Riccucci, and Carolyn Ban, "employees who challenge universal or random drug testing in the courts stand a fighting chance of success."[13]

The Challenge of Public Employee Organizations

In the public sector, employee organizations have taken a leading role in efforts to curtail mandatory random drug and alcohol testing of large numbers of federal workers. They have been active on all levels of the federal judiciary and frequently have had considerable success. In Congress, the unions have worked hard to block or limit the scope of legislation that would set up mandatory testing. Recently, the National Federation of Federal Employees (NFFE) successfully lobbied for the defeat of amendments to authorization bills that would have required drug tests for all applicants, new hires, and current employees of the Departments of State and Defense.

On the federal level, employee organizations have been most successful in curbing or blocking the implementation of sweeping drug-testing programs that do not "target" those positions in which the use of drugs might significantly threaten organizational performance, national security, or public safety. In a number of cases, they have effectively argued that drug-testing programs should be allowed only under conditions where the agency is able to demonstrate that "compelling reasons" exist for searches of job applicants and employees.

Targeting Positions

Following up on President Reagan's Executive Order 12564, which directed federal agencies to develop plans for achieving a drug-free workplace, Congress passed a law in 1987 requiring these agencies to have their plans certified by the Department of Health and Human Services.[14] The plan of the Department of Agriculture (USDA), certified in 1988, called for random urinalysis of certain motor vehicle operators, plant protection and quarantine officers (PPQs), and computer specialists. In addition, all USDA employees were subject to reasonable-suspicion urinalysis.

When this plan was challenged in district court by the NTEU, representing some 800 USDA employees, the court consolidated the suit with an action brought by the National Association of Agriculture Employees. Both unions sought injunctions against random testing, reasonable-suspicion testing, job applicant testing, and postaccident testing.

The U.S. Court of Appeals for the District of Columbia upheld the random testing program for USDA's motor vehicle operators in 1990, but it halted implementation of random testing for PPQs and computer specialists.[15] Its ruling was based on the Supreme Court's reasoning in *Railway Labor Executives* and *NTEU* v. *Von Raab*. The USDA position was that PPQs, like customs agents, could help drug smugglers, and it tried to convince the court that because computer specialists had access to sensitive information, random testing was justified for them also. The appeals court rejected both arguments in its decision that the functions of these employees did not create a government need that outweighed their privacy rights under the Constitution.

Thus, in this case, the appeals court applied the balancing test prescribed by the Supreme Court. It analyzed the job responsibilities of specific positions in the USDA, evaluated the agency's claims about the public's safety and welfare, and weighed these concerns against the privacy rights of the affected workers. In the court's judgment, the USDA's argument was convincing for motor vehicle operators but not for PPQs and computer specialists.

The message in this ruling is clear: Mandatory drug-testing programs are far more likely to survive judicial scrutiny if they carefully target positions that directly affect public safety and heath, national security, or effective law enforcement. Executive Order 12564 had recommended this approach, but most federal departments initially made only modest efforts to target positions. Many questionable positions were included, and in many instances the justifications offered to Health and Human Services were simply not credible. Under pressure from the federal courts to improve their targeting, federal agencies began to review their lists of jobs targeted for testing with an eye toward cutting them back.[16]

An example of the trend toward more precise targeting under judicial pressure is the U.S. Interior Department's drug-testing program. As originally designed, this program required random drug tests for about 17,000 employees, more than 25 percent of the department's work force. By January 1989, it had been successfully challenged in federal district court by the NFFE. In his ruling curtailing the plan, Judge Harold Greene described it as "bureaucracy run amok." The Interior Department then ordered a comprehensive review of the positions it had designated for testing. Ultimately, 11,000 positions were eliminated from the original testing pool, including over 3,000 teachers, education specialists, and guidance counsellors in the Bureau of Indian Affairs. The revised plan mandates drug testing only for workers in positions "substantially affecting public safety or national security, such as pilots, law enforcement personnel, and those with top security clearances."[17]

Demonstrating Compelling Reasons

The federal courts have consistently invalidated drug-testing programs when they have determined that public agencies have no compelling reasons for using them. An example is the decision of the Massachusetts District Court in *American Postal Workers Union, AFL–CIO, Boston Metro Area* v. *Frank* (1989).[18]

As part of a study to determine the correlation between the results of preemployment drug tests and job performance, the Postal Service administered drug tests to all applicants for career employment, starting in late 1986. The on-the-job performance of those who got jobs with the Postal Service was evaluated according to such criteria as absenteeism, discipline, injuries, and length of employment (turnover). Only the researchers and one data clerk had access to the drug test results.[19]

The American Postal Workers Union challenged this project, pointing to three problems. First, applicants who might receive false positives were given no opportunity to question the results, which is required in HHS plan certification rules. A physician with knowledge of substance abuse is to serve as medical review officer and make the final interpretation of positive test results. The physician must consider alternative medical explanations, taking into account conversations with the employee and other evidence. This review would give some protection in the well-known story of the worker who tested positive for heroin after having eaten poppyseed rolls.[20] Second, the union's negotiated agreement required the Postal Service to offer assistance to workers with substance abuse problems. Under the federal guidelines, these workers should be referred to an employee assistance program (EAP) and the employees' health insurance plan should provide coverage for treatment of drug abuse, but the Postal Service research design precluded making such offers to those who tested positive. Third, the union asserted that the anonymity of the test results increased the chance that workers using illegal drugs would be asked to operate machinery dangerous to themselves and coworkers.

Although Supreme Court rulings have tipped the balance in favor of the government on questions relating to the constitutionality of urinalysis drug testing for public employees in "safety-related positions," the Postal Service's effort to explore the relationship between drug use and productivity had gone too far, in the opinion of Judge John McNaught:

> I simply cannot extend the breadth of the Supreme Court decisions to persons seeking employment in an industry such as the Postal Service for the sake of research...drug testing for all job applicants to the United States Postal Service without individualized case suspicion is an unreasonable intrusion into the privacy of applicants, and thus, a violation of the Fourth Amendment.

Similarly, in *American Federation of Government Employees and National Treasury Employees Union* v. *Sullivan*,[21] the district court for the District of Columbia enjoined random testing of workers by the Department of Health and Human Services after accidents. It found the HHS plan, which allowed postaccident testing with no showing of fault and no evidence of drug-related conduct, "simply too invasive for the government's stated purpose." The court did approve random testing of motor vehicle operators and employees with top-secret security clearances.

Drug Test Accuracy and Interpretation

A major charge made by critics of drug testing is that the methods used are not 100 percent accurate, and a certain percentage of false positives must be expected. There is also doubt about the interpretation of results, which raises the issue of whether a confirmed positive result necessarily means that performance is or would be impaired.[22] False positives may at least initially cast unfair suspicion on employees and job applicants. If for no other reason, drug-testing policies should be designed to keep errors to a minimum.

Federal efforts to limit false positives have several components. In addition to the final review and interpretation by an experienced physician described above, the tests must be conducted by HHS-certified laboratories, and positive tests must be subjected to a second, more rigorous analysis. (Most state and local governments also require a second confirmatory test before an employee or job candidate who initially tests positive can be removed or denied employment.) Federal drug-testing programs also do not set especially sensitive cut points for the level of a drug that is considered sufficient to identify a drug abuser. The lower the cut point, the greater is the likelihood of false positive errors. The norms established by HHS are not lower than those generally adopted in other large drug-testing programs.[23]

Test accuracy depends on the quality of the laboratories doing the tests. A study of drug testing and the regulation of testing laboratories in the public and private sectors, published by the GAO in 1988, produced the following findings:

1. There was no nationwide regulation of the laboratories doing employee drug testing.
2. In 11 states, drug testing was controlled through statutes and regulations that specifically dealt with testing of employees.
3. In 15 other states, control was exercised through general med-

ical or chemical laboratory statutes and regulations that did not include specific drug-testing standards.

4. In 24 states there were no laws or regulations applying to drug testing of state or local employees. In these states, federal quality control was exercised through the Mandatory Guidelines for Federal Workplace Drug Testing Programs of the National Institute on Drug Abuse, which apply to all laboratories doing drug testing for federal employers.[24]

It is clearly in the employer's (as well as the employee's) best interest that broadly accepted standards regulating laboratory staffing policies and technical operations be in force. In an area as sensitive as mandatory drug testing, doubts about accuracy are likely to undermine the confidence of employees as well as the public in the integrity of the entire program.

The available research does suggest a correlation between a positive drug test and job performance. There is a tendency to higher rates of absenteeism, sick-leave use, turnover, and dismissal for cause among users of illegal drugs. The Postal Service study described above in relation to the *American Postal Workers Union* case revealed this pattern; the service estimated that it could save about $4 million a year in turnover and absenteeism costs by testing all applicants.

Issues in the Extent of Drug Testing

Critics of drug testing also argue that fewer rather than more positions should be targeted for testing. One line of reasoning that supports their contention that drug testing is already being overused is that "fishing expeditions" should not be substituted for testing based on "reasonable suspicion." For example, instead of random or universal testing of employees in safety or security-sensitive positions, employers should be required to show that there is a reasonable probability that a worker is using illegal drugs before testing may be authorized. Reasonable suspicion, according to this argument, should be based on an individual employee's behavior, not the position occupied.

Public employee organizations have consistently favored such suspicion-based testing, provided employees have the right to appeal any management decision to require testing. In the absence of overriding legislation, management and unions may negotiate the details of an agency's drug-testing program in some states.

A second line of criticism concerning the extent of drug testing focuses on direct and indirect costs. Random or universal drug testing can be very expensive and, in terms of the number of genuine positives or "hits" obtained, highly inefficient. A 1992 GAO report to the Civil Service Subcommittee of the U.S. House stated that drug use among federal workers and applicants was so rare (well under 1 percent) that each positive test cost taxpayers $77,000.[25] Another GAO report issued in May 1991 revealed that in less than a year, some 40 federal agencies had conducted over 31,000 tests, yielding just 169 positives.[26] In marked contrast, targeted testing using demographic factors and reasonable-suspicion criteria has produced far higher hit rates in the public as well as the private sector.

Given the testing costs involved, the potential for heavy expenses associated with legal challenges, the risk of widespread employee dissatisfaction, and the possibility that recruitment efforts will be negatively affected, random or universal testing programs should be approached cautiously. As Thompson, Riccucci, and Ban put it, "one lesson of federal drug testing seems clear: employers who are considering the initiation or expansion of drug testing should view the federal program as a flashing red light. Stop; proceed with caution if at all."[27]

INTERVENTION AND REHABILITATION PROGRAMS

The traditional view in personnel administration was that employers have no formal responsibility for workers' private lives. Accordingly, an employee whose job performance was being adversely affected by some personal problem was expected to deal with it without help from the organization. No matter the cause, continued substandard performance was grounds for dismissal, demotion, or other adverse action. This way of dealing with alcohol and drug abuse problems is losing ground to an approach in which employers are encouraged to provide services that can help workers overcome such problems.[28]

In contrast to earlier assumptions, it is now recognized that individuals are unlikely to escape the grip of an addiction to alcohol or drugs without outside help and support. In other words, it is unrealistic to expect that employees with such problems will be able to voluntarily "kick the habit" and improve their job performance just because they are told that their job or career is at risk. From a purely practical point of view, therefore, employers unwilling to invest in intervention and rehabilitation programs must accept the likely consequences: lower overall productivity, excessive use of sick leave and health insurance, and high rates of absenteeism and turnover. Social attitudes have also changed; employers are now expected to assume at least some responsibility for trying to help workers deal with psychological as well as physical illnesses.

Employee Assistance Programs

In the private sector, EAPs have been for some time the keystone of employers' efforts to intervene and assist workers with serious personal problems. As we noted in Chapter 10 in connection with AIDS, EAPs are workplace-centered programs established to help employees with a variety of personal problems, and alcohol and drug abuse is one of the most prevalent of such problems. EAPs usually have three phases: (1) identifying individual workers with a specific problem, (2) motivating them to recognize it and seek assistance, and (3) directly or indirectly providing counseling, medical treatment, and other forms of support intended to rehabilitate them.[29] Large cities, for example, may have internal employee assistance programs. Smaller municipalities are more likely to rely on external agencies such as hospitals and private practitioners. Rehabilitation or counseling services may be provided directly by city agencies, or employees may have to locate their own providers. According to Paul Cary, "Regardless of the format, a good treatment program should be designed to restore physical health, [and] produce permanent changes in behavior."[30]

EAPS, once a rarity in the public sector, now are provided by public employers in many jurisdictions. They are required in the federal service by OPM regulations under Executive Order 12564; all covered agencies must offer EAPs with high-level direction, emphasizing education, referral to rehabilitation, and coordination with available community resources.[31] EAP services are available to federal employees who voluntarily seek their help or those who have been determined by the employer to be abusing alcohol or drugs.

The policies of public employers with respect to the rehabilitation of workers who test positive for drugs vary. Under OPM regulations, federal agencies have considerable discretion. Support for the use of EAPs was provided in a study by the GAO on the actions of agencies when positive drug tests occur. Well over half of the employees in three agencies who tested positive and entered EAPs completed rehabilitation and remained in jobs targeted for testing.[32] Most local employers allow an employee at least one positive drug test without punitive action if the employee accepts appropriate help. [33]

ARBITRATORS AND DISCIPLINARY ACTION UNDER
NEGOTIATED AGREEMENTS

When a collective bargaining agreement is in place (see Chapter 8), arbitrators often play an important role in disciplinary actions related to cases of alcohol or drug abuse. Their decisions can in effect contribute important elements of the policies applied in such situations.

Negotiated agreements usually state that management may discipline employees only for "just cause." The agreement may provide for the dismissal of any employee who possesses or consumes alcohol or illegal drugs on the employer's property. If the employee files a grievance against such a dismissal under terms of the contract, the arbitrator holds a hearing and investigates the factual basis of management's case. The arbitrator may uphold, cancel, or modify the employer's disciplinary action. Typically, as noted in Chapter 8, such decisions are final and binding.

Important as such arbitration awards are, arbitrators' definitions of employers' responsibilities are more significant and far-reaching. Many arbitrators accept the proposition that alcohol or drug abuse is an illness that requires treatment as opposed to punishment, and they expect employers to try to provide such assistance. In practical terms, this approach may produce a decision that the employer *does not* have just cause for dismissal, since the employee is a sick person who is unable to change an addictive condition without positive support or treatment.

An analysis of arbitrators' decisions in discharge cases involving drug and alcohol abuse over a seven-year period, published by the Industrial Relations Research Association in 1991, revealed the following pattern:

1. Arbitrators are reluctant to give management broad powers to discharge workers who violate the employer's rules due to "chemical dependency." In their view, such dependency is an illness that should be treated medically, and once employees are "cured," they should be returned to their jobs.
2. Arbitrators may reduce the severity of a disciplinary action because management did not offer the grievant an opportunity to enter a rehabilitation program through an EAP or insurance coverage.
3. In conjunction with enrollment in an EAP, reinstatement often is conditioned upon an employee's participation in counselling sessions, group therapy, and support meetings such as Alcoholics Anonymous, or similar treatment for a

specified period after initial rehabilitation. Another condition of reinstatement is agreement to submit to periodic drug testing in the future.

4. Arbitrators favor reinstatement upon completion of an appropriate assistance program, but an employee who repeats the offense may be fired.

5. In discharge cases, arbitrators consider mitigating circumstances such as seniority. In over 25 percent of the cases where reinstatement was ordered, the grievant was given "one last chance" to change the behavior.

6. Disciplining workers for off-duty substance abuse requires the employer to establish a connection between that behavior and job performance.

7. Drug abusers are likely to be punished more severely than alcohol abusers.[34]

THE FUTURE OUTLOOK

As an employer, government has had some success in developing programs for responding to and controlling substance abuse by workers. Clearly, alcoholism and drug addiction are widespread in society, and the threats they pose to organizational performance and public confidence in government are also clear. Drug testing, especially targeted testing, is likely to be incorporated in employment relationships on all levels of government as the courts work out the constitutional ground rules employers must follow.[35] Employee organizations will continue to be active, both in the courts and at the bargaining table. EAPs have the potential to become standard features of substance abuse policies and programs. Creating a drug-free workplace in government is likely to continue to be a popular theme among politicians seeking to provide symbolic evidence that the nation's leadership is indeed serious about prosecuting "the war on drugs."

At minimum, the current state of affairs requires that public employers have rational and enforceable substance abuse policies in place. These policies must be able to withstand judicial scrutiny and, if necessary, be responsive to the constraints on management discretion imposed by negotiated agreements and arbitrators' awards. They should include the following components:

1. A clear explanation of the need for the policy, including the fact that substance abuse is not a problem restricted to certain categories of workers or demographic groupings.

2. A statement of the employer's position on the use and posses-
sion of alcohol and drugs by employees on and off the job
site.
3. A description of the conditions under which universal, random, and suspicion-based drug tests may be administered,
including the rationale for testing the incumbents in certain
categories of positions.
4. A statement of procedures to be used in order to minimize the
risk of false positives and interpret test results accurately.
5. Specification of disciplinary and other actions to be taken if
the terms of the policy are violated.
6. A description of the employer's position on intervention and
rehabilitation and the treatment opportunities available to
workers.
7. Provisions for a clearly defined appeals process under civil
service regulations, in addition to any procedures that may
exist for employees covered by negotiated contracts.

■

NOTES

1. Paul L. Cary, "Drugs and Drug Testing in the Workplace," in John
Matzer (ed.), *Personnel Practices for the '90s* (Washington, DC: International City Management Association, 1988), p. 183.
2. Robert Coulson and Mitchell D. Goldberg, *Alcohol, Drugs, and Arbitration*
(New York: American Arbitration Association, 1987), p. 7.
3. U.S. Bureau of the Census, *Statistical Abstract of the United States: 1992*,
112th edition (Washington, DC, 1992), Table 197.
4. Tim Bornstein, "Getting to the Bottom of the Issue: How Arbitrators
View Alcohol Abuse," *Arbitration Journal*, vol. 44, no. 4 (December 1989),
p. 46.
5. Peter Bensinger, "Dangers in the Workplace: What Lies Ahead," in Bureau of National Affairs, *Alcohol and Drugs Special Report* (New York,
1986), p. 126.
6. Frank J. Thompson, Norma M. Riccucci, and Carolyn Ban, "Drug Testing
in the Federal Workplace: An Instrumental and Symbolic Assessment,"
Public Administration Review, vol. 51, no. 6 (November–December 1991),
p. 516.
7. 109 S.Ct. 1402 (1989).
8. Ibid., p. 1410.
9. Ibid.

10. Ibid., pp. 1414–1415.
11. 109 S.Ct. 1384 (1989).
12. *NTEU* v. *Von Raab*, 49 CCH S.Ct. Bulletin (1989), pp. B1694–1702.
13. Thompson, Riccucci, and Ban, "Drug Testing in the Federal Workplace," p. 507.
14. See U.S. Department of Health and Human Services, "Mandatory Guidelines for Federal Workplace Drug Testing Programs," *Federal Register*, vol. 53 (April 11, 1988), pp. 11970–11989.
15. *Clayton Yeutter* v. *National Treasury Employees Union*, 918 F.2d 968 (DC Circuit), November 16, 1990.
16. Thompson, Riccucci, and Ban, "Drug Testing in the Federal Workplace," p. 519.
17. Jeff Sumberg, "NFFE Wins Interior Department Drug Testing Fight," *The Federal Employee*, vol. 76, no. 3 (March 1991).
18. C.A. No. 87–1264–Mc (D.C. Mass.), November 21, 1989.
19. Craig Zwerling, James Ryan, and Endel J. Orav, "The Efficacy of Pre-employment Drug Screening for Marijuana and Cocaine in Predicting Employment Outcome," *Journal of the American Medical Association*, vol. 264 (November 28, 1990), pp. 2639–2643.
20. Thompson, Riccucci, and Ban, "Drug Testing in the Federal Workplace," p. 519.
21. No. 88–3594, 90–0205 (D.D.C.), March 2, 1990.
22. Barry A. Hartstein, "Drug Testing in the Workplace: A Primer for Employers," *Employer Relations Journal*, vol. 12, no. 4 (Spring 1987), pp. 577–607.
23. Thompson, Riccucci, and Ban, "Drug Testing in the Federal Workplace," p. 518.
24. U.S. General Accounting Office, *Drug Testing, Regulation of Drug Testing Laboratories* (Washington, DC, September 1988).
25. U.S. General Accounting Office, *Employee Drug Testing: Estimated Cost to Test All Executive Branch Employees and New Hires* (Washington, DC, June 1992).
26. U.S. General Accounting Office, *Employee Drug Testing, Status of Federal Agencies' Programs* (Washington, DC, May 1991).
27. Thompson, Riccucci, and Ban, "Drug Testing in the Federal Workplace," p. 523.
28. Janet M. Spencer, "The Developing Notion of Employer Responsibility for the Alcoholic, Drug Addictive or Mentally Ill Employee: An Examination under Federal and State Employment Statutes and Arbitration Decisions," *St. John's Law Review*, vol. 53, no. 4 (Summer 1979), pp. 659–720.
29. William J. Sonnenstual and Harrison Trice, *Strategies for Employee Assistance Programs: The Crucial Balance* (New York: ILR Press, School of Industrial and Labor Relations, Columbia University, 1990), p. 1.
30. Cary, "Drugs and Drug Testing in the Workplace," p. 193.
31. U.S. Office of Personnel Management, "Federal Personnel Manual Letter 792–16, Establishing a Drug-Free Federal Workplace," *Federal Register*, vol. 54 (April 6, 1989), pp. 14024–14033.

32. U.S. General Accounting Office, *Action by Agencies when Employees Test Positive for Illegal Drugs* (Washington, DC, 1989).
33. Cary, "Drugs and Drug Testing in the Workplace," p. 193.
34. Helen Elkiss and Joseph Yaney, "Recent Trends in Arbitration of Substance Abuse Grievances," *Proceedings of the 1991 Spring Meeting,* Industrial Relations Research Association, pp. 556, 560.
35. See Robert N. Roberts and Marion T. Doss, Jr., "The Constitutional Privacy Rights of Public Employees," *International Journal of Public Administration*, vol. 14, no. 3 (1991), pp. 315–356.

Sexual Harassment   12

Sexual harassment in the workplace is a serious problem that public employers are now expected to recognize and respond to as a matter of law and policy.[1] This is not a new phenomenon. Working women have always had to deal with sexual harassment to some extent; moreover, sexual harassment of men by women is not unheard of, and gays may be victimized by either or both sexes. Sexual harassment is now understood to be a widespread and costly form of discrimination public management must address through formal policies, disciplinary procedures, training programs, and finding ways of eliminating it from the workplace.[2]

The reasons for the spotlight now shining on this previously dark corner of the workplace are not hard to identify.[3] First, women not only now represent nearly half of the civilian labor force, they are moving into traditionally male job categories, including managerial positions.[4] In the courts, cases of blatant harassment by male employees resisting the "desegregation" of their exclusive enclaves (e.g., police and fire departments) have received particular attention. Second, social attitudes are changing. Traditional definitions of sex or gender roles and power relations between men and women in society are breaking down, and behaviors once considered at worst impolite or unfortunate are now simply not acceptable in many settings.

A third reason for the new attention to sexual harassment is that in conjunction with shifting social values, the political climate has changed significantly. In the 1992 national election, for example, women doubled their representation in the U.S. House, from 24 to 48 members, and their share of senatorial seats grew to six. Women were at least equally successful on the state and local levels of government. In response to their growing political influence, women's viewpoints now get far more consideration than they did even a few years ago, and this reality is reflected in court rulings, legislation, rules promulgated by agencies such as the EEOC, and personnel policies on all levels of government.[5]

DEFINING SEXUAL HARASSMENT IN THE WORKPLACE

The Equal Employment Opportunity Commission (EEOC) is responsible for enforcement of Title VII of the Civil Rights Act of 1964. Along with the federal courts, the EEOC has interpreted Title VII to mean that sexual harassment in the workplace is a form of sexual discrimination. In other words, sexual harassment is illegal; violators may be prosecuted and held liable for damages. For the public employer, sexual harassment charges made by workers or clients are serious legal matters.

The EEOC Guidelines

To establish what behaviors or practices constitute sexual harassment, the EEOC issued the following guidelines in 1980:

> Harassment on the basis of sex is a violation of Sec. 703 of Title VII. Unwelcome sexual advances, requests for sexual favors, and other verbal or physical conduct of a sexual nature constitute sexual harassment when (1) submission to such conduct is made either explicitly or implicitly a term or condition of an individual's employment, (2) submission to or rejection of such conduct by an individual is used as the basis for employment decisions affecting such individual or (3) such conduct has the purpose or effect of substantially interfering with an individual's work performance or creating an intimidating, hostile, or offensive working environment.[6]

Items (1) and (2) of the EEOC's guidelines are straightforward and have evoked little controversy. They prohibit employers from making submission to unwelcome sexual behavior a condition of

employment or reacting to workers' negative responses to such behavior with personnel actions such as firing or denying pay raises.
This is often called *quid pro quo harassment*. Item (3) relates to the creation of a second type of sexual harassment called a *hostile or offensive
working environment*. This type is far broader in application, and it
does not require the plaintiff to prove that she or he was denied a tangible benefit such as a job or promotion. All that has to be established
is that the defendant's behavior toward the plaintiff created a hostile
or offensive working environment. Most sexual harassment charges
in government are based on the hostile-environment argument.

The Supreme Court Definition of a Hostile Environment

The EEOC's inclusion of category (3) violations was a "radical departure from the case law on the subject,"[7] but the U.S. Supreme Court
unanimously upheld its position in a landmark case, *Meritor Savings
Bank* v. *Mechelle Vinson et al.* (1986).[8] The principal point the Court
made in *Meritor* v. *Vinson* was that Title VII is violated if serious and
continuing unwelcome sexual behavior creates a hostile or abusive
work environment, even if the victim is not denied any material benefits.[9]

In this case, Mechelle Vinson charged her male supervisor with
four years of sexual harassment, including fondling, psychologically
coerced sexual relations, and rape. After her dismissal for taking "excessive sick leave" in 1978, Vinson brought action against the supervisor and the bank in U.S. district court. The supervisor denied
allegations of sexual activity and asserted that her charges were in
response to a business-related dispute. In its defense, the bank
claimed that it was unaware of any sexual harassment and, if it had
taken place, it was without the bank's consent or approval. The district court ruled against Vinson, stating that if she and her supervisor
had a sexual relationship, "it was voluntary and had nothing to do
with her continued employment at the bank, and that therefore [she]
was not the victim of sexual harassment."[10]

The Court of Appeals for the District of Columbia reversed the
district court's decision against Vinson. Since the district court had
not considered the issue of hostile-environment sexual harassment,
the appeals court remanded the case, noting that employers are "absolutely" liable for sexual harassment practiced by their supervisory
personnel.[11]

Hearing the case on appeal, the Supreme Court agreed with the
appeals court, stating that "unwelcome sexual advances that create

an offensive or hostile working environment violate Title VII." As to the supervisor's and the bank's contention that there was no violation because Vinson had suffered no loss of a tangible benefit, the Court disagreed. Congress, the Court said, intended to "strike at the entire spectrum of disparate treatment of women" in terms of employment. The EEOC guidelines, while not binding on the courts, "do constitute a body of experience and informed judgment to which courts and litigants may properly resort for guidance."[12] Accordingly, the case was sent back to district court for further proceedings consistent with the Supreme Court's opinion.

Meritor v. *Vinson* also focused on employer liability under varying circumstances. Meritor Savings Bank had argued that it should not be held liable because it had a written policy against discrimination, and Vinson had not used an existing grievance procedure. The Court disagreed with both claims: The policy was vague and did not specifically address sexual harassment, and the grievance procedure discouraged complaints. The Court, however, did not fully resolve the issue of employer liability. Writing for the majority, Chief Justice William Rehnquist noted that while employers are absolutely liable for acts of their supervisors when economic benefits are involved, some limits might be placed on employer liability when hostile work environments were the issue.[13]

Further Definitions

Because the terminology of the EEOC guidelines is ambiguous, various state and local governments have made their own interpretations of such concepts as "verbal or physical conduct of a sexual nature." One of the first to do so was the city of Madison, Wisconsin, which amended its Equal Opportunity Ordinance in 1980 to provide a more specific definition of sexual harassment for managers and supervisors. The amendment provides examples of unwelcome verbal and physical conduct "which shall include but not be limited to, deliberate or repeated unsolicited gestures, graphic materials, verbal or written comments." This language, in combination with other language specifying that sexual harassment is a form of "misconduct... subject to remedial action which may include the imposition of discipline," established conditions under which the EEOC's broad terminology could be made operational by the city. Jeri Spann describes how, in Madison,

> ...grossly offensive language, graphic and written materials as well as inappropriate physical conduct, all winked at, denied or unseen for

years have been elevated to the canon of recognized "don'ts," such as poor work performance. Thus the issue of sexual harassment has been officially transferred out of the realm of advocacy and politics and into the realms of ordinary management responsibility and employee competence.[14]

Other attempts to define what constitutes sexual harassment also have been made in various cases heard in federal district and appeals courts. Two of these examples, and one case that is to be heard by the Supreme Court, are described in the next section.

PROVING SEXUAL HARASSMENT CHARGES

The Equal Employment Opportunity Commission is authorized to investigate and conciliate disputes involving sexual harassment in the workplace. A worker who wants to make a charge of sexual harassment is to file a complaint with the EEOC, and the agency, after investigation, is to decide whether it will sue on the worker's behalf. In practice, however, the commission has filed suits in only a small percentage of cases that have been brought to its attention (in 1990, only 50 of the 5,964 complaints it received). Most sexual harassment suits therefore are brought to trial by private lawyers, who often bypass the EEOC complaint.[15] The EEOC process was strengthened, however, by a provision of the 1991 Civil Rights Act that allows for the payment of compensatory and punitive damages; formerly, the claimant was entitled only to back pay and reinstatement in a job.

The standards of proof required in the proceedings of courts, as well as quasi-judicial bodies such as human relations commissions, are formidable. It is in practice difficult to sustain charges of sexual harassment. The adjudicator often is forced to rely exclusively on the credibility of plaintiffs, defendants, and witnesses who do not have firsthand knowledge of the facts, and physical or documentary evidence may be sparse or nonexistent.

Hostile-environment sexual harassment is usually more difficult to prove than quid pro quo cases, but its effects are no less severe. The EEOC guidelines state that to establish this kind of harassment, evidence should reveal persistent requests or demands for sexual favors and persistent refusals, and other evidence of a sexual nature that demeans or humiliates the victim and creates an offensive work environment. There are many circumstances that may result in charges of hostile-environment sexual harassment. The two examples that follow illustrate the importance of establishing a pattern of conduct.

Finley Downs and the FAA

Finley Downs was demoted from his position as supervisory aviation safety inspector and reassigned by the Federal Aviation Administration (FAA). The FAA specified five charges for this adverse action, including:

1. Discrimination based on sex by reassigning a particular duty from a female to a male inspector.
2. Sexual harassment by engaging in a pattern of abusive and offensive sexual behavior directed to female employees. . . .
3. Sexual harassment by suggesting or inferring that sexual favors by females are the basis for employment, training or promotional opportunities. . . . [16]

The Merit Systems Protection Board denied Downs's petition for review, but in 1985 the U.S. Court of Appeals held that neither quid pro quo nor hostile-environment harassment had been proven.

The incidents used by the FAA to build the case against Downs included statements he made concerning the appearance and sexual behavior of a female coworker, two incidents where he touched her hair, and a joke he made about a nonemployee's tight clothing. The appeals court found these incidents insufficient to demonstrate the pervasiveness of conduct needed to support a claim of sexual harassment through creation of an intimidating, hostile, or offensive workplace. In its decision, the court said that to establish a claim of sexual harassment, the "offensive conduct must be sufficiently pervasive so as to alter conditions of employment, and must be sufficiently severe and persistent to affect seriously the psychological well-being of an employee."[17]

Considering the record as a whole, the court concluded that, even if true, these charges were not enough to demonstrate a pattern of sexual harassment. For such a pattern to be established, the behavior must be routinized to the point that it becomes a condition of employment. Furthermore, there was no evidence that Downs's conduct "interfered with an employee's work" or caused serious psychological damage. Accordingly, the court reversed the MSPB decision that upheld the adverse action against Downs.

Lois Robinson and JSI, Inc.

In a 1991 case with the opposite outcome, a federal district court judge ruled that graphic pictures of female nudes displayed in a workplace could be a form of sexual harassment. Lois Robinson, the female plaintiff in this lawsuit, had worked for seven years as a welder at Jacksonville Shipyards, Inc. (JSI). All of the supervisory and managerial personnel were men; the company, in fact, was described as a "boys club" in which many members were interested in the photographic arts. Robinson found the pictures offensive and asked that they be removed on several occasions. According to her complaint, she and other women at JSI were often subjected by male employees to comparison with the pictures, and they routinely faced a barrage of sexually oriented comments, including invitations to perform sexual acts. Offensive sexual jokes and pranks designed to humiliate, sexual nicknames assigned by male coworkers, sexually explicit graffiti, and unwanted sexual "touching" were described as endemic to the workplace.

Robinson brought suit against JSI, its president, and any supervisor who had authority over her or played a part in the handling of her complaints. She maintained that this hostile work environment discriminated against her as a woman and that she had missed work and overtime pay because of its damaging psychological effects. JSI, in turn, argued that a reasonable woman would not be offended by the pictures, that the pictures alone did not support a claim of hostile-environment harassment, and that the court could not order their removal because that would violate the men's First Amendment right to free speech.

Judge Howell Melton found that the facts did establish that there was hostile-environment sexual harassment at JSI. He agreed with Robinson's contention that she had been subjected to a pattern of unwelcome sexual conduct and determined that management knew (or should have known) about the harassment and failed to take appropriate remedial action. In his opinion he stated that a reasonable woman would find conditions at JSI to be abusive, and he found JSI corporately liable for sexual harassment. Managers responsible for the company's sexual harassment policies were also held liable but the president was not, because he had not directly participated in creating the hostile environment. Robinson was not granted monetary relief under Title VII, however, on the grounds that she had failed to prove with "sufficient definiteness" how much she had lost. This aspect of the case is still in litigation.[18]

Teresa Harris and Forklift Systems

The nation's courts continue to differ in their decisions on what constitutes sexual harassment. More definitive action may come from the Supreme Court, which agreed in 1993 to hear arguments in the case of Teresa Harris versus Forklift Systems, Inc., the most recent sexual harassment case to come before it. The Court will decide whether Harris, who stayed on the job despite two years of sexually derogatory remarks from her boss at Forklift Systems, can win reversal of a lower court's finding that she was offended by conduct that would have offended a reasonable victim, but she had not suffered severe psychological injury. A decision in this case is expected in 1994.[19]

POLICIES IN THE PUBLIC SECTOR

Public employers, as well as corporations such as JSI and Forklift Systems, are responsible for doing everything reasonably possible to prevent sexual harassment. A fundamental part of such an effort is an explicit policy statement that incorporates the EEOC guidelines, establishes an administrative procedure for initiating and dealing fairly with complaints, and describes clearly the penalties for violations. The policy should specifically identify a member of top management who is to be responsible for monitoring the program.[20] The potential liability of executives, supervisors, and others also should be explained, including the provision of the Civil Rights Act of 1991 under which victims of sexual harassment may receive up to $300,000 in compensatory and punitive damages.

To be as clear and definitive as possible, sexual harassment policies should provide descriptions of unacceptable behaviors. The St. Paul, Minnesota, City Council revised its policy in 1988 to include the following list of actions that demean the dignity and worth of the individual and could be grounds for a complaint of sexual harassment.

1. Threatening actions against someone if sexual favors are not performed.
2. Intimating, by way of suggestion, a desire for sexual relations or physical contact.
3. Making suggestions about invitations to social events outside the workplace, after being told such suggestions are unwelcome.
4. Using offensive terms that have a sexual nature.
5. Using sexually degrading words to describe a person.
6. Making jokes or remarks of a sexual nature in front of people who find them offensive.
7. Using sexually suggestive objects.

8. Displaying pictures that embarrass or offend in the work-place, including posting "dirty" pictures.
9. Prolonged staring or leering at a person.
10. Whistling so as to attract attention to a person.
11. Engaging in uninvited physical contact, as in touching, hug-ging, patting, or pinching.[21]

Managers and supervisors must be trained to recognize and re-spond to problems quickly and effectively. In Madison, Wisconsin, training programs on how to prevent sexual harassment have been a part of the city's affirmative action program since 1981, and its expe-rience strongly suggests that training designed to stop problems be-fore they become sexual harassment complaints should be required of all employees. The programs should include descriptions of prob-lem behaviors and examples of inappropriate written materials and verbal conduct, explained in terms of the EEOC guidelines and court rulings. It is important to make sure that trainees understand com-plaint procedures, which should take into account the rights of both complainants and respondents.[22]

Michigan was the first state to implement statewide or agency-level sexual harassment policies in 1979, followed by over 40 states by the late 1980s. State policies generally incorporate the EEOC guidelines and definitions of sexual harassment. A number of states, such as Montana, have comprehensive training programs that in-clude films, brochures, posters, and self-report questionnaires to ex-amine employees' attitudes toward sexual harassment. Training in other states may consist only of efforts to disseminate a stated policy or the mention of sexual harassment in orientation sessions for new employees.[23]

About 85 percent of cities with populations over 100,000 have in-stituted sexual harassment policies since 1980, and most of them have some kind of formal training program in place. Typically, the central personnel office or board has responsibility for conducting this training. A national survey of large cities published in 1989 indi-cated that affirmative steps were being taken as protection against potential liability suits and damaging publicity. The authors con-cluded, "City officials evidently feel that it is important to develop clear policies prohibiting sexual harassment and... to develop griev-ance procedures to resolve disputes. By resolving sexual harassment complaints internally through formal grievance procedures, cities may avoid litigation and outside intervention... by state and federal agencies or the courts."[24]

THE FUTURE OUTLOOK

By all accounts, sexual harassment is still one of the most underreported forms of discrimination in the workplace. Nevertheless, growing public awareness and media attention have created an environment in which those who believe they are victims of sexual harassment can be expected to take advantage of the remedies available to them. In the public sector, the trend to increasing numbers of sexual harassment complaints on all levels of government is likely to continue.

The elimination of all forms of illegal discrimination has been a major responsibility of public personnel administration for almost 30 years, since passage of the Civil Rights Act of 1964. The specific challenge of dealing with and preventing sexual harassment in the workplace is a newly recognized dimension of that ongoing responsibility. Like racial, ethnic, gender, age, or any other kind of discrimination, sexual harassment is a manifestation of deeply rooted social and psychological conditions that extend far beyond organizational boundaries.[25] For this reason, Spann maintains that for most large organizations, "the complete elimination of sexual harassment is simply not a realistic goal in the short term. Workplaces mirror the cultures from which they draw their values, their resources and their employees, and despite obvious advances, American culture remains racist and sexist to a significant extent."[26] This reality does not, however, relieve public employers of their moral and legal obligations to make a genuine, sustained effort to create a workplace free of all forms of discrimination, including sexual harassment.

■

NOTES

1. Connie Kirk-Westerman, David M. Billeaux, and Robert E. England, "Ending Sexual Harassment at City Hall: Policy Initiatives in Large American Cities," *State and Local Government Review* (Fall 1989), pp. 100–105.
2. Dennis L. Dresang and Paul J. Stuiber, "Sexual Harassment: Challenges for the Future, " in Carolyn Ban and Norma Riccucci (eds.), *Public Personnel Management: Current Concerns—Future Challenges* (New York: Longman, 1991), pp. 114–125; U.S. Merit Systems Protection Board, *Sexu-*

al Harassment in the Federal Workplace: Is It A Problem? (Washington, DC, 1981).

3. For examples of recent media attention, see Bob Cook, "Growing Awareness: Anita Hill Says the Workplace Today Is a Slightly More Tolerable Place," *Chicago Tribune*, March 7, 1993, sect. 6, pp. 11; and Richard Morin, "Sexism Common at Capitol," *Washington Post* syndicated article, February 22, 1993.
4. U.S. Bureau of the Census, Statistical Abstract of the United States: 1992, 112th edition (Washington, DC, 1992), Tables 615, 629.
5. Donna M. Stringer, Helen Remick, Jan Salisbury, and Angela B. Ginorio, "The Power and Reasons Behind Sexual Harassment: An Employer's Guide to Solutions," *Public Personnel Management*, vol. 19, no. 1 (Spring 1990), pp. 43–52.
6. Equal Employment Opportunity Commission, "Discrimination Because of Sex under Title VII of the Civil Rights Act of 1964: Adoption of Final Interpretive Guidelines," *Federal Register*, vol. 45 (November 1980), pp. 74676–77.
7. Robert W. Martin, Jr., "Sexual Harassment: Improving the 'Atmosphere' in the Workplace," *The Review*, Center for Employment Relations and Law, Florida State University, vol. 1, no. 4 (Summer 1980), p. 32.
8. 106 S.Ct. 2399 (1986).
9. Maria Morlacci, "Sexual Harassment Law and the Impact of *Vinson*," *Employee Relations Law Journal*, vol. 13 (Winter 1987–88), pp. 501–519.
10. *Meritor Savings Bank* v. *Vinson*, 477 U.S. 57, 91 L. Ed. 2d 49; 106 S.Ct. 2399, June 19, 1986, p. 53.
11. Ibid., pp. 53–54.
12. Ibid., p. 58.
13. Morlacci, "Sexual Harassment Law," pp. 513–515.
14. Jeri Spann, "Dealing Effectively with Sexual Harassment: Some Practical Lessons from One City's Experience," *Public Personnel Management*, vol. 19, no. 1 (Spring 1990), pp. 59–60.
15. Tamar Lewin, "A Case Study in Sexual Harassment and the Law," *The New York Times*, October 11, 1991, p. A17.
16. *Finley Downs* v. *Federal Aviation Administration*, 775 F.2d 288, October 18, 1985, p. 290.
17. Ibid., p. 292.
18. See Tamar Lewin, "Nude Pictures Are Ruled Sexual Harassment," *The New York Times*, January 23, 1991 and "Ruling on Pinups as Sexual Harassment: What Does It Mean?" *The New York Times*, February 8, 1991.
19. Joan Biskupic, "Court to Define Harassment," *Washington Post* syndicated article, March 3, 1993.
20. Robert K. Robinson, Delaney J. Kirk, and James D. Powell, "Sexual Harassment: New Approaches for a Changed Environment," in John Matzer, Jr. (ed.), *Personnel Practices for the '90s: A Local Government Guide* (Washington, DC: International City Management Association, 1988), p. 207.
21. Center for Employment Relations and Law, Florida State University, *The Review*, (October 1988), p. 1.

22. Spann, "Dealing Effectively with Sexual Harassment," p. 66.
23. Cynthia S. Ross and Robert E. England, "State Government's Sexual Harassment Policy Initiatives," *Public Administration Review*, vol. 47, no. 3 (May–June 1987), pp. 259–260.
24. Kirk-Westerman, Billeaux, and England, "Ending Sexual Harassment at City Hall," p. 104.
25. Stringer et al., "Power and Reasons behind Sexual Harassment."
26. Spann, "Dealing Effectively with Sexual Harassment," p. 67.

Issues in Pay Administration: Comparable Worth and Pay for Performance

13

The concepts of comparable worth and pay for performance are part of pay policy and administration on all levels of government. The issue of pay equity for women emerged in the 1970s, when attention began to be directed to their historic concentration in the lower-paying jobs of the public as well as private sectors. The result has been a significant gap between the average earnings of women and those of men. Alice Cook describes the term *comparable worth* as "a *means* of measuring the breadth of this gap and providing a tool for narrowing it."[1]

The idea of pay for performance (PFP) has a longer history, since it is a central element of the merit principle that was a hallmark of Civil Service Reform I. The modern version of pay for performance emerged during the late 1970s, along with the emphasis in Civil Service Reform II on increasing efficiency and productivity through more effective human resources management techniques (see Chapter 2).

THE CONCEPT OF COMPARABLE WORTH

It has been illegal in the United States to pay women less than men for the same work since passage of the federal Equal Pay Act of 1963.

The norm of equal pay for equal work, however, does not address issues concerning the value placed on jobs traditionally occupied by women. About 80 percent of women in the civilian labor force are concentrated in 20 of the Labor Department's 427 job categories, and women working full time earn about 70 cents for every dollar earned by men (see Chapter 7). Women's groups, with strong support from some unions, legislators, and public officials, maintain that the labor force is characterized by occupational segregation, as a result of which women are shunted into low-paying, dead-end jobs.[2] In the occupational category of managerial and professional specialties, for example, women made up 46 percent of the work force in 1991, but they represented 95 percent of the registered nurses, 74 percent of the elementary and secondary schoolteachers, 83 percent of the librarians, and 68 percent of the social workers, all comparatively low-paid positions in this category. At the other end of the pay spectrum, they represented just 8 percent of the engineers, 10 percent of the dentists and 20 percent of the physicians, 19 percent of the lawyers and judges, and 26 percent of the natural scientists.[3]

Since segments of the labor market dominated by women are undervalued, the effect on wages paid in the public sector is inevitable. When governments conduct prevailing-rate surveys (see Chapter 7), they perpetuate a systemwide pattern of discrimination against women.[4] Advocates of comparable worth argue, therefore, that public employers should implement a policy of equal pay for work of equal value, instead of merely satisfying the requirement of equal pay for equal work. This approach, they believe, would be a better way to deal with the traditionally low wages paid for work in the occupations dominated by women.

Job-Factor Point Value Systems

One way the concept of comparable worth is applied to try to deal with gender-based pay disparities is by establishing the relative value or worth of every job to the employer or to society. Jobs can be assigned numerical values using a point system that is based on the skills, education, effort, and responsibility necessary to do the work, as well as the conditions under which the job must be performed.[5]

Advocates argue that such an approach allows employers to compare different kinds of jobs (e.g., a secretary and a garbage collector) pay workers according to each job's point value. Therefore, the comparable-worth method relies on objective job evaluations to produce a hierarchy of positions that accurately reflects their relative worth *to the organization*. Robert Mulcahy and Jon Anderson identify

12 job-content factors that could be examined: knowledge required, consequences of error, effort required, job complexity, amount of discretion, contacts within and outside the organization, hazards, stress, physical effort, surroundings/environment, personnel authority, and personnel supervised.[6]

In the public sector, job evaluations that have used job-factor point value systems often reveal that for jobs predominantly occupied by women, the point totals are higher than would be suggested by what is paid in them, compared to the totals for better-paid jobs dominated by men. Advocates of comparable worth maintain, therefore, that women are the victims of the subjective position classification methods that are prevalent in the public sector.[7] In short, a key component of the comparable-worth argument is that gender-based wage differences are at least in part the result of arbitrary and inaccurate job evaluation methods.

THE DEBATE OVER COMPARABLE WORTH

The desirability of improving the objectivity of job evaluation techniques in the public sector is not particularly controversial. Nevertheless, the issues raised while trying to implement reforms pose the potential for conflict between racial and ethnic or gender groups in the organization. The factors used and the weights they are given in the job evaluation system can greatly affect the outcomes with regard to relative worth and pay. As J. Donald Treiman notes, "Certain weighting schemes are likely to be relatively advantageous to particular social categories—men versus women, whites versus blacks, and so on." He suggests, therefore, that the choice of factors and factor weights in job evaluation systems is not so much a technical issue as it is "an expression of the values underlying notions of equity."[8]

The most hotly debated aspect of comparable worth is the idea that market factors should be disregarded in establishing relative worth and pay in organizations. All other things being equal, pay policies based on comparable-worth concepts would substitute *administratively* determined pay rates for the prevailing rates generated by the supply-demand forces of the labor market.

Advocates of comparable worth contend that administratively determined rates are necessary because prevailing rates perpetuate patterns of social and economic discrimination against women. Critics, on the other hand, argue that while the goal of fairness and pay equity for women is commendable, administratively imposed pay scales would be very costly and highly inefficient. In practical terms, public employers would be placed in the position of having to raise the pay of many employees substantially, while lowering the pay of others would be impossible for political and labor market supply reasons. There is considerable debate over how much this would cost taxpayers, but upward pay adjustments throughout the public sector inevitably would be expensive. In addition, employers' costs associated with job evaluations and pay administration would increase greatly.

From the standpoint of classical economics, a more fundamental and long-term problem would be politically imposed distortions of the labor market. In other words, comparable worth would force employers to overpay for skills in ample supply and to underpay for scarce and essential human resources.[9] Such economic inefficiencies, critics argue, are not justified by the prospect of eliminating whatever part of the pay gap between men and women is caused by discrimination. Opponents of comparative worth stress their view—widely accepted in the United States—that the money value of a job or task cannot in practice be based on the abstract concept of inherent worth; it can only be based on labor prices that "clear" an open market. Systemic and intentional discrimination against women or racial and ethnic minorities should be removed through legal and administrative means. If this can be accomplished, the market should function even more efficiently, and it should be allowed to do so.

Proponents and opponents of comparative worth also disagree on the fundamental question of whether or not women are intentionally segregated or they are in fact concentrated in certain occupations. The term *occupational segregation* describes a situation in which a particular class of workers, in this case women, are, for a variety of socioeconomic, cultural, and political reasons, forced or channeled into low-paying jobs. From this perspective, comparable worth is a necessary intervention to allow women as a group to escape wage discrimination in occupations where they predominate.[10]

Opponents of comparable worth (e.g., the business community in general) dispute the idea that women are occupationally segregated. They assert that the true condition is one of *occupational concentration*, which results from the free choice of women to plan their lives differently from men. According to this argument, many women expect to leave the work force for some period to have children or care for their families. Because they do not anticipate uninterrupted work careers, they voluntarily choose not to invest in the education, training, and career development required to qualify for higher-paying jobs. Thus, the argument goes, it is these choices, not discrimination, that accounts for most of the pay gap between women and men.[11]

This point of view is challenged by advocates of comparable worth who point to the rapid rise in the percentage of married women with children under age six who are participating in the labor force, from 18.6 percent in 1960 to 59.9 percent in 1991. They also point to the growing representation of women among college students earning degrees, as a measure of their intent to pursue careers. The percentage of bachelor's and master's degrees earned by women rose about 10 percent from 1971 to 1989, when it reached slightly above 50 percent of all these degrees awarded. Even more impressive was the rise in the same period of the percentage of doctorates awarded to women, from 14.3 percent to 36.5 percent of all such degrees.[12]

Pursuing their own line of reasoning, critics maintain that if the position of women in the labor force is a matter of choice, not discrimination, occupational concentration would end if women would prepare for and seek the same careers as men. In fact, they say, if comparable worth were implemented on a large scale, there might well be even greater concentration, because women would have less of an economic incentive to qualify for other occupations that have been male-dominated and better-paying. Needless to say, advocates of comparable worth strongly disagree, primarily because they see discrimination as playing a central role in creating and maintaining the wage gap between male- and female-dominated occupations.

COMPARABLE WORTH IN THE COURTS

Attempts to validate the theory of comparable worth in the courts have not received a warm reception. The Department of Justice has maintained that the comparable-worth argument does not establish a cause for action under federal law, and the EEOC has consistently turned aside complaints based on such arguments. In *County of Washington* v. *Gunther* (1981)[13] the Supreme Court did rule that this county in Oregon was intentionally discriminating against women because it was paying female matrons less to guard women prisoners than it was paying male guards to watch men. The Court, however, did not endorse the concept of comparable worth.

Subsequent decisions by federal appeals courts have allayed public employers' fears that failure to do a job evaluation study could leave them open to successful charges of intentional discrimination. Currently, plaintiffs seeking remedies under Title VII of the 1964 Civil Rights Act are required to prove that their employers have intentionally discriminated against them. The courts also have a long and continuing tradition of allowing employers to counter wage discrimination claims by arguing that their pay systems are based on the realities of the labor market.[14] These were the arguments used in the Ninth Circuit Court of Appeals to strike down a district court order issued in 1983 requiring Washington State to immediately bring pay for all workers in predominantly female job categories up to their "evaluated worth."

The Washington State Experience

The State of Washington was the first to recognize the inequality in payment of its women employees. In 1974 a civil service study had concluded that men and women were being paid differently. The state then initiated a comparable-worth study, and in 1976, funds were appropriated to implement needed pay adjustments. Efforts to rectify the situation and provide pay equity for women ran into difficulty the following year, however, when the newly elected governor blocked the appropriation. Eventually, the U.S. district and appeals courts were drawn into the controversy.

The issue was pursued by employee organizations, and in 1981 the American Federation of State, County, and Municipal Employees (AFSCME) and the Washington Federation of State Employees filed sex discrimination charges with the EEOC. When the commission failed to act, AFSCME filed suit the following year in federal district court.[15] In December 1983, Judge Jack E. Tanner ruled that in setting pay the Washington State government had been guilty of sex discrimination under Title VII of the Civil Rights Act of 1964. The court found intentional discrimination because the comparable-worth study commissioned by the state had found a difference of about 20 percent in compensation between mostly male and mostly female job classifications. The state was ordered to pay thousands of women employees the salaries they were entitled to under a comparable-worth plan adopted by the state but only partially implemented.

A major setback for supporters of comparable worth was the reversal on appeal of this ruling by a three-judge panel of the Ninth Circuit in 1985. Judge Anthony Kennedy, now a Supreme Court justice, wrote the decision for the unanimous panel. In terms anticipating the Supreme Court's reasoning in *Ward's Cove* (1989) (see Chapter 2), Kennedy stated that *discriminatory intent* had not been established; moreover, it "could not be inferred from statistical evidence, even when joined with the defendant's study showing that the jobs in question were of comparable value."[16] According to the court, paying market rates could not be interpreted as intent to discriminate, and the free market was not a "suspect enterprise." In Bill Shaw's words, the court's position was that intent to discriminate "means more than mere awareness of consequences" and the plaintiff "must prove this element of its case with evidence that the employer chose its wage policy *because of* its effect on the protected class, not merely *in spite* of its effect."[17]

In an attempt to avert further appeals, an out-of-court settlement was reached between AFSCME and Washington State four months after the appeals court decision was announced. Under the agreement, over $100 million in pay raises were to be paid to nearly 35,000 state workers, most of them women earning less than $14,000 a year at that time. Although the settlement was far smaller than the initial district court decision had provided for, it was greeted by unionists and women's advocates as a victory in securing recognition of the principle of comparable worth.

THE FUTURE OF COMPARABLE WORTH

The appeals court's reasoning in the Washington State case is a precedent that continues to present serious difficulties in the pursuit of pay equity or comparable worth through the courts. Subsequent rulings by the Supreme Court, such as *Ward's Cove*, have offered even less encouragement, and it remains to be seen if the Civil Rights Act of 1991 will make any difference (see Chapter 2).

In light of the federal courts' stance to date, efforts to advance the cause of comparable worth in the future are likely to be focused on legislation, executive initiatives, and negotiated labor-management contracts. In addition to substantial legislative and administrative progress in the states and localities during the 1980s, comparable worth had successes at the bargaining table.[18] In 1985, for example, the City of Los Angeles and AFSCME negotiated a settlement under which some $12 million was allocated to close the pay gap that existed between the three entry-level positions that were then dominated by women and the three entry-level positions dominated by men.[19]

It is unlikely that the debate over comparable worth will "go away" in the near future. It encompasses key policy issues that divide employers, elective officials, political parties, women's organizations, and even the unions. While unions with large male memberships have historically shown little interest in improving women's pay,[20] there are about 20 unions that have consistently raised this issue in collective bargaining negotiations.[21] As the political influence of women on all levels of government grows, the pressure on many public employers to close or eliminate the wage gap between men and women is likely to increase accordingly.

PAY FOR PERFORMANCE IN THE PUBLIC SERVICE

One of the major reasons for the rush to implement pay for performance (PFP), or merit pay systems, under Civil Service Reform II has been public pressure for more bureaucratic accountability and productivity. In James L. Perry's words, pay for performance is "a message from politicians and the public that the governed are in control and things are as they should be. At the same time, it is a way for administrators to communicate that they are responsive to important external constituencies and that they are doing something about perceptions of lagging performance."[22]

Using PFP schemes to raise productivity has been a basic element of management thinking in the United States since the late 1800s. The early scientific managers were well known for their efforts to develop systems that tightly linked factory workers' output to their pay. The current emphasis on merit pay in government, which emerged in a climate of fiscal stress, concentrates on raising the productivity of white-collar workers by tying pay to performance.

Although some states and localities were experimenting with PFP before passage of the Civil Service Reform Act in 1978, Title V of that act was a highly visible break with traditional pay practices in the public sector. Borrowing from private-sector practices, it tied salary increases for grades 13–15 managers to their performance ratings. Since 1978, PFP programs have been adopted by over 20 states and many local governments.[23] In the late 1980s, well over 25 percent of the major U.S. cities reported that they were using performance appraisals to allocate rewards for managerial and nonmanagerial personnel.[24]

Pay-for-Performance Programs

Pay-for-performance plans take a variety of forms, including bonuses, shared cost savings, and performance-based wage and salary increases. Individual as well as group performance incentives are used, but individual bonuses and base-pay increases are by far the most common in the public sector. In some jurisdictions, only supervisory and managerial personnel are covered; in others, PFP is restricted to nonmanagerial personnel. In some states and localities, both groups are covered by the same or different systems. In other words, *pay for performance* is a generic term that applies to a wide variety of monetary incentives programs.

No matter the form it takes, the widespread popularity of PFP plans in managerial circles is based on the proposition that they remedy a fundamental flaw in traditional systems by making pay *contingent on performance*, as opposed to grade and seniority. Logically, they accept the psychological model of motivation set forth in expectancy theory (see Chapter 3), which is the basis for the idea that pay should be treated as a management tool because it can be a powerful source of day-to-day control over employee behavior. The idea is that traditional systems of pay administration, which rely on membership-based rather than individual inducements, do not give supervisors the kind of discretion and flexibility they need to use pay as an effective motivator.[25]

Other organizational advantages attributed to PFP programs include the following enumerated by Thomas Rollins:

1. They increase the probability that superior performers will feel valued and equitably compensated for their efforts.
2. They focus management's attention on the importance of accurate performance appraisals using preestablished, measurable standards and objectives.
3. They give supervisors a means of pressuring poor performers to either improve or leave.
4. They encourage supervisors and subordinates to communicate clearly about goals and expectations.
5. They improve the capacity of organizations to allocate limited financial resources effectively.[26]

Despite these possible benefits, the experience in the public sector with pay-for-performance programs strongly suggests that simplistic applications of expectancy theory are unlikely to be successful, for a variety of reasons. Overemphasis on external rewards such as pay, for example, may undermine intrinsic sources of individual motivation (such as self-esteem and contributing to organizational achievements). Employees' attention and concern may not be directed to organizational goals, and merit pay for individuals as opposed to groups may promote interpersonal competition and conflict in situations where jobs require coordination and collaboration.

Another potential problem is that the highly specific performance contracts between supervisors and subordinates associated with PFP impose damaging limits on organizational flexibility, because they may encourage employees to concentrate on meeting contract terms while neglecting other important responsibilities. Moreover, performance appraisal techniques, instruments, and procedures cannot always be trusted to provide valid distinctions among levels of performance, especially for professional-technical and managerial jobs. And, within public budget constraints, the funds needed to support PFP programs may not be forthcoming, which could lead employees to be cynical or suspicious of management's intentions.[27]

Overall, the experience with pay for performance in the public sector provides ample reason for caution and careful evaluation. The report of a study by the National Academy of Sciences issued in 1991 included the conclusion that there is no solid empirical evidence that PFP or merit pay programs are effective.[28] These findings were also noted in the 1991 report of the Pay-for-Performance Labor-Management Committee established under terms of the Federal Employees Pay Comparability Act. In this report to the OPM, the committee advised that "Governmentwide implementation of any new pay-for-performance system for General Schedule employees should be preceded by a period of extensive and comprehensive experimentation involving a variety of programs that are tailored to the contextual conditions of Federal agencies."[29] The same year, and in a similar vein, a committee established to evaluate the federal Performance Management and Recognition System reported finding "virtually no empirical evidence that the PMRS has increased individual or organizational productivity."[30] The recommendations of these committees are discussed at the end of this chapter, but clearly, findings such as these provide little justification for an across-the-board imposition of PFP in the public service.

THE FEDERAL EXPERIENCE WITH MERIT PAY

Merit pay in the federal government has been by far the most extensively described and evaluated of these programs. The federal experience with merit pay or pay for performance illustrates a number of the problems with such systems, and the lessons learned by federal policymakers can be of potential value to states and localities contemplating them.

The Merit Pay System

The Merit Pay System (MPS) created by the CSRA in 1978 is usually seen as the first federal effort to implement PFP (see Chapter 5). However, there had been incremental efforts to strengthen the link between pay and performance, starting in 1949 with the Commission on Organization of the Executive Branch, known as the first Hoover Commission. This commission recommended that employees were to get within-grade increases only when their supervisors certified that they had earned them. The Classification Act of 1949 established the ten-step pay ranges for each of the General Schedule (GS) grades, and the Performance Rating Act of 1950 required agencies to set up performance appraisal systems with three summary ratings (outstanding, satisfactory, and unsatisfactory). Initially, within-grade step increases were tied to seniority, and there were no monetary rewards for those receiving an outstanding performance rating.

The first legislative attempt to connect pay with performance was the Incentives Awards Act of 1954, which authorized recognition and cash payments for superior accomplishments, suggestions, inventions, or other personal efforts. The Federal Salary Reform Act of 1962 required that an "acceptable level of competence" standard be used in granting within-grade increases, and it also stressed rewarding exceptional performances with quality step increases (QSIs) to base pay.[31] By 1977, however, the staff working on the proposed civil service reform act under President Carter had concluded that the linkage between pay and performance in existing plans was at best weak; within-grade increases were all but automatic, and cash awards and QSIs were seldom used.

Under the merit pay plan mandated by the CSRA, GS 13–15 employees (managers and supervisors) were included and placed in a General Management (GM) pay plan designation. The pay range for GM employees' grades was "open"; that is, there were no preset rates for steps within the grade. A distinctive feature of this plan was that these employees were guaranteed only half the annual comparability adjustments received by GS workers. All other funds available for pay increases were placed by agencies into merit pay pools. Within each agency, the GM employees had to compete with one another, on the basis of their performance ratings, for merit increases paid out of these pools, while those in GS positions continued to receive full comparability adjustments as an entitlement. Otherwise, agencies were given considerable discretion to develop their own merit pay systems.

The intention of the framers of the CSRA was to make this the first step in the Merit Pay System, to be followed by an extension of merit pay to all federal executive branch personnel if the experience with the GM level proved successful. However, serious problems developed even before the system was to become effective throughout the federal service in October 1981. The system suffered its first official setback with a decision by the comptroller general that resulted in a substantial reduction in the funds available for merit pay purposes. Moreover, many GM employees had complained that they were receiving "meaningless" pay increases, resulting in lower total pay than their GS counterparts.[32] With these funding cuts, unhappiness with the MPS spread rapidly. In the mid-1980s, the GAO reported that support for the MPS was very weak, and about half of the GM group said they wanted to return to the General Schedule. GAO studies found that over 75 percent of the respondents believed that merit pay had not motivated them to perform better.[33]

Researchers Jone L. Pearce and James L. Perry, who studied attitudes toward merit pay in five agencies, reported in 1983 that employees were no better motivated under merit pay than they were under previous compensation policies. They observed, "It is not that federal managers do not value pay as a reward....These managers report that effort is *less* likely to lead to a good performance rating, and therefore these managers believe that merit pay does not encourage them to perform their jobs well or contribute to their agencies' effectiveness." Their conclusion was that the results of the merit pay experiment at grades 13–15 did not warrant extending coverage to the rest of the General Schedule.[34]

Why did a program intended to motivate better performance fail so badly? One reason was that agency appraisal systems were put into effect under a very short deadline and without pretesting. Many GM employees believed that the performance standards for their positions were not correct or that the ratings they received were inaccurate. Then the requirement that no more money be spent on merit pay than had been expended under the previous system set a restrictive upper limit on the pay increases that managers and supervisors could achieve with superior performance ratings. Fixed limits on merit pay pools created conditions under which one employee's gain was another's loss, a win-lose situation which tended to generate trivial differences in rewards. For each agency, as the number of superior performers increased, their individual pay raises decreased. In other words, many employees came to believe that outstanding performance does not lead to meaningful pay raises.

In response to these conditions, pay pool administrators modified the distributions of performance ratings in order to achieve higher payouts for those receiving the highest (outstanding) ratings, but this undermined confidence in the objectivity and fairness of the MPS. The phenomenon of such "managed ratings" raised the question: If the ratings are accurate, why should they be manipulated? Budgetary constraints and rigidities further aggravated suspicions about how the Merit Pay System was being administered. All in all, the system was implemented in an atmosphere of hostility toward public employees, an attitude cultivated by the Reagan administration and shared by many in Congress who opposed fully funding the system.

The Performance Management and Recognition System

In 1984, Congress responded to these problems with the Merit Pay System by abolishing it, instituting in its stead the Performance Management and Recognition System (PMRS), which is currently in force. The PMRS represents return to a more centralized approach to federal pay administration; many of the flexibilities in the Merit Pay System were eliminated in order to restore pay equity across agencies and between GS and GM personnel. Under the PMRS, all GM employees who receive performance appraisals of fully successful must be given full annual comparability and merit increases of 1 percent, and GM employees rated outstanding are given raises of 3 percent. Those rated one level below fully successful are guaranteed one-half of the comparability increase, and those rated unsatisfactory receive no adjustment. The PMRS also encourages the use of cash bonuses or performance awards to recognize exceptional performance.

The original PMRS legislation contained a five-year sunset provision, and when Congress evaluated the system in 1989, it heard evidence of major discontent with the current system but no consensus as to what should replace it. The PMRS was extended for 18 months with some minor changes, including a requirement that agencies were to develop performance improvement plans (PIPs) for all employees rated below fully successful. In light of the continuing problems with merit pay for managers, an extension of pay for performance to the entire federal white-collar work force was removed from the Pay Comparability Act of 1990, and the Pay-for-Performance Labor-Management Committee was established by Congress to study the issue. In early 1991, Congress extended the PMRS through September 30, 1993, and another committee, the PMRS Review Committee, was established to study the system and make recommendations to the director of the OPM on policy for a fair, effective pay-for-performance system for federal managers.

The conclusion of the PMRS Review Committee report issued in November 1991 was that the system had failed to meet three basic criteria, not unlike the failings that had flawed the Merit Pay system.

First, performance ratings were suspect and not perceived as accurate. Second, there was doubt about the extent to which real differences in performance were linked to meaningful payouts. Third, many GM employees saw the system as unfair in its administration as well as its outcomes.

Recommendations on Merit Pay and PFP

The two committee reports on pay for performance issued in 1991 both included recommendations for improving provisions for merit pay or PFP in the federal service. The PMRS Review Committee made some 38 recommendations over a wide range of topics, including improved performance appraisal processes, expanded system coverage, increased funding of merit increases, and training for GM-grade employees and their supervisors. Overall, the committee expressed support for the *concept* of pay for performance, and to improve the PMRS it favored an incremental approach rather than the creation of an entirely new system. The committee also urged Congress to allow federal agencies greater flexibility to expand and adapt pay-for-performance programs to serve their particular structure, culture, and objectives.[35]

The Pay-for-Performance Labor-Management Committee's report was equally cautious about creating a new merit pay program. In light of the existing state of knowledge and research, it evaluated the GS system for measuring and rewarding performance as "a workable pay-for-performance system." The committee noted that GS employees must be rated satisfactory to receive within-grade increases, and quality step increases are available. It suggested therefore that federal agencies should make better use of the resources available to them:

> What is often lacking in managing the General Schedule system is a commitment to use the flexibilities that are authorized under current regulations governing performance and incentive awards to recognize employee accomplishments. Rather than replacing one base pay adjustment system with another, the Federal Government may be well served by a renewed focus on, and dedication to, improved management of the current General Schedule system.[36]

Other recommendations of the Pay-for-Performance Committee included:

1. Providing full and adequate funding so that employees will see payouts as meaningful.

2. Giving federal agencies the authority to design and administer individual pay-for-performance programs to fit their specific "needs, objectives, workforce characteristics, and organizational culture."

3. Taking actions designed to assure fairness and to prevent adverse impact on any "class of employees."

4. Creating mechanisms through which employees are able to participate in the design, implementation, and evaluation of pay-for-performance programs.

The OPM is currently evaluating the reports of both committees, and recommendations for policy changes and new legislation may be forthcoming in the Clinton administration. In any case, it is obvious that the thinking about pay for performance in the federal government has changed greatly since the early 1980s. The design and successful implementation of merit pay systems is now understood as a difficult, long-term challenge.

■

NOTES

1. Alice H. Cook, "Pay Equity: Theory and Implementation," in Carolyn Ban and Norma M. Riccucci (eds.), *Public Personnel Management: Current Concerns—Future Challenges* (New York: Longman, 1991), p. 101. Emphasis in the original.

2. Paula England, "Socioeconomic Explanations of Job Segregation," in Helen Remick (ed.), *Comparable Worth & Wage Discrimination* (Philadelphia, PA: Temple University Press, 1984), pp. 28–46.

3. U.S. Bureau of the Census, *Statistical Abstract of the United States: 1992*, 112th edition (Washington, DC, 1992), Table 629.

4. Laura L. Vertz, "Pay Inequalities between Women and Men in State and Local Government: An Examination of the Political Context of the Comparable Worth Controversy," *Women & Politics*, vol. 7, no. 2 (Summer 1987), pp. 43–57.

5. Sami M. Abbasi, Joe H. Murrey, Jr., and Kenneth W. Hollman, "Comparable Worth: Should You Reexamine Your Compensation Program?" in John Matzer, Jr. (ed.), *Pay and Benefits: New Ideas for Local Governments* (Washington, DC: International City Management Association, 1988), p. 30.

6. Robert W. Mulcahy and Jon E. Anderson, "The Bargaining Battleground Called Comparable Worth," *Public Personnel Management*, vol. 15, no. 3 (Fall 1986), pp. 241–242.

7. Richard W. Beatty and James R. Beatty, "Some Problems with Contemporary Job Evaluation Systems," in Remick (ed.), *Comparable Worth & Wage Discrimination*, pp. 59–78.
8. J. Donald Treiman, "Effect of Choice of Factors and Factor Weights in Job Evaluation," in Remick (ed.), *Comparable Worth & Wage Discrimination*, pp. 88–89.
9. M. Anne Hill and Mark R. Killingsworth (eds.), *Comparable Worth: Analyses and Evidence* (New York State School of Industrial and Labor Relations: ILR Press, 1989).
10. Elaine Sorensen, "The Wage Effects of Occupational Sex Composition: A Review and New Findings," in Hill and Killingsworth (eds.), *Comparable Worth*, pp. 57–79.
11. Myron Lieberman, "The Conversion of Interests to Principles: The Case of Comparable Worth," *Journal of Collective Negotiations*, vol. 15, no. 2 (1986), pp. 145–152.
12. U.S. Bureau of the Census, *Statistical Abstract of the United States: 1992*, Tables 620, 279.
13. 452 U.S. 161 (1981).
14. Neil E. Reichenberg, "Pay Equity in Review," *Public Personnel Management*, vol. 15, no. 3 (Fall 1986), pp. 213–214.
15. *AFSCME et al.* v. *State of Washington et al.* (1983), No. C82-465T, United States District Court for the Western District of Washington.
16. *AFSCME* v. *Washington*, 770 F2d. 1401 (1985).
17. Bill Shaw, "Comparable Worth and Its Prospects: *AFSCME* v. *State of Washington*," *Labor Law Journal* (February 1987), p. 107.
18. Reichenberg, "Pay Equity in Review," pp. 225–228.
19. Ibid., p. 118.
20. Helen LaVan, Marsha Katz, Maura S. Malloy, and Peter Stonebraker, "Comparable Worth: A Comparison of Litigated Cases in the Public and Private Sectors," *Public Personnel Management*, vol. 16, no. 3 (Fall 1987), pp. 283–284.
21. Cook, "Pay Equity," p. 110.
22. James L. Perry, "Linking Pay to Performance: The Controversy Continues," in Ban and Riccucci (eds.), *Public Personnel Management*, p. 80.
23. John M. Greiner, "Motivational Programs and Productivity Improvement in Times of Limited Resources," *Public Productivity Review*, vol. 10, no. 39 (Fall 1986), pp. 81–102; U.S. General Accounting Office, *Pay for Performance: State and International Pay-for-Performance Systems* (Washington, DC, October 1990).
24. David N. Ammons and Arnold Rodriguez, "Performance Appraisal Practices for Upper Management in City Governments," *Public Administration Review*, vol. 46 (September–October 1986), pp. 460–467; Robert E. England and William M. Parle, "Nonmanagerial Performance Appraisal Practices in Large American Cities," *Public Administration Review*, vol. 47 (November–December 1987), pp. 498–504.
25. Gerald T. Gabris and Kenneth Mitchell, "Merit Based Performance Appraisal and Productivity: Do Employees Perceive the Connection?" *Pub-*

lic Productivity Review, vol. 9, no. 4 (Winter 1985), pp. 311–327.

26. Thomas Rollins, "Pay for Performance: The Pros and Cons," in Matzer (ed.), *Pay and Benefits*, pp. 5–8.

27. Gilbert B. Siegel, "The Jury Is Still Out on Merit Pay in Government," *Review of Public Personnel Administration*, vol. 7, no. 3 (Summer 1987), pp. 3–15; U.S. General Accounting Office, *Pay for Performance* (Washington, DC, 1990), pp. 23–24; James L. Perry, "Merit Pay in the Public Sector: The Case for a Failure of Theory," *Review of Public Personnel Administration*, vol. 7, no. 1 (Fall 1986), pp. 57–69; Gerald T. Gabris, Kenneth Mitchell, and Ronald McLemore, "Rewarding Individual and Team Productivity: The Biloxi Merit Bonus Plan," *Public Personnel Management*, vol. 14, no. 3 (Fall 1985), pp. 231–244; Gerald T. Gabris, "Can Merit Pay Systems Avoid Creating Discord between Supervisors and Subordinates?: Another Uneasy Look at Performance Appraisal," *Review of Public Personnel Administration*, vol. 7, no. 1 (Fall 1986), pp. 70–89.

28. George T. Milkovich and Alexandra Wigdor, *Pay for Performance: Evaluating Performance Appraisal and Merit Pay*, National Academy of Sciences, National Research Council (Washington, DC: National Academy Press, 1991).

29. Pay-for-Performance Labor-Management Committee, *Strengthening the Link Between Pay and Performance* (Washington, DC, November 1991), pp. i–ii.

30. Performance Management and Recognition System Review Committee, *Advancing Managerial Excellence: A Report on Improving the Performance Management and Recognition System* (Washington, DC, November 5, 1991), p. 14.

31. Ibid., pp. 1–2.

32. Ibid., p. 3.

33. U.S. General Accounting Office, *A 2-Year Appraisal of Merit Pay in Three Agencies*, report to the Chairwoman, Subcommittee on Compensation and Employee Benefits of the House of Representatives (Washington, DC, March 26, 1984).

34. Jone L. Pearce and James L. Perry, "Federal Merit Pay: A Longitudinal Analysis," *Public Administration Review*, vol. 43, no. 4 (July–August 1983).

35. Performance Management and Recognition System Review Committee, *Advancing Managerial Excellence*, pp. 49–52.

36. Pay-for-Performance Labor-Management Committee, *Strengthening the Link*, p. ii.

Public Personnel and Work-Family Issues

14

As the demographic composition of the American work force changes, public personnel administration is pressured to keep pace (see Chapter 1). Two of the most rapidly growing segments of the work force are women and older workers, and the traditional family structures and employment patterns upon which many personnel policies have been based are rapidly becoming things of the past. If public employers are to compete successfully for human resources and to manage them effectively, personnel policies and practices must adapt to these new realities. The challenge is to adopt and put into practice public personnel policies that fully address work-family issues such as flexible work schedules and locations, family leave, child care, and elder care.

WORK AND THE CHANGING AMERICAN FAMILY

Data on the demographics of the work force are collected by the U.S. Bureau of the Census Current Population Surveys in terms of the civilian labor force (CLF), defined as all civilians in the noninstitutional population 16 years and over who are classified as either employed or unemployed. A significant change since 1950 has been the increase in the proportion of all women who are participating in the CLF. In 1990, about 57 million women were working or looking for jobs, up over 200 percent since 1950; the increase for men was 55 percent. Over the same period, the proportion of women participating in the labor force grew from 33 to 60 percent, while the male participation rate fell from 86 to 76 percent. The Bureau of Labor Statistics (BLS) predicts that these trends will continue, and by the year 2005 the female participation rate will reach as high as 66.1 percent and the male participation rate will fall as low as 72.9 percent.[1]

The number of dual-income families in the CLF has also expanded significantly. In 1990, about 70 percent of the men in the CLF had wives who also worked, compared to about 32 percent in 1960. Another important demographic shift has been the substantial increase in the number of working mothers. Less than 20 percent of married women with children under the age of six worked in 1960; by 1990, 59 percent were in the labor market, as were 49 percent of single mothers and 64 percent of mothers who were widowed, divorced, or separated. The percentages were higher for mothers with school-age children (ages 6–17); in this category, the labor force participation rate was 74 percent of married mothers, 70 percent of single mothers, and 80 percent of widowed, divorced, or separated mothers.[2]

For public as well as private employers, many of the assumptions that dominated human resources policies for decades are no longer valid. Marriage and childbirth occur later in life than they did in the 1950s and 1960s, and there are more single-parent families. Older people are more likely to live alone and to depend on their adult children for help of one kind or another. The traditional family in which the man worked and the woman stayed home to have children and care for the family is now a relatively small segment of the society—well below 20 percent of all families.[3] Nevertheless, with a few exceptions, personnel policies on all levels of government continue to be based on the assumption that the work force is a homogeneous one in which traditional family arrangements prevail.

Until recently, public employers gave little thought to questions about the fit between personnel policies such as those governing benefits and working hours and the needs or preferences of workers. As the General Accounting Office notes in a 1992 report on the changing work force, many workers therefore must try to manage personal responsibilities from the office or work site, and "their ability to keep family concerns isolated from work has been rendered an historical artifact."[4] The conclusion is that federal and nonfederal (private-sector and state/local) personnel policies are often unresponsive to the new realities of family life in the United States:

Employees trying to balance family and work responsibilities have often found traditional employment policies unaccommodating. For example, workplace stress is heightened for parents when an inflexible work schedule conflicts with school hours or day care arrangements. In the absence of backup child care, parents must often miss work when a child is sick at home or regular day care arrangements break down. Workers can also be faced with agonizing choices between parenthood and job security if there are no assurances that their jobs will be waiting for them after they take time off for the birth, adoption, or care of children.[5]

From the employer's standpoint, these kinds of problems have important organizational as well as social implications. Today's workers are likely to need or want a balance between their on- and off-the-job responsibilities, and the research has suggested that the employer's responsiveness to these concerns is an important factor in its ability to recruit or retain workers and to improve productivity.[6] Since traditional employment practices have not been able to meet the challenge of helping workers achieve a balance between work and family life, attention has focused on the need for new, more creative approaches.

The Response of Employers

There are signs that both public- and private-sector employers are beginning to respond to this challenge. For example, the proportion of state and local government employees who are eligible for child-care assistance grew from 2 percent to 9 percent between 1985 and 1989,[7] and new resources are being developed to meet the need. Thus, while social values and demographic patterns are beyond the control of employers, responsive personnel policies designed to exploit emerging opportunities are certainly possible. A variety of new programs and techniques to improve the response of personnel systems to work-family issues is being used in many corporations and governments. They include flexible work programs, family-leave policies, child-care assistance, and provisions for elder care.

FLEXIBLE WORK PROGRAMS

Most public personnel systems provide for standardized work schedules and benefits that apply to all employees and cannot be tailored to individuals' personal or family situations. Flexible work programs are intended to allow a better fit between organizational requirements and individual employees' needs and preferences. Programs that have been introduced in various jurisdictions include part-time work and job-sharing, alternative schedules, flexible workplaces, and flexible benefits.

Part-Time Work and Job-Sharing

Provisions for part-time work respond to the situations of employees who want to (or must) spend more time with their families than the normal 40-hour week allows. The BLS defines part-time employment as working less than 35 hours a week.

An effort to expand part-time opportunities in the federal service was the Federal Employees Part-Time Career Employment Act, passed in 1978. The act recognizes that "many individuals in our society possess great productive potential which goes unused because they cannot meet the requirements of a standard workweek," and it summarizes the advantages of part-time employment as follows:

1. Helps older workers make the transition into retirement.
2. Opens employment opportunities for disabled and other workers who need a reduced workweek.
3. Gives parents a chance to balance family responsibilities with the need to earn additional income.
4. Supports students' efforts to finance their educations or vocational training.
5. Provides a basis for higher productivity and job satisfaction while reducing turnover rates and absenteeism.
6. Enhances management's flexibility in meeting work requirements and addressing shortages in certain occupational categories.
7. Benefits society by reducing unemployment and retaining the skills of experienced and trained people.[8]

In this early federal effort to address the changing nature of the work force, part-time positions are defined as those involving a 16- to 32-hour workweek. Agencies are required to prorate contributions to health insurance premiums for part-time workers and to set up part-time employment career programs. The Office of Personnel Management is given responsibility for providing technical assistance to agencies and for periodic evaluations and reports to the president and Congress.

This legislation was passed in order to correct what Congress saw as serious weaknesses in the government's approach to part-time employment by calling for agencies to "make a substantial good faith effort to set goals which would represent meaningful progress and to move toward them." In 1986, however, the GAO concluded that neither the OPM nor the agencies had fulfilled their duties under the act. In 1991, the Merit Systems Protection Board noted that a few agencies, such as the Department of Veterans' Affairs and the OPM, had established formal programs, but most part-time positions in the federal service had probably been created in response to requests from individual full-time employees, rather than as part of a planned program or policy.[9]

The available evidence suggests that part-time workers are as productive as their full-time counterparts, and personnel costs are not significantly higher. Federal agencies report no serious difficulty recruiting part-time employees. The MSPB, noting that opportunities to expand the number of part-time jobs do exist throughout the federal service, and nothing prevents federal managers from hiring several part-time employees to fill previously full-time positions, concluded that the limited progress in this area was the result of "bureaucratic inertia."[10]

The term *job-sharing* refers to a form of part-time work in which two or more employees share the responsibilities of one full-time position by splitting work days or weeks. In addition to sharing a job on the basis of time, workers may also divide the job tasks, depending on their skills and expertise. A single job's salary and benefits are typically split among those doing the work. Job-sharing is a more complicated form of part-time work because it combines the efforts of two or more employees in order to fill one full-time slot. For this idea to work, there must be at least two employees in the same agency who are personally and professionally compatible and who want to share one job.[11]

Under the Part-Time Career Employment Act, in 1990 Congress required the OPM to set up a formal job-sharing program in which it is expected to function as a clearinghouse through which persons looking for job-sharing opportunities are matched with positions that may be filled under such an arrangement. The OPM's pilot automated registration project, called the OPM Connection, covers the cities of Boston, Chicago, Los Angeles, and Washington, D.C. The project matches employees looking for job-sharing partners, and the team then can apply for full-time vacancies announced by agencies.[12] Federal agencies are also supplied with the names of workers interested in part-time and shared job opportunities. As of early 1991, about 800 employees were sharing jobs, but a significant expansion of this approach to part-time employment is considered to be unlikely, primarily because of the coordination and scheduling complexities involved.

In the long term, public employers are likely to benefit greatly from part-time employment programs. In 1991, about 25 percent of working women in the United States were on part-time schedules, but only 10 percent of the men were working part-time.[13] Because of economic, social, and demographic changes, a far larger percentage of the work force may be working part-time in the future. As the MSPB has observed, "The increasing role of women in the work force, and the government's increasing need for women to fill critical jobs, both argue for creating more part-time positions."[14] Most high-level part-time federal employees (GS 11–15) are women; the overall percentage of part-time positions in these grades increased from 10 percent in 1978 to over 20 percent in 1991.[15]

Alternative Work Schedules

Alternative work schedules (AWS) are now found on all levels of government. The various forms are modifications of the traditional 9:00-to-5:00, five-days-a-week schedule. Two basic forms are widely used. In one, called *flexitime* in the federal government, the work day is divided into two kinds of time: core time and flexible time. All workers must be on the job during core time, but flexible time allows for variations in starting and stopping times. Core time, for example, might be from 10:00 a.m. to 3:00 p.m.; in flexible time, some workers might arrive at 7:00 a.m. and leave at 3:00 p.m., while others start at 10:00 a.m. and stop at 6:00 p.m. All employees work an eight-hour day and must account for the time they are scheduled to be on the job.

The other basic form of AWS offers a variety of options for workers who want work schedules that regularly free up a day or two for personal or family use. The OPM defines this as *compressed time*, an 80-hour biweekly basic work requirement which is scheduled for less than ten full workdays.[16] The 80-hour requirement is fulfilled in a variety of ways; according to the MSPB:

> ...there are "5-4/9" workweeks (5 days one week and 4 days the next week), 4-day workweeks, and 3-day workweeks. Each of these requires the employee to work, under a fixed schedule, more that 8 hours per day. As a result of working these longer days, the employee is able to work fewer than 10 days in each 2-week pay period.[17]

BLS reports for 1989 indicated almost 20 percent of full-time federal workers were on flexible work schedules; the figures for state and local workers were 13 and 6 percent, respectively. In contrast, about 12 percent of workers in the private sector were taking advantage of AWS systems. These systems appear to have strong support among federal workers. A 1991 GAO survey revealed that 40 percent of the respondents were on flexible work schedules, and almost half reported that they would like even more flexibility. One measure of the popularity of AWS is the GAO's finding that only 13 percent of those *not* using flexible schedules said they did so "on their own volition," and over 40 percent said "being allowed to work flexible schedules would make them more likely to stay with the federal government."[18] A year earlier, the MSPB had found that almost half of those who answered its survey of federal employees listed flexible work schedules as a reason for staying.[19]

As a trendsetter in the use of alternative work schedules, the federal government can offer useful guidance to states and localities. The first flexible work schedules were established by the Bureau of Indian Affairs and the Social Security Administration during the early 1970s. Both agencies began their AWS experiments in an effort to deal with tardiness, low productivity, poor morale, and, in the case of the SSA, extensive leave-taking without pay. For both, the results were positive.

AWS programs were not technically legal, however, until 1979, when the Flexible and Compressed Work Schedules Act of 1978 became effective. This legislation created a three-year experimental AWS program intended to evaluate its effects. The responsibility for setting up, managing, and evaluating the program was given to the OPM; evaluation was required in six areas: (1) efficiency of government operations, (2) impact on mass transit and traffic, (3) energy consumption, (4) service to the public, (5) opportunities for full- and part-time employment, and (6) responses of individuals and families. The highly favorable results found by the OPM led to passage of the Federal Employees Flexible and Compressed Work Schedules Act of 1982, which established AWS as an ongoing program and imposed a three-year sunset provision. By the end of this period, strongly positive evaluations by the OPM, the GAO, Congress, and others had set the stage for passage in 1985 of Public Law 99-196, which made AWS a permanent program.[20]

Considering the federal government's 20-year experience with alternative work schedules, the MSPB concluded in 1991:

> ... it is clear that AWS programs are having a meaningfully positive effect on agency operations and employees.... agencies should be looking for more opportunities to expand use of AWS and to better publicize its availability. Since the Federal Government is already a leader in this benefit area, it makes sense to capitalize on this fact, and to use it as a marketing tool in recruitment efforts.[21]

Flexible Workplaces

Flexible workplace and *flexiplace* are terms describing several forms of paid employment and employer-employee relationships in which the location of the work site is shifted away from the traditional primary office. These include work done at home or at satellite offices and telecommuting or teleworking, in which sophisticated communication and computer systems are used to carry out work assignments from remote locations.[22]

The idea of designating an employee's home as an official work site is not new to the public sector. In 1957, the U.S. comptroller general authorized federal agencies to pay employees for work done at home if the agencies could verify and evaluate performance, the work could really be done at home, and it made sense from an agency perspective to use the home as a work site. Such arrangements were used on an informal basis to deal with special situations, but no organized federal flexiplace program existed until 1990.

Current thinking about flexible workplaces stresses several potential benefits. According to a 1990 report of the President's Council on Management Improvement (PCMI), flexiplace has the potential to help by:

> ... attract[ing] and retain[ing] employees in critical occupations and positions, such as technical and scientific researchers or computer programmers; targeting new labor markets such as severely handicapped individuals; reducing space and associated costs; or enabling agencies to better conduct the organization's work by allowing increased flexibility in the location of the work site.[23]

The federal service's limited exposure to flexiplace has suggested that it is a concept worth exploring. The best-known initiative was the Federal Flexible Workplace Pilot Project, established in 1990 under guidelines set forth by the PCMI. This project is overseen by the General Services Administration (GSA) and the OPM, which evaluated the project at its conclusion in January 1992. Participating workers were allowed to work in their homes for specified portions of each payroll period, and agencies were authorized to pay for telephones and equipment in employees' homes. A satellite workstation, equipped with facilities needed to support telecommuting by up to 200 workers, was a part of the project plan.

By 1992, around 550 workers were participating in the project, mostly from the Environmental Protection Agency, the Equal Employment Opportunity Commission, and the Departments of Agriculture and Health and Human Services. Although this is very small number of cases upon which to base firm conclusions, the GAO reported some early indications that the federal flexiplace initiatives could improve productivity and lower costs. In the EEOC, productivity among investigators, measured by the number of interviews conducted, increased under the program. Similarly, allowing Defense Investigative Service special agents and industrial security specialists to work out of their homes eliminated the need for office space at government facilities and produced cost savings.[24] The OPM also reported favorable results in focus group meetings for participants; 90 percent of employees and 70 percent of supervisors said they considered flexiplace a desirable work arrangement.[25]

Flexible Benefits

Flexible benefits programs are becoming increasingly popular as a response to changing workers' needs and rapidly rising health-care costs. The term *cafeteria benefits* applies to programs in which employees are able to select benefits from a "menu" of alternatives that usually includes health insurance, dental care, life insurance, and other programs such as flexible spending accounts, which shelter from taxes income spent on medical care or care for dependents. Flexible benefits provide choices between taxable and nontaxable compensation and among nontaxable benefits.[26]

Flexible benefits are of special help for the growing number of dual-income families, because the two workers are allowed to construct benefit packages that complement rather than duplicate each other. The MSPB has found such plans desirable because they allow employees to tailor their benefits to their personal or family situations. The board notes that "In the past employers often structured their benefit plans assuming the traditional family structure of working husband and homemaker wife. As a result, the needs of single parents, working women, two-earner couples, and others whose needs don't match this traditional model weren't being met."[27]

As health-care and other costs continue to escalate, flexible benefits programs may also be attractive to employers because they offer some degree of cost control.[28] Employers control the level of core benefits that all workers receive, and they are able to set the total value of the additional coverage that can be selected from the menu. For employees, consequently, the tradeoff is often between greater flexibility and lower total benefits.

FAMILY-LEAVE POLICIES

The United States has been one of the few industrialized nations that did not guarantee employees the right to take time off from their jobs

to attend to family matters. This changed on February 5, 1993; the
Family and Medical Leave Act was the first legislation signed by
President Bill Clinton. Two earlier versions of the bill had been
passed by Congress but vetoed by President Bush on the grounds
that they would undermine productivity and were an unjustified intrusion by government in the operation of the marketplace.

The act, which takes effect in August 1993, applies only to companies with at least 50 employees and provides for a maximum of 12
weeks of unpaid leave from work each year for the birth or adoption
of a child, the care of a seriously ill child, spouse, or parent, or the
employee's own serious illness. Employers must maintain health insurance coverage for workers on leave and place them in the same
job or an equivalent when they return.

The argument for family leave is clearly stated in the introduction to the vetoed 1989 version of the bill (HR 770):

> H.R. 770 addresses a profound change in the composition of the
> workforce that has had a dramatic effect on families. Sixty percent of all
> mothers are currently in the labor force, which is three times what it
> was thirty years ago. In the great majority of families today, all of the
> adult members work. The role of the family as primary nurturer and
> care-giver has been fundamentally affected by a new economic reality.
> Families are struggling [to] find a way to carry out the traditional role of
> bearing and caring for children and providing the emotional and physi-
> cal support to their members during times of greatest need. When fami-
> lies fail to carry out these critical functions, the social costs are
> enormous.[29]

Family Leave in the Public Sector

Family leave is one area of employee benefits in which the public
sector has generally been ahead of the private sector. Before passage
of the federal law, some 40 states had mandated certain family-leave
rights for their employees.[30] In 1992, for example, Georgia enacted
legislation providing state workers with 12 weeks of family leave
during any 12-month period; leave is to be unpaid unless "the eligible employee obtains approval from the employer to utilize accrued
annual or sick leave."[31] Similarly, local governments, including cities
such as Denver, Seattle, and Los Angeles and Dade County, Florida,
have made family-leave rights available to their employees. Dade
County's Family Leave Ordinance requires municipalities with 50 or
more workers to allow 12 weeks of unpaid leave every two years.[32]

Federal workers generally are not guaranteed unpaid leave or
the use of accrued annual leave for family purposes, but agency

heads do have the discretion to make these decisions. Although workers are usually granted the family leave they request, in some instances requested leave without pay has been denied. There are a number of federal agencies that have given employees the right to family leave. Employees in the GAO are guaranteed up to six months for births and adoptions in addition to their sick or annual leave, and they are assured the same or comparable positions upon their return. The Tennessee Valley Authority allows up to ten weeks during a 24-month period for births, adoptions, and serious family illnesses and continues to pay the employer's share of benefit costs.[33]

Policies with regard to the use of sick leave may also be made more flexible in order to deal with family illnesses. One approach is to allow workers to use all or some of their sick leave to care for a sick family member, as in Ventura County, California, where non-managers can use up to half of their annual sick-leave days as parental leave. Government workers in over 40 states can use sick leave to care for ill dependents. In general, the federal policy on sick leave is that it can be used only for an employee's own illness, unless a family member has a *contagious* disease such as chicken pox. The employee could not use sick leave to care for a child who breaks a leg or contracts cancer.[34]

Leave-Sharing Programs

Programs that allow workers to share or pool their leave days were an innovation in the public sector. The Federal Employees Leave Sharing Act of 1988 authorizes federal agencies to allow employees to donate annual leave (but not sick leave) to coworkers who have used up their paid leave and face a family medical emergency that requires extended absence from work resulting in loss of income. Six agencies are also experimenting with leave banks, which allow employees to donate annual leave to a pool from which they may draw in case of their own medical emergencies. In 1990, the OPM reported that 77 percent of federal installations they had surveyed were using leave-sharing programs, and 60 percent of them allowed donations to workers who needed time off to care for sick family members. Both leave-sharing and pooling are experimental, and the legislation has a 1993 sunset provision. Based on its evaluation, the OPM is to recommend whether or not these programs should be continued.

An MSPB survey reported in 1991 revealed that over 22,000 employees had donated leave to over 8,000 coworkers, for an average amount of four or five weeks. The Department of the Army calculated that almost 500,000 hours of annual leave had been donated by its personnel. In the MSPB's estimation, a substantial need among federal employees for some form of short-term disability coverage, beyond current sick-leave provisions, was apparent. It was also apparent that federal employees "feel a responsibility to help coworkers faced with emergency medical problems, and have responded with heart-warming generosity."[35]

Although the MSPB report indicated that federal agencies "view the leave transfer program as a success story, and are happy to have it as a part of their benefits package," it did raise several questions. Since the federal leave-sharing program is voluntary and depends on the generosity of workers, there is no assurance that paid leave will actually be available to all who might need it. And, to the MSPB, it "seems unusual for the country's largest employer to be offering a fringe benefit to some of its employees which is funded by other employees. We wonder whether this approach to short-term disability protection represents the image that the Federal Government wants to present to current and prospective employees." The conclusion was that leave-sharing is certainly better than nothing, but the OPM should consider contracting for some kind of short-term disability insurance that workers could buy at group rates to protect themselves. This would allow the leave-sharing program to focus on emergencies involving family members and dependents.[36]

Leave-sharing and pooling are also found in state and local governments. Under Georgia law, for example, local boards of education are authorized to establish and set policies and procedures for a sick-leave bank or pool of voluntarily contributed employee sick-leave days. Participating employees may make equal contributions and are entitled to draw sick-leave days from the pool in accordance with the board's policies.

CHILD-CARE PROGRAMS

For single-parent families and those in which both parents work, child care is one of the most pressing issues. A 1988 Census Bureau report revealed that there were about 9.5 million children under five years of age whose mothers were working.[37] Many families have difficulty arranging reliable, affordable, trustworthy child care, and, according to Fran and Charles Rodgers, "those with the most difficulty also experience the most frequent work disruptions and the greatest absenteeism."[38] Since the availability of child care has a significant impact on workers' productivity, public as well as private employers have a vested interest in helping meet this need.

Employers' Efforts to Assist

The efforts of both public and private employers to provide child-care assistance to their workers have only begun to meet the need. On the whole, however, public employers have been more responsive for some time. The BLS reported in 1988 that less than 2 percent of the companies surveyed sponsored day-care centers, compared to over 9 percent of the public employers.[39] An editorial in *The New York Times* in 1989 noted that the federal government was setting a good example with on-site day care for congressional employees, child-care referrals provided for Internal Revenue Service workers, and day-care facilities sponsored across the country by the General Services Administration.[40]

The extent of child-care help offered by employers may look better on paper than it is in practice. Surveys tend to overestimate the cooperation of employers because they do not differentiate between the availability of programs and the practicality for workers of using them, due to such factors as cost, convenience, and supervisors' attitudes. The surveys also consider any type of assistance a child-care program. A recent survey by Hewitt Associates, a benefits consulting firm, for example, indicated that 74 percent of large companies contacted said they were offering some type of child-care assistance. Most of the efforts, however, were not actual facilities or financial help. Resource/referral services, often just a list of potential child-care providers, were offered by 41 percent of the companies, and 93 percent provided dependent-care spending accounts, which allow employees to shelter from taxes up to $5000 of their annual salaries to pay for child care.[41]

Programs in the Public Sector

Public employers have taken the lead in providing actual child-care facilities at or near the workplace for their employees. They have also introduced a variety of initiatives, including the referral services and spending accounts favored in the private sector, as well as financial assistance in the form of vouchers and subsidies.

Community Child-Care Resources and Referrals

Through their employee assistance programs or outside contractors, many public agencies provide information and support to workers needing child care. These services range from simply making lists of providers available to actively helping employees locate and select an appropriate child-care facility. In New York State, the program contracts with local child-care providers who go to the work site to provide workers with information and referrals. In the federal service, basic agency-level information and referral services are fairly common, but more extensive programs contracted for by a number of agencies have been discontinued because the costs were not justified by the level of use.

Beyond information and referrals, public employers may be able to increase the availability and quality of child-care services in their communities by allocating funds to train child-care workers, to enhance existing facilities, or to help existing programs satisfy accreditation standards. A number of local governments have implemented innovative technical assistance, planning, interagency coordination, and subsidy programs designed to support the development of the child-care resources required to meet all citizens' needs, including those of public employees.[42]

Child-Care Centers for Public Employees

Child care can be a very expensive proposition, especially for workers at the lower end of the pay scale. In many areas, parents must expect to pay $3,000 or more annually per child for full-time day care. Some families find the cost outweighs the benefits of a second income; in the typical family, child care may be the fourth largest expense, after housing, food, and taxes.[43] In general, public employers do not offer workers direct financial assistance, but some, including the federal government, do subsidize child care by providing space for facilities rent-free, negotiating discounts with private providers, and covering initial membership fees and costs associated with joining child-care networks.

Federal agencies are authorized to use public funds for space and services for child-care facilities, provided that the space is available, it will be used for child-care services to a group composed of at least 50 percent federal employees, and federal employees will be given priority access. Many agencies have established on-site operations, either on their own or in conjunction with other agencies.[44] According to the MSPB, federal agencies are able to charge between 5 and 20 percent less than other centers for equivalent services. Even with the subsidy, the cost to federal workers is not low, however; in 1990 the weekly cost ranged from $65 in Ogden, Utah, to $165 in Boston. Moreover, there are not enough federal child-care centers to meet the demand from workers.[45]

Somewhat different approaches to child care are used by the states of New York and California. New York State provides free space for child-care centers in state buildings, and the centers charge employees sliding fees based on income. New York had some 50 centers serving over 3,000 children in 1991. In California, grants have been made to nonprofit corporations to set up centers on state property; as of 1991, about 20 had been established. For new state buildings holding 700 or more employees, California requires a child-care needs assessment. If a need is found to exist, child-care space must be provided. In both of these states, state workers are given priority use of the centers, but other employees are allowed to use them on a space-available basis.[46]

On the local level, an interesting example is the pilot child-care program in the City of Los Angeles Department of Power and Water. This program was started in 1987 as a cooperative effort between the DPW and bargaining units represented by the electrical workers, service employees, and engineers and architects unions. The DPW contracts with existing child-care centers for spaces in their facilities and subsidizes employees' costs at the rate of $25 for each employee using these placements. It has also sponsored a flexible spending account which allows workers to shelter income set aside for child care from federal and state taxes. An innovation is the reservation of spaces at a facility for the care of not-seriously-ill children; the DPW subsidy for these services cuts the cost to workers by over 75 percent. Additional features of the program include a service to assist in the placement of children with special needs and parenting classes sponsored by the department. At an estimated annual cost of $200,000, the program was expected to more than pay for itself through increased productivity and lowered turnover.[47]

Fairfax County, Virginia, provides another example of innovation in the area of child care. Since 1988, Fairfax County has offered a child development program as an employee benefit. According to its sponsors, the program has allowed the county to respond to many of the child-care needs of its employees, "enhancing the benefits for existing employees and attracting qualified new employees to county government in a highly competitive metropolitan labor market."[48] The county's first Employee Child Care Center, intended to serve over 70 children, is headed by a director with a Ph.D. in child development. There are 4 lead teachers, 12 full- and part-time teachers, and a full-time cook, all qualified county employees attracted by competitive salaries and benefits. In addition to the center's normal activities, it provides a program for employees whose regular child-care providers are temporarily not available. A second child-care center at a new government complex was designed to handle over 90 children. Fairfax County was given a 1989 Achievement Award by the National Association of Counties for its employees' child-care program.[49]

ELDER-CARE PROGRAMS

The number of persons in the United States 65 years old and over is rapidly increasing, from about 20 million in 1970 to 32 million in 1991.[50] The proportion of the population age 65 or older was over 10 percent in 1990 and is expected to more than double by the year 2030. By the year 2010, in fact, there will be about 6 million people over the age of 84.

The elderly population includes many who take care of themselves and others who are able to do so with the help of in-home medical care and social services. For a steadily growing group of workers, however, balancing work and family concerns will involve caring for elderly parents, relatives, or friends. In all likelihood, this caregiver group will be composed largely of women and older workers. The MSPB notes that in these situations:

> ...certain kinds of employees are more likely to be caregivers than others, given the demographic realities surrounding elder care. For example, employers whose workforce is older than average probably have more caregivers among their workers than employers with a young staff. Similarly, employers with greater than average numbers of female workers may find a disproportionate number of their employees have elder care responsibilities.[51]

Public employers such as the federal government fit the description of those projected to be hit hardest by their employees' need to provide elder care. The proportions of female and middle-aged workers in the public sector are relatively high, and the projected trend is for steady increases.[52] Many workers are members of what has been called "the sandwich generation"; they are "increasingly finding themselves caught between the needs of their children on the one hand and of their aging parents on the other."[53] For these employees, child-care responsibilities may be followed by a potentially even longer-term commitment to elder care, with comparable effects on productivity and turnover for the employer. For public employers in the labor market of the future, indifference to the needs of workers providing elder care or anticipating the need to do so would surely be a competitive disadvantage.

For the most part, public-sector responses to elder-care needs have come in the form of educational programs and resource/referral networks. The former are designed to help prepare employees for elder-care responsibilities, and the latter are intended to assist in finding the services that elderly dependents may require. In 1990, the GAO found that about 25 percent of federal civilian and military installations had some kind of elder-care information and referral service in place. The Social Security Administration, for example, reported that it was putting its headquarters employees in contact with elder-care resources in the Baltimore, Maryland, area.[54] The Justice Department sponsored Dependent Care Fairs for its Washington, D.C., employees to provide information on community resources for child care and elder care, and the OPM developed a resource/referral handbook to give agencies information on elder-care resources in the states.

Several agencies are evaluating the feasibility of on-site elder-care centers. The IRS plans a pilot test of several adult day-care centers intended to provide respite or occasional care for elderly dependents, but questions about the legality of governments using space and appropriated funds for this purpose must first be resolved.

Otherwise, attention has focused on the possibility of changing or liberalizing leave policies, much along the lines discussed above in reference to family leave. The MSPB considers that one of the most useful benefits an employer can provide to employees with elder-care problems is the option of taking additional time off from their jobs as these responsibilities require.[55] Since an employee's paid leave may be used up, one approach would be for employers to arrange for group policies for long-term care insurance covering dependents as well as workers.

PROSPECTS FOR THE FUTURE

Solving the problems and issues faced by public employers as a result of the changing demographics of the American population and the need of employees to balance their work and family concerns will require a comprehensive reform of the institutions and policies that govern the workplace.[56] While personnel agencies are certainly in a position to exercise leadership on the organizational level, personnel problems caused by the problems of the larger society, such as those afflicting the U.S. health-care, social insurance, and welfare systems, are public policy issues that must be addressed by the nation's political leadership.

The relatively new issue of elder care is a good example. Public employers are not equipped to provide direct services for the elderly dependents of their employees, but all concerned will suffer if affordable and reliable systems for delivering elder care are not developed. Within limitations, individual public agencies may be able to stimulate and support the development of such resources, as they have done to some extent in the child-care area. Nevertheless, the most enlightened and responsive personnel initiatives will achieve only marginal improvements if they do not have a strong foundation in public policies on all levels of government.

■

NOTES

1. U.S. General Accounting Office, *The Changing Workforce: Demographic Issues Facing the Federal Government* (Washington, DC, March 1992), p. 23.
2. Bureau of National Affairs, Inc., *101 Key Statistics on Work and Family for the 1990s* (Washington, DC, 1989); U.S. Bureau of the Census, *Statistical Abstract of the United States; 1992*, 112th edition (Washington, DC, 1992), Table 620.
3. Bureau of National Affairs, *101 Key Statistics*, p. 29.
4. U.S. General Accounting Office, *The Changing Workforce: Comparison of Federal and Nonfederal Work/Family Programs and Approaches* (Washington, DC, April 1992), p.11.
5. Ibid.
6. Dana E. Friedman, *Linking Work-Family Issues to the Bottom Line* (New York: Conference Board, 1991).
7. U.S. General Accounting Office, *Changing Federal Workforce*, p. 12.
8. Public Law 95-437, 92 Stat. 1055, October 10, 1978.
9. U.S. Merit Systems Protection Board, *Balancing Work Responsibilities and Family Needs: The Federal Civil Service Response* (Washington, DC, November 1991), pp. 40–42.
10. Ibid.
11. Ibid., p. 43.
12. U.S. General Accounting Office, *Changing Workforce: Comparison of Work/Family Programs*, p. 78.
13. U.S. Bureau of the Census, *Statistical Abstract of the United States: 1992*, Table 626.
14. Jennifer McEnroe, "Split-Shift Parenting," *American Demographics*, vol. 13, no. 2 (February 1991), p. 52.
15. U.S. Office of Personnel Management, *Federal Staffing Digest*, vol. 3, no. 3 (December 1991), pp. 6–7.
16. U.S. Office of Personnel Management, *Federal Personnel Manual*, FPM Supplement 990–2, September 30, 1980, pp. 620–624.
17. U.S. Merit Systems Protection Board, *Balancing Work Responsibilities and Family Needs*, p. 33.

18. U.S. General Accounting Office, *The Changing Workforce: Comparison of Work/Family Programs*, pp. 78–79.
19. U.S. Merit Systems Protection Board, *Working for America: A Federal Employee Survey* (Washington, DC, June 1990), p. 29.
20. U.S. General Accounting Office, *Alternative Work Schedules for Federal Employees* (Washington, DC, July 19, 1985).
21. U.S. Merit Systems Protection Board, *Balancing Work Responsibilities and Family Needs*, p. 37.
22. Ibid., p. 48.
23. President's Council on Management Improvement, Human Resources Committee, "Guidelines for Pilot Flexible Workplace Arrangements," (Washington, DC, January 1990), p. 3.
24. U.S. General Accounting Office, *Changing Workforce: Comparison of Work/Family Programs*, p. 82.
25. U.S. Office of Personnel Management, "If It's Wednesday, It Must Be Home, " *Federal Staffing Digest*, vol. 3, no. 3 (December 1991), p. 7.
26. U.S. General Accounting Office, *Changing Workforce: Comparison of Work/Family Programs*, pp. 26–27.
27. U.S. Merit Systems Protection Board, *Balancing Work Responsibilities and Family Needs*, p. 59.
28. Ian Allen, "Financing and Managing Public Employee Benefit Plans in the 1990s," *Government Finance Review*, vol. 4, no. 5 (October 1988), pp. 32–33.
29. Family and Medical Leave Act of 1989, 101st Congress, H.R. 770, April 13, 1989, p. 2.
30. Jason DeParle, "U.S. Loses Lead to States on Family Leave Policies," *The New York Times*, September 21, 1991, p. 8y.
31. Official Code of Georgia, Senate Bill 831, Title 45, Chapter 24 (1992), p. 4.
32. Center for Employment Relations and Law, *Employment Relations Bulletin*, vol. 10, no. 6 (Tallahassee: Florida State University, February 1992), p. 1.
33. U.S. General Accounting Office, *Changing Workforce: Comparison of Work/Family Programs*, p. 84.
34. Ibid.
35. U.S. Merit Systems Protection Board, *Balancing Work Responsibilities and Family Needs*, p. 56.
36. Ibid., p. 58.
37. U.S. Bureau of the Census, *Statistical Abstract of the United States: 1992*, Table 600.
38. Fran Sussner Rodgers and Charles Rodgers, "Business and the Facts of Family Life," *Harvard Business Review*, no. 6 (November–December 1989), p. 123.
39. U.S. Bureau of Labor Statistics, *Child-Care Benefits Offered by U.S. Business Establishments* (Washington, DC, January 15, 1988), p. 4.
40. "Family-Friendly Employers," *The New York Times*, September 13, 1989, p. A30.
41. Amy Saltzman, "Family Friendliness," *U.S. News & World Report*, February 22, 1993, pp. 60–61.

42. Claudia Rhoades, "Local Initiatives for Child Care," *MIS Report*, vol. 21, no. 11 (Washington, DC, International City Management Association, November 1989), pp. 1–16.

43. Ibid., p. 1; and Linda Thiede Thomas and James E. Thomas, "The ABCs of Child Care: Building Blocks of Competition," *Sloan Management Review*, vol. 31, no. 2 (Winter 1990), p. 36.

44. U.S. General Accounting Office, *Changing Workforce: Comparison of Work/Family Programs*, pp. 85–86.

45. Alison N. Starr (ed.), "Federal Child Care Centers: More Than Before—But Still Not Enough and Still Costly," *Employee Benefits Review*, vol. 3, no. 3 (Washington, DC, March 1990).

46. Edward L. Suntrup, "Child-Care Delivery Systems in the Government Sector," *Review of Public Personnel Administration*, vol. 10, no. 1 (Fall 1989), pp. 52–54.

47. Ibid., pp. 51–52.

48. Gail Bjorklund, Roberta Owens and Ellen A. Tuyahov, "Child Care: An Employee Benefit for Fairfax County Workers," *Government Finance Review* (August 1989), p. 19.

49. Ibid., pp. 22–23.

50. U.S. Bureau of the Census, *Statistical Abstract of the United States: 1992*, Table 39.

51. U.S. Merit Systems Protection Board, *Balancing Work Responsibilities and Family Needs*, pp. 24–25.

52. Howard N. Fullerton, Jr., "New Labor Force Projections, Spanning 1988 to 2000," *Monthly Labor Review*, November 1989, pp. 7–9.

53. Ken Dychtwald, *Age Wave: The Challenges and Opportunities of an Aging America* (Los Angeles: Jeremy P. Tarcher, 1989), p. 298.

54. U.S. General Accounting Office, *Comparison of Work/Family Programs*, pp. 88–89.

55. U.S. Merit Systems Protection Board, *Balancing Work Responsibilities and Family Needs*.

56. William B. Johnston, *Workforce 2000: Work and Workers for the 21st Century* (Indianapolis: Hudson Institute, June 1987), p. xxv.

The Future of Public Personnel in the United States

15

The 1990s are likely to be a decade of transformation for public personnel administration in the United States, as we suggested in the preface to this text. The goal of public personnel systems will still be to develop a strong human resources base for the agencies through which governments function. We anticipate, however, that how it goes about doing this will change considerably.

ONGOING TRENDS

Several trends that developed during the preceding decade are likely to continue through the 1990s. Fiscal and political pressures to get more done with fewer resources may force governments to consider all the ways contracting-out might be used as a cost control measure. Because of the same pressures, much of the debate over alternative personnel policies will be focused on questions of economic costs and benefits, and the emphasis on efficiency is unlikely to change.

Many of the tasks currently assigned to the civil service will not change, but changes in how they are performed will be necessary as new technologies and organizational structures requiring higher levels of skill and more extensive training and education are developed.

A growing proportion of government jobs will require personnel who are highly professionalized and prepared to constantly upgrade their skills in order to keep pace with the intellectual and technical demands of their positions. Recruiting, developing, and retaining managerial and supervisory talent will become vital functions of personnel specialists in a public sector marked by increasingly complex, interdependent organizational arrangements.

In all likelihood, flexibility and adaptability will gradually replace routinization and standardization as hallmarks of the modern public personnel system. During the 1990s, the lessons learned from experiments with simplified position classification structures, streamlined hiring procedures, pay-for-performance systems, and new approaches to pay and benefits will certainly have major effects on personnel policies and practices in many jurisdictions.[1]

Another shift in emphasis is the trend to delegation and decentralization in public personnel systems. The human resources management point of view is likely to persist, but the traditional regulatory functions of personnel agencies will probably be deemphasized and shifted to specialized units like the Merit Systems Protection Board. Tensions between the managerial and regulatory responsibilities of personnel systems must be expected to grow as authority for basic personnel decisions is increasingly placed in the hands of line managers. In an analysis of recent "simplification" initiatives by the Office of Personnel Management, the MSPB correctly noted that "shifting decisions to line managers speeds the decision-making process...[and] requires managers to bear direct responsibility for compliance with law and regulation."[2]

While many aspects of personnel administration could be decentralized or delegated without posing a major threat to the merit principle, the MSPB notes that giving managers the discretion to make fundamental personnel decisions "has the *potential* for the injection of favoritism and other nonmerit factors."[3] Clearly, one of the challenges of the 1990s will be the creation of effective oversight and evaluation mechanisms to reassure all concerned that the merit principle will be protected. Another challenge that will require creative policy leadership and commitment from personnel specialists is to make progress toward the long-standing goals of equity, equal opportunity, and procedural fairness in human resources management.

The causes of the "quiet crisis" in the American public service described in Chapter 1 will have to be addressed to equip it to meet the many demands being placed on it by the public. The recommendations of the Volcker Commission in 1989 applied to the federal civil service, but they could be used to upgrade the image of public service in general and to reform personnel practices to deal with the problems confronting public agencies on all levels of government. Long-delayed investments in human resources can no longer be avoided if the United States is to have the high-quality public work force it needs on the local, state, and federal levels. Building the political support necessary to authorize these investments, as the Volcker Commission stated, should be a high priority for the nation's political leadership.

THE STATE OF THE ART

In all probability, the technical capacities of public personnel systems will continue to lag behind the demands placed on them. Valid selection tests and performance appraisals are key objectives of many reform proposals, but they have been very difficult to realize, in large measure because knowledge is incomplete and resources are limited. In many jurisdictions, efforts to validate selection tests and to improve performance evaluation systems have taken place only after public employers were forced to act by employee organizations and the courts.

Obviously outmoded and ineffective classification and pay systems have been caught in a kind of political-administrative gridlock that must be broken if new approaches are to be tested and implemented during the 1990s. The OPM's renewed interest in sponsoring the research and demonstration projects on modernizing federal classification authorized by the Civil Service Reform Act of 1978 is a positive sign in this regard.[4]

A broad issue to be addressed is whether government should be committed to serving as a "model employer." Should the public sector try to take the lead in providing benefits such as parental leave, child care, and flexible working conditions? Should it set an example for the rest of the society in the areas of equal opportunity, pay equity, and meaningful jobs for the disabled? Would efforts to be a model employer undermine organizational performance or would they provide a solid foundation for excellence in the long term? Must efforts to meet employee needs be justified in terms of cost savings or improved productivity, or should initiatives such as those described in Section III be considered intrinsically worthwhile, to be pursued if resources are available? The answers to these questions will surely have a major impact on the future of public personnel.

As is so often the case, leadership by public personnel specialists and their organizations is needed to overcome bureaucratic inertia and a "wait until someone forces us to change" attitude. Policies and practices may become proactive, as opposed to largely reactive, in the 1990s; in any case, external forces such as the changing demography of the labor force and shifting political priorities will make change necessary to some extent. For public personnel specialists, the important question is: Will they use their expertise and experience to inform and shape these changes, or will they be swept into a future they did little to create or prepare for? We should know the answer to this question by the year 2000.

■

NOTES

1. U.S. Merit Systems Protection Board, *Delegation and Decentralization: Personnel Management Simplification Efforts in the Federal Government* (Washington, DC, October 1989).
2. Ibid., p. 4.
3. Ibid., p. 21.
4. U.S General Accounting Office, *Federal Personnel: Status of Personnel and Demonstration Projects*, Briefing Report to Congressional Requesters (Washington, DC, September 1987); U.S. General Accounting Office, *Federal Personnel: Observations on the Navy's Personnel Management Demonstration Project*, Report to the Chairman, Subcommittee on Federal Services, Post Office, and Civil Service (Washington, DC, May 1988); U.S. Merit Systems Protection Board, *Federal Personnel Management Since Civil Service Reform: A Survey of Federal Personnel Officials* (Washington, DC, November 1989).

Suggested Readings

Ammons, David N. *Municipal Productivity*. New York: Frederick A. Praeger, 1984.

Barrett, Jerome T. *Labor-Management Cooperation in the Public Service*. Washington, DC: International Personnel Management Association, 1985.

Barzelay, Michael. *Breaking through Bureaucracy*. Berkeley, CA: University of California Press, 1992.

Burton, John F., ed. *Industrial Relations Research Series: Proceedings of the Forty-Third Annual Meeting*. Washington, DC: Industrial Relations Research Association, December 28–30, 1990.

Coulson, Robert. *Alcohol, Drugs, and Arbitration*. New York: American Arbitration Association, 1987.

Donahue, John D. *The Privatization Decision*. New York: Basic Books, 1989.

Eddy, William B., ed. *Handbook of Organizational Management*. New York: Marcel Dekker, 1983.

Franklin, Grace, and Ripley, Randall B. *C.E.T.A.: Politics and Policy, 1973–1982*. Knoxville: University of Tennessee Press, 1984.

Gael, Sidney. *Job Analysis: A Guide to Assessing Work Activities*. San Francisco: Jossey-Bass, 1983.

Gruenfeld, Elaine F. *Performance Appraisal: Promise and Peril*. Ithaca, NY: School of Industrial and Labor Relations, Cornell University, 1981.

Heclo, Hugh. *A Government of Strangers: Executive Politics in Washington*. Washington, DC: Brookings Institution, 1977.

Johansen, Elaine. *Comparable Worth: The Myth and the Movement*. Boulder, CO: Westview Press, 1984.

Kaufman, Herbert. *The Administrative Behavior of Federal Bureau Chiefs.* Washington, DC: Brookings Institution, 1981.

Kearney, Richard C. *Labor Relations in the Public Sector.* New York: Marcel Dekker, 1984.

Kingsley, J. Donald. *Representative Bureaucracy: An Interpretation of the British Civil Service.* Yellow Springs, AR: Antioch Press, 1944.

Krislov, Samuel, and Rosenbloom, David H. *Representative Bureaucracy and the American Political System.* New York: Frederick A. Praeger, 1981.

Landy, Frank J. *Psychology of Work Behavior,* 3rd ed. Homewood, IL: Dorsey Press, 1985.

Morrisey, George L. *Performance Appraisals in the Public Service: Key to Effective Supervision.* Reading, MA: Addison-Wesley, 1983.

Mosher, Frederick. *Democracy and the Public Service.* New York: Oxford University Press, 1968.

———. *The GAO: The Quest for Accountability in American Government.* Boulder, CO: Westview Press, 1979.

National Academy of Public Administration. *The Future Role of the Office of Personnel Management.* Washington, DC, 1988.

Nigro, Felix A. "Public Personnel Administration: From Theodore Roosevelt to Ronald Reagan," *International Journal of Public Administration,* vol. 6, no. 1 (March 1984).

Phillips, Jack J. *Handbook of Training Evaluation and Measurement Methods.* Houston: Gulf, 1983.

President's Council on Integrity and Efficiency. *Compendium of Publications on Fraud, Waste, and Abuse Indicators.* Washington, DC, June 30, 1988.

Prince, Carl E. *The Federalists and the Origins of the U.S. Civil Service.* New York: New York University Press, 1977.

Rabin, Jack; Vocino, Thomas; Hildreth, W. Bartley; and Miller, Gerald J., eds. *Handbook on Public Personnel Administration and Labor Relations.* New York: Marcel Dekker, 1983.

Reichenberg, Neil E. *Drug Testing in the Workplace.* Alexandria, VA: International Personnel Management Association, n.d.

Robson, Mike, ed. *Quality Circles in Action.* Brookfield, VT: Gower, 1985.

Rosenbloom, David H. *Public Law and Public Administration: Bench and Bureau in the United States.* New York: Marcel Dekker, 1983.

Schiesl, Martin J. *The Politics of Efficiency.* Berkeley, CA: University of California Press, 1977.

Schroder, William B., ed. *Measuring Achievement: Progress over a Decade.* San Francisco: Jossey-Bass, 1980.

Sealander, Judith. *As Minority Becomes Majority: Federal Reaction to the Phenomenon of Women in the Work Force, 1920–1963.* Westport, CT: Greenwood Press, 1983.

Stanley, David T. *The Higher Civil Service.* Washington, DC: Brookings Institution, 1964.

Stewart, Debra W., and Garson, G. David. *Organizational Behavior and Public Management.* New York: Marcel Dekker, 1983.

Strauss, George; Gallagher, Daniel G.; and Fiorito, Jack, eds. *The State of the Unions*. Madison, WI: Industrial Relations Research Association, 1991.

Suleiman, Ezra N. *Politics, Power, and Bureaucracy in France: The Administrative Elite*. Princeton, NJ: Princeton University Press, 1974.

Suskin, Harold, ed. *Job Evaluation and Pay Administration in the Public Sector*. Chicago: International Personnel Management Association, 1977.

Task Force on the New York State Public Workforce in the 21st Century. *Public Service through the State Government Workforce: Meeting the Challenge of Change*. Albany, NY: Rockefeller Institute, 1989.

Taylor, Frederick W. *The Principles of Scientific Management*. New York: Harper and Row, 1911.

Thompson, Frank J., ed. *Classics of Public Personnel Policy*, 2nd ed. Pacific Grove, CA: Brooks/Cole, 1991.

U.S. Commission on Civil Rights. *Toward an Understanding of Stotts*. Washington, DC, 1985.

U.S. General Accounting Office. *Description of Selected Systems for Classifying Federal Civilian Positions and Personnel*. Washington, DC, July 13, 1984.

————. *Human Resource Management: Status of Agency Practices for Improving Federal Productivity*. Washington, DC, June 1987.

————. *Federal Employees: Trends in Career and Noncareer Employee Appointments in the Executive Branch*. Washington, DC, July 1987.

————. *Federal Productivity: DOD's Experience in Contracting Out Commercially Available Activities*. Washington, DC, November 1988.

————. *Federal Workforce: Implementation of the Executive Exchange Program Voluntary Services Act of 1986*. Washington, DC, March 1989.

————. *Senior Executive Service: Training and Development of Senior Executives*. Washington, DC, September 1989.

————. *DOD Revolving Door: Few Are Restricted from Post-DOD Employment and Reporting Has Some Gaps*. Washington, DC, February 1990.

————. *Employee Conduct Standards: Some Outside Activities Present Conflict-of-Interest Issues*. Washington, DC, February 1992.

U.S. House Committee on Post Office and Civil Service. *History of Civil Service Merit Systems of the United States and Selected Foreign Countries*. Report to the 94th Congress, 2d Session. Washington, DC, 1976.

U.S. Merit Systems Protection Board. *The Senior Executive Service: Views of Former Federal Executives*. Washington, DC, October 1989.

————. *Senior Executive Service Pay Setting and Reassignments: Expectations vs. Reality*. Washington, DC, October 1990.

Van Riper, Paul. *History of the United States Civil Service*. New York: Harper and Row, 1958.

Volcker, Paul A. *Public Service: The Quiet Crisis*. Washington, DC: American Enterprise Institute, 1988.

Walker, John W. *Human Resource Planning*. New York: McGraw-Hill, 1980.

White, Leonard D. *The Federalists: A Study in Administrative History*. New York: Macmillan, 1948.

————. *The Jeffersonians: A Study in Administrative History, 1801–1829*. New York: Macmillan, 1951.

————. *The Republican Era: 1869–1901, A Study in Administrative History*. New York: Macmillan, 1958.

Wigdor, A., and Garner, W., eds. *Ability Testing: Uses, Consequences, and Controversies*. Washington, DC: National Academy Press, 1982.

Willborn, Steven L. *A Comparable Worth Primer*. Lexington, MA: Lexington Books, 1986.

Wilson, Woodrow. "The Study of Administration." *Political Science Quarterly*, vol. 56 (1941).

Zack, Arnold M., ed. *Arbitration in Practice*. New York: American Arbitration Association, 1984.

————. *Public Sector Mediation*. Washington, DC: Bureau of National Affairs, 1985.

Index

THE NEW PUBLIC PERSONNEL ADMINISTRATION
Edited by Gloria Reardon, Belvidere, Illinois
Internal design by Willis Proudfoot, Mt. Prospect, Illinois
Cover design by Lesiak/Crampton Design, Inc., Chicago, Illinois
Production supervision by Kim Vander Steen, Palatine, Illinois
Composition by Point West, Inc., Carol Stream, Illinois
Printed and bound by Braun-Brumfield, Inc., Ann Arbor, Michigan
Paper, Springhill
The text is set in Palatino